The City of London
and its
Livery Companies

"WHITTINGTON REDIVIVUS."

The New Progressive Dick W. "WHAT ARE THE BELLS SAYING, PUSSY? 'TURN *AGAIN*, WHITTINGTON, LORD MAYOR OF LONDON,'—OR IS IT 'TURN *OUT*'?"

The City of London and its Livery Companies

'We must remember that this country is not governed by logic, but by Parliament'.
                                                                    Benjamin Disraeli

'But logic has its limits and the position of the City lies outside them'.
              Herbert Commission on Local Government in Greater London

I. G. Doolittle

The Gavin Press

JS 3648

First Edition 1982

© 1982 I. G. Doolittle

British Library Cataloguing in Publication Data

Doolittle, I.G.
 The City of London and its livery companies.
 1. London (England)—Guilds
 I. Title
 338.6'32'094212   HD6462.L7
 ISBN 0-905868-11-0

Published by The Gavin Press, Dorchester, Dorset
Typeset by Preface Ltd., Salisbury, Wilts
Printed in Great Britain by The Dorset Press, Dorchester, Dorset

CONTENTS

LIST OF ILLUSTRATIONS FROM 'PUNCH'

Certain figures were regularly used to represent the City in *Punch's* cartoons. **Gog and Magog** were the giants who featured in rather confused myths about a Trojan foundation of London and their statues still preside over the Guildhall; the **Turtle** derived from the turtle soup which traditionally began City feasts (hence the expression 'turtledom'); and the **Griffin** stood, and stands, guard on the boundaries of the Square Mile.

All the illustrations are reproduced by permission of the Bodleian Library,
Oxford (class-mark N.2706 d.10).

PREFACE

This book traces the reasons for the survival of the City of London and its Livery Companies. There have been many attempts to undermine or abolish these ancient institutions, but all have failed. Why should this have been so? The answer possesses its own intrinsic interest, since the story is a colourful and sometimes dramatic one. It also has a certain topicality, because the City and its Guilds retain their fascination and still arouse controversy. Finally, it has some academic relevance, since the subject is intimately connected with the history and development of London as a whole. Whether I have done justice to all these themes is another matter. All I can claim is that no-one has attempted the task before.

ACKNOWLEDGEMENTS

I have contracted a number of debts in writing this book. Dr. Ken Young's pioneering work on London's politics and government was invaluable and he added a personal service by letting me see a copy of *Metropolitan London* (written jointly with Patricia L. Garside) in advance of publication. Mr. John Davis was generous with his intimate knowledge of the subject. Dr. Francis Nicholson gave me permission to cite his thesis on *'The Politics of English Metropolitan Reform'*. The Chairman of the City of London's Policy and Resources Committee, Mr. Wixley, and the Deputy Town Clerk, Mr. Rowley, talked to me about the City's present position. Dr. Valerie Pearl read Chapter I; Mr. John Prest and Dr. Blair Worden helped with specific points; and Professor Donald Olsen, Dr. Roland Quinault, Dr. Francis Sheppard and Mr. William Thomas assisted in other ways. I am grateful to them all.

The Bodleian Library, Oxford, kindly gave permission for the use of the twenty-three *Punch* illustrations, reference N.2706 d.10, and the Town Clerk of the City of London, Guildhall, granted permission for the use of the City Arms on the cover of this book.

CHAPTER I

PROLOGUE (1625–1835)

This great concourse of all sorts of people
The story begins in the early seventeenth century when London enjoyed a
position of overwhelming importance in national life. Its population was
growing furiously and numbered well over a quarter of a million, ten times
the size of the next largest town. Immigrants from all corners of the country, and the continent, poured into the metropolis to swell the already
swollen ranks and replace the many victims of disease and malnutrition.
This 'great concourse of all sorts of people drawing near unto the City' [1]
added fuel to a combustible mixture of industry and enterprise. There was
certainly no shortage of work for the newcomers. Many found employment
in the bustling life of the Port, for London's commerce was no longer
exclusively directed towards the cloth marts of Europe, but now turned its
face to the Levant and the East. Indeed London was fast becoming the
entrepôt of Europe. There was trade too with the rest of the kingdom.
Foodstuffs of all kinds arrived to feed the growing multitude, and in return
London 'exported' a wide range of specialist and luxury goods. In fact,
London was as much an industrial as a commercial centre, and the ship-
building and house-building trades (for obvious reasons) flourished in
these years.

Nor was London's pre-eminence confined to economic matters. In many
other facets of life – political, legal, religious and cultural – London led the
way. So much so that it aroused both jealousy and fear. There was jealousy
from the provinces, where the 'outports' (as London's rivals significantly
were called) denounced the capital's stranglehold on trade, and the *menu
peuple* feared for their supplies of grain in the face of competition from
London merchants. Fear was born of the insecurity of rulers, such as James
I, who declared that London would soon devour England, and the anxieties
of the theorists who, prone to conceive of the 'commonwealth' as analog-
ous to the human body, were affronted by the growth of this monstrous
head. As early as the 1570s a Londoner felt constrained to write a discourse about the City of London 'by way of an apology (or defence) against
the opinion of some men, which think that the greatness of that City
standeth not with the profit and security of this realm'. [2]

The proud, unthankful, schismatical, rebellious, bloody City of London
The centre of this profusion of energy was the famous square mile, the six
hundred and seventy acres governed by the ancient Corporation. Indeed, it
was still true to say that the City of London *was* London. On demographic

grounds alone this was a plausible proposition: 130,000 inhabitants, possibly half the total population of the metropolis, lived cheek-by-jowl within
the confines of the City. On other grounds it was even more obvious. The
personal wealth of the City's magnates and the depth of its own coffers
gave the Corporation a position of extraordinary influence in the councils
of the nation. At a time when the monarchy was in dire financial straits and
found Parliament in uncompromising mood, the wealth of Guildhall
assumed the guise of a political cure-all.

Both James I and Charles I relied heavily on the City and its guilds for
financial assistance, and the constitutional crisis of 1640 owed not a little to
the City finally calling a halt to the repeated demands. As Civil War
approached, Parliament's Puritan allies seized control of the City for the
Cause. This proved vital for, deprived of his capital and his creditors,
Charles slid almost inexorably towards defeat. Little wonder that a royal-
ist pamphleteer expostulated in 1643: 'If posterity shall ask who would
have pulled the Crown from the King's head, taken the government off its
hinges, dissolved monarchy, enslaved the laws, and ruined their country;
say, 'twas the proud, unthankful, schismatical, rebellious, bloody City of
London'.[3]

For the final word on the importance of the City in the early seventeenth
century, we need look no further than the Lord Mayor's Show. The fes-
tivities attendant on the Lord Mayor's installation now reached their pin-
nacle of extravagance and expense in what has been described as their
Golden Age.[4] The traditional pageant presented by the guilds at Midsum-
mer gave way to a lavish Mayoral Show in which both the Corporation and
the Companies participated. Some of the most celebrated dramatists of the
day – Dekker, Middleton, Munday and Webster – were employed to create
elaborate allegorical fantasies. The absurdity of these spectacles varied
from year to year, but their ostentatious splendour never altered. Through
them the City and the Livery Companies proclaimed to the nation their
power and prestige.

The nation needed little persuading. Contemporaries were only too well
aware of the opportunities afforded by the City's trade and commerce, and
many came up from the provinces to seek their fortune. Their hopes were
vividly reflected in the tale of Dick Whittington, and it can be no coincidence that it was in the early seventeenth century that the tale of the future
Mayor and his mythical cat first gained currency. The career of one of the
City's most illustrious sons, who made a fortune in trade, lent money to
kings, served three times as Mayor and left noble benefactions to worthy
causes, served an enduring inspiration to succeeding generations of citizens. The myth was based on a tantalising reality.

But if these years represented the high-point of the City's fortunes, they
marked a turning-point too; and it is with the subsequent difficulties con-
fronting the Corporation and its Companies that this history is concerned.

As a preliminary to the enquiry it is obviously essential to dwell briefly on the way in which the City and the Livery Companies conducted their affairs. Without some knowledge of the arcane delights of the constitutions of these bodies, much of what follows will be inexplicable. On one level, there are idiosyncratic terms which have to be explained; and, on another, the privileges embodied in these constitutions formed the battleground for the struggles shortly to be related. It was, after all, on its unique rights and liberties that the City's pre-eminence was based. One of the Corporation's nineteenth-century supporters, Lord Chief Baron Kelly, was said once to have spoken of 'the duty of ever maintaining unimpaired and, if possible, unquestioned, the high and ancient privileges of the City of London, as with them, and under them, it has become the first and greatest City in the world'.[5]

High and ancient privileges
The City's constitution was the confused creation of a long history of turbulence and expansion. By the start of the seventeenth century, however, it had reached a point of equilibrium, and the system which had evolved by then is still recognizable today. At the head of a pyramidal structure stood twenty-six Aldermen, who each represented one of the City's wards. These were wealthy and powerful men, who were elected for life; and from their number the Lord Mayor was chosen each year. It was on these men that much of the day-to-day adminstration of the square mile devolved. To some extent this entailed supervising the extensive estates and interests of the Corporation itself; but it also involved regulating a host of public services, including the enforcement of law and order, the control of commerce in the Port of London, the conservancy of the lower reaches of the Thames, the supervision of the public markets and the provision of street-lighting and water supplies.

Some of these duties were shared with the next rank in the hierarchy, Common Council. To this court were returned each year some two hundred and thirty representatives from the wards. They helped the Aldermen in some tasks, it is true, but their participation in City government was intermittent and circumscribed. It was not until the eighteenth century that, as a consequence of the increasing pressure of work and a final rejection of the Aldermen's claim to a veto over their proceedings, they began to play a regular part in administration. In the seventeenth century Common Council was important chiefly for the independent politics of its members. They gave sensitive expression to the views of the citizens at large, and they had the capacity to embarrass the more conservative Aldermen.

More radical still were the politics of Common Hall, the last of the City's three main courts. This was the forum of the Liverymen, or those who had assumed the 'clothing' or Livery of certain privileged Companies. There were approximately four thousand Liverymen at the start of our period, but this number grew substantially in later years and it oscillated between seven and eight thousand during the eighteenth century. These gatherings in Common Hall were theoretically concerned only with the election or nomination of City officers, particularly the Lord Mayor, the Chamberlain (or treasurer), one of the two Sheriffs and the four M.P.s. In practice, however, Common Hall could occasionally be the scene of a vigorous outburst of anger against the City's leaders or the national government of the day. If the City's constitution was archaic and complex in form, it was also volatile and almost democratic in operation. This may have seemed a source of conflict and bitterness in the early centuries of the Corporation's life, but in later more 'progressive' times it was to prove an invaluable source of strength. It prevented the Corporation from becoming moribund and incapable of change, and it soothed the indignation of the radicals.

Below Common Hall came those citizens who were members of the Corporation only by virtue of their freedom. No-one could buy or sell goods in the square mile without being free of the City. This and other regulations, together with the Corporation's privileged trading position, made the freedom a prerequisite for business success in these years. It conferred political privileges too. It was the freemen householders in each ward who elected the Aldermen and Common Councilmen; and of course the freedom represented the starting-point for the long and arduous climb up that rickety ladder of City preferment outlined above.

From the City we turn to the Livery Companies. These corporations too had an ancient past, with the antecedents of some stretching back to the twelfth century and their incorporation by royal charter beginning in the fifteenth century. There were about seventy Companies in the seventeenth century, fifty of whom had been granted the right to bestow their Liveries on certain of their members. But the figures fluctuated a good deal, as new Companies were formed, others were subsumed or simply faded away, and still more were granted Liveries for the first time. There is a similar complexity attached to the Companies' constitutions, and many peculiarities confront the observer. Nonetheless some general features can be identified and deserve a short description.

In some respects Company government resembled its counterpart at Guildhall. At the head of our model Company stood the Master and two or three Wardens, a *cursus honorum* of annually elected officers. Either on their own or in conjunction with a Court of twenty or so Assistants, the officers carried out the administrative tasks: controlling the trade or craft through apprenticeships and inspections of work; providing for Company finances by letting the corporate estates and levying fines on members; and assisting needy dependants through the disbursement of the legacies of former members. Below the Assistants were placed the Liverymen who were eligible (usually by order of seniority) for the Court when a vacancy occurred. Then came a much larger body of freemen (increasingly known as the yeomanry), from whom were drawn (on payment of a fine) the Liverymen as and when need, often financial need, arose. At the bottom of this oligarchical hierarchy there was a substantial and ill-defined group of journeymen (sometimes known as the commonalty), who were obliged to submit to the Company's rules governing their work.

Before this descriptive interlude can be brought to a close it is necessary to consider the relations between the City and the Companies. In this instance too the early seventeenth century marked the culmination of a long and halting process. When a Lord Mayor claimed at this time that he was master of all the Companies, he was unconsciously announcing the final assimilation of the guilds into City government. This was not the result of coercion, but a recognition of mutual interdependence. For its part the City needed the wealth of the Companies and their members in its efforts to meet the financial demands of the Crown, as well as their control of trade in its attempts to maintain the freedom. On their side the Companies relied on the social and political prestige of Guildhall to encourage traders to submit to the requirements of the freedom on which the craft regulations depended, and they needed the arbitration of the Court of Aldermen to settle their domestic disputes. Of course, the relationship was not without its problems. There was bitterness, for instance, when the Corporation required Companies to contribute to the Crown loans in the years preceding the Civil War. For the most part, however, a combination of self-interest and mutual respect kept the two parties together; and, naturally enough, as their shared difficulties increased and threats to their existence arose, so the relationship grew more intimate. As common friends or common enemies their fortunes are inextricably linked in the story which follows.

The Great Refusal
From the static picture of privilege and power, we move on to the volatile process of change and decay. At the very moment when the City stood at the peak of its prestige, the subsequent decline was already under way. In fact, the two developments shared the same root cause – population. For if the City's wealth and authority were based on the enormous increase in London's population, then the same phenomenon undermined them. The City could no longer accommodate the capital's teeming thousands within the limits of its jurisdiction. Immigrants began to settle in colonies outside the City walls, both north and south of the river. Nor was this by any means a purely involuntary affair. Men of all sorts came to realise the advantages of life in the suburbs. The affluent could escape the grime and over-crowding of the square mile, the enterprising and industrious could avoid the restrictions on trade, whilst the disreputable could find refuge from the law.

These developments posed an obvious threat to the well-being of both the City and its Livery Companies. If traders were allowed to practise their crafts without supervision then the City's unique position as a protected market could be fatally undermined. The freedom would lose its efficacy and men would no longer be obliged to serve Guildhall or Company offices. All this received graphic emphasis in a petition which the City presented to the Privy Council in 1632. This included a rehearsal of matters of general concern – the influx of beggars and loose persons, profiteering, the destruction and contamination of the water supply, the danger of plague, and so on – which were doubtless intended to ensure the document's favourable reception. But the kernel of the address was surely to be found in the portentous declaration that:[6]

... the freedom of London which is heretofore of very great esteem is grown to be of little worth, by reason of the extraordinary enlargement of the suburbs, where great numbers of traders and handicraftsmen do enjoy, without charge, equal benefit with the freemen and citizens of London.

The problems caused by this growth and shift in population were compounded by related changes in the economy. Trade could no longer be subjected to the kind of regulations the City fathers wished to impose. Companies found themselves beset by internal conflicts based on the new divisions between trader and craftsman, employer and workman; they also had to compete with other Companies for the control of new or changing industries. Despite a spate of new incorporations encouraged by the impecunious early Stuarts, the guilds simply could not cope. They began to lose touch with their trades; and, since the 'custom of London' permitted a freeman to choose any retail trade he pleased whatever his Company and since also the freedom could be acquired by inheritance and redemption as well as apprenticeship, the process, once started, gathered its own momentum. Repeated attempts to reverse the trend all eventually proved ineffectual, and the Companies began their slow and halting transformation from trading fraternities into charitable clubs. Professor V. Pearl and Dr. J.R. Kellett have quite properly warned against ante-dating and exaggerating this economic decline, but the long-term trend is undeniable.

This transformation, like the City's decline, was doubtless inevitable; but the process could certainly have been retarded, and might well have taken a different course, had effective action been taken to deal with the problem of the suburbs. The answer, of course, was for the City to assume responsibility for its extra-mural outlaws; and this was a solution only too obvious to contemporaries. In the year following the presentation of the petition noticed above, the Privy Council asked the City 'whether they would accept of part of the suburbs into their jurisdiction and liberty for better government'.[7] But after a number of meetings the proposal was rejected. A similar suggestion made early in 1634 met with the same fate. Thwarted in this way Charles I pressed on without the City, and in 1636 he established a 'New Incorporation' in the suburbs. It is true that the King had no serious intention of creating a political rival to the City and that his motives were largely social and financial, but the effects of his scheme were far-reaching nonetheless. The new body posed an immediate threat to the City and its freedom. Not only was it given the right to press freemen to submit to its regulations, but it also attempted to impose jurisdiction over certain areas to which the City itself laid strong claim. Disputes between the two rivals, ancient and *parvenu*, were inevitable, and a series of acrimonious exchanges took place. They were concluded only when the arrival of Civil War evidently brought an end to the life of the infant corporation. There the matter rested until the Restoration when the question was raised once more. Guildhall remained as implacable as ever and Common Council resolved *nem. con.* 'that they conceived the incorporating of the suburbs of London distinct from the City to be destructive to the interests and trade of the City . . .'[8] In the face of this intransigence the proposal met its last defeat and no more was heard of incorporating the suburbs.

Of course, the problem of London's extra-mural development remained. Immigrants continued to invade the settlements in the East End and south of the river, whilst the trickle of citizens leaving the square mile for more salubrious areas broadened into a stream. The consequence of these trends, multiplied many times, we see today: a depopulated City surrounded by sprawling and overflowing suburbs. It takes little imagination to realise the importance of the Corporation's decision in the 1630s, when it declined to accept responsibility for those living outside its walls. If it had done so, it would have undertaken the duties of the London County Council two hundred and fifty years before that body appeared; and in so doing it would have started a new and exhilarating chapter in its history. It would have been spared the rivalry of those authorities which at length had to be created for the government of the suburbs and it would have been protected from the attacks of the reformers in the democratic age. It is therefore scarcely surprising that the resolutions of the 1630s have been dubbed 'The Great Refusal'.[9]

What then were the reasons for this momentous self-denial? We may legitimately question whether the Guildhall officials could have envisaged the events of centuries to come, but it is clear that their decision was not lightly made. It entailed, after all, the possible creation of a rival corporation and the potential destruction of the City's trading privileges. The fact that these threats never materialised was entirely fortuitous, and the City could well have had cause to rue its 'refusal'. Logic in the apparent madness can be presumed, and it is to be found in the difficulty of governing the slum-ridden and unruly suburbs. The Aldermen found themselves already hard-pressed by their mounting civic duties, and they had no wish to devote

more time and money to the thankless task of trying to control the rack-
eteers, vagabonds, rogues and criminals who had congregated outside their
walls. The effort was likely to prove a profitless drain on the resources of
both the City and the Aldermen. So an essentially negative approach was
adopted. All care would be taken to impose the freedom on traders in the
suburbs and to prevent the establishment of a rival authority there, but no
administrative responsibility would be assumed.

This attitude is best illustrated in the important case of Southwark. Here
a series of royal charters gave the City extensive rights to certain manorial
lands and liberties south of London Bridge. Following the grant of the
entire 'Borough' in 1550, the City created a new ward ('Bridge Ward
Without') and installed an Alderman there. At first the Alderman seems to
have undertaken his duties with energy and purpose; this, at least, is
implied by the speed with which incumbents transferred (after an obligatory three years) to less demanding wards. But after a short while the office
degenerated into a sinecure. From the 1630s onwards the ward was simply
a resting-place to which senior Aldermen could 'retire'; it had neither
voters nor Common Councilmen. (Bridge Without is now amalgamated
with Bridge Ward proper, and the number of Aldermen is consequently
twenty-five not twenty-six.) The City had baulked at making effective provision for Southwark's government. In fact, it may be doubted whether the
City had ever seriously entertained the notion of accommodating its found-
ling in the family home. Even in 1550 it appears to have been more
concerned to exclude rival jurisdictions from the burgeoning suburb than
with extending its own authority.

So it was that in this atmosphere of caution and timidity expansion was
eschewed and the bewildering developments outside the gates ignored. It
was not long, of course, before the City and the Companies found themselves left behind by the economic advances and social changes taking
place around them. At first imperceptibly, and then with frightening speed,
the medieval corporations of the square mile were left high and dry by
'progress'. It is, therefore, to the seventeenth century that we must first
turn in our attempt to chart the decline – and the subsequent survival – of
the Corporation and its guilds.

A place that hath much advanced and is drawn dry
The first threat to the existence of the City took the unlikely form of
insolvency. For much of the seventeenth and eighteenth centuries the Corporation and the Companies lived in a state of financial embarrassment,
and the prospect of bankruptcy was a recurrent reality. The fact that
ancient and well-endowed corporations reached such a pass is striking
testimony to the efforts of man and God. Into the first category fall the
repeated demands of governments of all persuasions in the early seventeenth century. It would be tedious to catalogue the loans and contracts

which litter the City records of these years. Suffice it to say that James I, Charles I and Parliament in turn made the most unscrupulous claims on the personal and corporate wealth of the square mile. Even Clarendon, who characterised the City as 'the sink of the ill-humours of this kingdom', acknowledged that it 'was (by the Court) looked upon too much of late time as a common stock not easily to be exhausted, and as a body not to be grieved by ordinary acts of injustice'.[10] This verdict receives emphatic confirmation from a courtier's observation in 1640:[11]

As for my Aldermen, methinks he would not be much out that compared them to nuts, they must be cracked before one can have any good of them, and then too at first they appear dry and choky, but bring them to the press, they yield a great deal of fat oil.

How unfair then for the parliamentary puritans in the 1620s to lampoon Guildhall as 'Yield-all',[12] and how much more accurate the City's own version of affairs when it described itself in a submission to Parliament in 1643 as 'a place that hath much advanced and is drawn dry'.[13] The trans-actions were complex and the final balance-sheet will never be known, but the City undoubtedly was left considerably out of pocket.

The Corporation's difficulties were shared by the Companies, who were often obliged to contribute to the loans levied *via* Guildhall. Again the net outcome is hard to uncover and varied from Company to Company, but despite passing on some of the burden to individual members Companies found themselves saddled with irrecoverable debts. The expedients em-ployed, including the sale of plate and expensive borrowing, give credence to the repeated and plaintive pleas for repayment.

Concentration, however, on these controversial dealings should not be allowed to disguise the more fundamental problems attached to corporate finances in the square mile. After all, the demands from Government would not have been so crippling had not deep-seated difficulties already conspired to undermine the financial health of the Corporation and its Companies. The growing reluctance to take up the freedom meant that membership fees and trading fines could no longer be maintained at former levels, and the drift away from the square mile precluded the imposition of further burdens on those who remained. For the same reasons tenants had to be treated with circumspection, and there was no possibility of effecting substantial increases in rents. Income then was necessarily static; whilst expenditure, by contrast, could not be checked. The Companies found it particularly difficult to make worthwhile economies since they relied increasingly on their entertainments to attract new members (who could no longer be coerced by trading restrictions alone). The Corporation faced similar problems, but also possessed a dilemma peculiar to itself. It may have renounced any formal obligation to the capital as a whole, but the growth in population, trade and industry placed an increasing strain on the services adminstered at Guildhall. Outgoings rose as resources dwindled, and by 1649 crisis loomed large. The Interregnum was a propitious time for change, and a determined effort at reform was made. But for various reasons the schemes proved abortive, and during the early years of the Restoration the situation worsened rapidly. Expenditure stood at roughly twice the average income and liabilities far outstripped assets.

So vast an expense
Such was the situation in 1666. A compound of immediate demands and long-term difficulties made the City and the Companies insecure and vulnerable. Certainly the Corporation can scarcely be blamed for regarding the Fire – that 'most horrid, malicious, bloody flame' (as Pepys vilified it)[14] – as an unqualified calamity. City officials were acutely aware that they could not undertake the task of reconstruction without assistance. They were stating no more than the bald truth when they lamented that the City had 'no common stock, nor revenue, nor any capacity to raise within itself anything considerable towards so vast an expense'.[15]

The *cri de coeur* did not go unheeded and Parliament directed that certain dues on coals entering the Port should be devoted to the rebuilding. The initial provisions were far from adequate, but after some alteration of the statutes by Parliament and a dubious interpretation of them by the City, the coal dues eventually met the entire bill of £730,000. Nonetheless the City by no means emerged unscathed from the catastrophe. It may have been protected from the immediate effects, but it had still to cope with the longer-term consequences. It was one thing, for instance, to replace the charred and tottering buildings; it was quite another to fill them with people again. The speed with which the rebuilding took place is remarkable, but it did not prevent many traders from acquiring a taste for the unfettered life of the suburbs, or merchants from finding more attractive accommodation in the West End. To persuade such men to return to a City whose regulations were no longer obligatory and whose offices were expensive was no easy task. The City was only too aware of this reluctance, and in 1673 it conducted a census of its rehabilitated domain. This revealed a total of over 3,400 houses which had been rebuilt and remained empty. The situation was improved somewhat by means of a combination of compulsion and concession which encouraged some errant citizens to return, but this was no more than a temporary check on the exodus which continued its inexorable trend in later years.

There was one other way in which the City's already precarious position was undermined by the Fire. In order to encourage rebuilding tenants had to be granted long and generous leases. This had the effect of preventing any substantial increase in income from rents for the forseeable future. The City was thus denied one of the few means at its disposal of improving the revenue from its inflexible resources.

Of course, these same problems applied equally to the Companies, who relied on their property income to compensate for the dwindling returns from membership fees and craft controls. Such difficulties were made almost insuperable by the widespread destruction of the Companies' Halls. Forty-four of these precious and valuable structures were consumed by the flames, and no less than forty-one were rebuilt by their owners. This feat was only accomplished at a colossal cost to the Companies and their members. All kinds of desperate measures had to be used, including mortgages of plate, personal subscriptions and calls on the livery. Some Companies were even forced to relinquish property. The Merchant Taylors, for example, were obliged to raise £5,000 from the sale of lands in Lombard Street and Cornhill, which they had regarded, with understandable pride, 'as the richest jewel of their estate'.[16] Such expedients left a legacy of indebtedness from which succeeding generations could not easily escape.

Sell their lands?
This spectre of bankruptcy which haunted the corporations of the square mile was much more than a vague and intermittent possibility. In one case, and this the most important, it became an immediate and ugly reality. In the face of a mounting financial crisis the Corporation had felt it necessary to plunder certain trust monies which freemen had deposited in the Chamber for the use of their orphaned children. Retribution for this short-sighted decision was not slow to arrive. The debt to the orphans alone rose to some £750,000 and, shortly after the Glorious Revolution and despite a series of desperate expedients, the Corporation had to admit defeat. It appealed to Parliament for relief. This was a move attended by the deepest misgivings for it entailed the sacrifice of the City's cherished independence. The Corporation's future lay at the mercy of the politicians.

The worst was certainly expected, and extraordinary humiliations were contemplated. At one stage, for instance, it seemed likely that the City's finances would be placed in commission, with no more than a modest allowance for running costs. No wonder the Corporation expostulated vehemently against the proposal, and it must have been deeply relieved when the scheme was defeated in committee. On another occasion the City was even prepared to sell its entire rent-roll, except for those lands encumbered with charitable obligations. There were sceptics, of course, who would not accept the sincerity of the City's intentions. 'Sell their lands?', cried one fictitious orphan to another, 'they'd as soon sell their charter'.[17] But the pamphleteer was wrong. Detailed arrangements for raising an anticipated £70,000 were made, and the money was to be offered to Parliament as a token of good faith. A bill was prepared and placed before a committee of M.P.s. It was only then that the proposal foundered and calamity averted.

These bleak plans may have failed, but the problem of the Corporation's finances remained. For some time, in fact, it appeared that the conflicting pressures of the interested parties would produce a debilitating *impasse*. At length, however, a solution was found, and for this two factors seem to have been responsible. The first was the liberal use of bribes, or (as one observer dubbed them) 'wonder-working guineas'.[18] Some time later it was discovered that the Speaker, Sir John Trevor, had accepted a gift of one thousand guineas from the Corporation. He was expelled from the House, together with another M.P., John Hungerford, who as chairman of the committee dealing with the Orphans' affair, had been given a similar, though a much smaller, *douceur*. Then there was the case of the Marquess of Normanby whose preferential lease of a prime site in one of the City's estates was almost certainly connected with these same proceedings. Allied to bribery was political loyalty. The City was protected from the attacks of its creditors and enemies by the partisan affection of the Whig M.P.s. In the heady years which followed the overthrow of James II and his Tory tyranny the Whigs looked back with nostalgic gratitude to the City's opposition to the Stuart kings. This was a debt which they felt honour-bound to discharge. They did so by passing the Orphans' Act of 1694, which provided for the establishment of a fund from which interest payments could be made to holders of Orphans' stock. To this fund were allotted a number of fees and dues, as well as a substantial yearly sum from the City's own resources.

A hard bargain

This was certainly a settlement which allowed the City to escape from the disasters depicted above; but it by no means represented a guarantee of future solvency. For some years after 1694 the fund was not buoyant enough to meet its commitments; and the City itself found great difficulty in sustaining its annual charge. Until 1710 at least the measure fully deserved its later characterisation by a City Solicitor as 'a hard bargain'.[19] Then the regular growth in receipts from one of the fund's sources of revenue – the trusty coal dues – began to produce a healthy surplus. The City was shortly able to pay off not only the interest but some of the principal debts as well – much to the chagrin of the creditors, who came to regard the fund as a snug and secure investment. This, in fact, was a view shared by Parliament, which allowed the City to extend the life of the fund and use it as security for raising revenue to effect a number of expensive 'improvements' in the square mile.

But this is to leap too far ahead. The metamorphosis of the Orphans' fund from a hasty rescue operation to a gilt-edged stock did not take place until the 1760s. It is also important to recognise that the City's ordinary revenue was in no way affected by the Act of 1694, save that it was now burdened with an annual contribution to the fund. The millstone of the Orphans' debt had been removed, but the Chamber had still to solve its own perplexing and long-standing problems. For some time it was not at all clear that the struggle would be attended by success. The inflexibility of the

finances was such that officials could only suggest piecemeal and ineffectual reforms which would do little to improve matters. They can scarcely be
blamed for inviting proposals from outsiders, but they would certainly have
been foolish to have given serious attention to the crack-brained and
dangerous schemes which ensued. Fortunately they did not, though they
had to withstand much vilification from the unscrupulous and litigious
'improvers'. Instead they limped along with the aid of good husbandry and
minor changes, and waited for leases to lapse. A number did so in the
1710s, and others followed in the 1730s. The influx of entry fines which
resulted undoubtedly helped to postpone disaster and the introduction of
shorter terms ensured a more regular income in the future. But the prevailing slump in the London property market – in part a consequence of the
coincident expiration of so many post-Fire building leases – restricted
the demands the Corporation could make on its tenants. There was little
that could be done to prevent a recurrence of deficits, and in the 1740s
insolvency seemed closer than ever.

The threat was particularly disturbing because the Orphans' Act had
provided that an increase in the Corporation's contribution to the fund as
well as the cessation of a proportion of the coal dues should take effect
from 1750. This black prospect prompted the City once more to throw
itself on the mercy of Parliament. Once again it was political allegiance
which decided the issue. There were grumbles, it is true, from some peers,
but it only required the Duke of Newcastle to point to the City's loyalty
during the Forty-Five rebellion to quell all opposition and rally the Whig
faithful. The City's increased commitment was substantially reduced and
the coal dues maintained at their former level for another term.

With this assistance the City could face the future with equanimity;
bankruptcy had been averted. Prosperity, however, was still out of reach
and depended on a substantial leap in revenue from an extraneous source.
This, remarkably enough, is precisely what occurred in the years which
followed. The windfall came from an estate known as Conduit Mead,
which covered some twenty-seven acres in the Oxford Street and Regent
Street area. The land had been granted to the Corporation as part of a
'Royal Contract' in 1628 and for long it was considered important only as a
source of water. In 1666 it was leased to the Earl of Clarendon for no less
than ninety-nine years at a negligible rent, and in 1694 (as we have noted)
the Marquess of Normanby was given the best part of the site for a further
hundred years on the back of the earlier grant. There the land remained, in
legal limbo, until the early eighteenth century when the West End became
a fashionable place to live. The speculators descended on the estate and the
City had to watch helplessly as enormous profits were seized from the
development of its land. Of course, it looked forward eagerly to the expiration of the original lease in 1765, but as that day approached problems
arose. Would the absence of a building convenant in Clarendon's lease

prompt tenants to let their houses decay unless assured of renewal? How much could be demanded of future lessees in the light of the widespread depression of property prices? Faced by such anxieties the City adopted a policy of safety-first. It allowed existing tenants to renew their leases many years before the expiry date – a move which attracted colourful, though unjustified, charges of corruption. Worse still, it gave tenants the right to renew their leases *in perpetuity*. At first a limit of ninety-six years was placed on such renewals, but this clause was dropped in Common Council.

It is tempting to attribute this 'remarkable omission'[20] to a clerical over-sight of monumental proportions; but it is clear that the decision was born of careful deliberation, and it is entirely in keeping with the policy adopted in the City's other estates. Of course, the long-term consequences of the decision were calamitous. The City has been able to resume no more than a fraction of the original leases and there are many tenants today paying eighteenth-century prices for prestigious accommodation in one of the most coveted areas of the West End. The fact that the Property Act of 1925 converted perpetually-renewable leases into two thousand-year terms affords the City little comfort! But these developments should not be allowed to disguise the immediate benefits which accrued from the renew-als of the 1750s. After all, one of the reasons for offering such favourable, indeed over-favourable, terms was the hope that the imposition of heavy entry and renewal fines would help to extricate the City from its financial embarrassment. So it transpired. The finances were transformed, and the City was able to make its final escape from bankruptcy. It even proved possible to reclaim Normanby's lease of part of Conduit Mead for £24,000 (a suitably costly retribution). It was, then, with understandable flam-boyance that a Chamberlain told a finance committee in 1762 that a number of pending renewals would 'enable the City to do anything they may have occasion for'.[21] This, of course, was an exaggeration and deficits did not disappear entirely from the Chamber's accounts. But there was to be no repetition of the crises which had punctuated the preceding decades. The City's financial future, after a century-long struggle, was secure.

A similar, though less spectacular, tale of recovery can be told in the case of the Companies. Here we must distinguish between the experiences of the larger and smaller Companies. This divide corresponded closely to the traditional separation of the Great Twelve – who were accorded a place of special prestige in Guildhall affairs – from their lesser counterparts. The Twelve derived much of their revenue from their substantial rent-rolls, and they naturally found the post-Fire years difficult times. Dues from mem-bers offered little hope of worthwhile compensation, because few of the great Companies still maintained control over their crafts and because they could not afford to make men even more reluctant to undertake the already expensive offices by further increasing the fines. They were obliged to adopt instead a series of temporary measures – including (in the case of the Mercers) an annuity scheme of breath-taking incompetence – which enabled them to survive until their building leases began to expire. Then they could reap some benefit from the increase in property values which (after the mid eighteenth-century trough) assumed dramatic proportions as the nineteenth century approached. When this occurred the great Companies could afford to raise their fines and become exclusive, fashionable societies. Their future was assured.

On the other hand, the smaller Companies escaped from their dilemma by a different route. They could look forward to no resolution of their difficulties from their property returns, which were too meagre to offer lasting relief. Instead they turned to their members for help. The fines of these Companies were low enough to attract those who were interested only in securing a vote in Guildhall elections or participating in City life. An influx of freemen redemptioners or a call on the Livery could be invaluable in the fight against insolvency. How valuable may be judged from the assiduous assistance given to these market forces. The Chamberlain's officials were encouraged by gratuities to direct newly-admitted freemen towards certain enterprising Companies. Other Companies offered similar incentives to their own officers – a temptation which proved too much for the Musicians' clerk, whose profiteering appears to have led to his dismissal in 1770.

Still more Companies decided to revive their controls over trade. These smaller societies could still affect an interest in the health of their crafts, and they used this as the pretext for asserting an exclusive right to enlist all those working in their nominal trades. A spate of such regulations were issued by Common Council at this time. That these entailed no genuine concern for economic matters may be understood from the concurrent relaxation of the traditional restrictions on the number of apprentices as master might employ. A 'closed shop' could no longer be maintained; Companies were concerned only with their financial positions. In this task they were largely successful. After a long, and sometimes bitter, struggle for members most of the smaller Companies were able to weather the storm. The political and social attractions of Guildhall were usually sufficient to ensure a steady inflow of members. Only those Companies without Liveries were faced with grave difficulties, and even some of these were able to arouse enough support for a successful application to the Aldermen to remedy the deficiency. In these various ways the lesser Companies survived the problems of the decades which followed the Fire, and for the most part they were able to share the confidence of their larger brothers as the Age of Reform approached.

The pomp and grandeur of the most august city in the world changed face in a moment
We have now traced the course of the financial threats to the City's survi-

val. It remains to consider the menace from Crown and Parliament. Legislative and judicial action, after all, could overturn the most established privileges and liberties. This danger was obvious enough in the applications to Parliament in 1694 and 1748, as we have just noticed. In these cases, of course, the City was able to benefit from the favourable regard of a majority of the M.P.s; but there was always the possibility of a quite different reception. At the beginning of our period such antagonism was generally inspired by the City's unnerving independence of Government and its habitual association with the Opposition of the day. Later, of course, the pattern was reversed. The City's radicalism waned and its oligarchical privileges became the target of democratic wrath.

The chronicle begins with an exception which proves this rule. Amid the bustle and drama of the King-less Commonwealth (1649-53), the Rump Parliament, under pressure from the army, asked its 'Committee for Corporations' to consider 'how Corporations may be settled as may be suitable to, and agreeable with, the government of a Commonwealth and how their respective charters may be altered and renewed to be held from and under the authority of this Commonwealth'.[22] Livery Companies were amongst those obliged to submit their charters for inspection. This naturally caused great consternation. When the Grocers received their summons in December 1652 the Wardens were asked to act with caution, to try to release only a copy of the charter and to withhold the original 'unless peremptorily required'.[23] The situation was made still more delicate when members of the commonalty took their grievances to the Committee. The Assistants of the Founders' Company, for example, were accused of arbitrary misgovernment and forced to counter-petition with denunciations of their opponents' 'levelling minds and proud imperious wills';[24] while the Saddlers' Court was the subject of a sustained polemic against all 'combinations and factions' whether in 'Guildhalls, Corporations, fraternities, Common Councils, Assistants or committees . . .'[25] Nothing tangible, however, appears to have resulted from these exchanges. The Assistants procrastinated to good effect. In April 1653 Cromwell dissolved the Rump and the 'Committee for Corporations' was no more. But short-lived though it was, the episode made it clear that the Companies', and the City's, future depended on the politicians.

The next assault was instigated by Charles II as part of his attempt to secure the succession of his Roman Catholic brother, the future James II. To this policy the City was implacably opposed. Its Low Church and parliamentary zealots leant staunch and influential support to those who wished to exclude James from the throne. The campaign culminated in the triumphant acquittal of the leader of the exclusionist Whigs, the Earl of Shaftesbury, in November 1681, when a City jury returned a verdict of *ignoramus* to the bill (alleging high treason) before it. This was certainly no miscarriage of justice, for the charges were manifestly unsound; but the

King and his ministers were maddened by the rebuff. They decided to attack the source of the defiance – the Corporation's powers and privileges (which included the right to elect the Sheriffs who selected the London and Middlesex juries). In January 1682 the City was served with a writ of *Quo Warranto* to determine by what warrant it exercised its jurisdiction. Two breaches of the charter were alleged, but these were intended to do no more than give legal substance to what was essentially a political confrontation.

At this point it is important to emphasise the limits of Charles's intentions. He was concerned simply with the City's personnel, not with its administration. He sought to oust his opponents and use his supporters to control the selection of juries, the enforcement of law and order, and the conduct of elections. But, of course, this could only be done by revoking the City's charter, and this left the Corporation exposed and helpless. Had Charles lived longer, and James remained on the throne, it is difficult to see how the City could have emerged unscathed from its charterless ordeal.

The first move in this perilous game was delayed by the ministers' attempt to arrange a voluntary surrender of the charter. After a successful, if brazen, intervention in the Shrieval election of 1682, the Government hoped that (with the Tory Sheriffs vigorously enforcing the laws against the Dissenters) the Common Council elections of December would produce a majority in favour of compliance. They did not, and the King decided to proceed with the threatened legal action. The case was heard in King's Bench between February and June 1683, but for all the learned expertise and erudition mustered on behalf of the defendants, the result was never in doubt. A pliable Bench gave solemn judgement in favour of the Crown. At once the City made a formal request for royal pardon and received an intimation that the verdict would not be 'entered' (and so be given force of law) if the King were allowed to exercise an extensive control over the City's elections and appointments. At first it was decided to accept this ultimatum, but after taking counsel's advice Common Council resolved by 103 votes to 85 not to surrender the charter. This was thought to have the important legal effect of limiting the King's authority to that of a *custos* (or guardianship) over the City's government, which left the City's lands, offices and liberties intact.

But such comfort must have seemed rather hypothetical in the face of stark reality. For all practical purposes the City had lost its precious independence and become (in the words of a contemporary) no more than 'a large village'.[26] Royal ministers now held sway at Guildhall; or, as Judge Jeffreys sardonically remarked, 'The King of England is likewise King of London'.[27] In fact, it was the notorious Jeffreys himself who became the virtual governor of the City. Alderman Sir James Smith reported that:[28]

... he had the title of Lord Mayor, but my Lord Chief Justice Jeffreys

usurped that power, that they had no access to the King, nor any message or direction from him as to any business but by the lord, that whatever was well done in the City was attributed to his influence and contrivance, that himself and the Aldermen were looked upon as his instruments, and that upon all occasions his lordship used them contemptibly and not according to the dignity of the City.

Outside observers put the affair into a more general context. John Evelyn, for example, noted the removal of 'eight of the richest and prime Aldermen' as well as the installation of the Lord Mayor and Sheriffs as mere *'custodes* at the King's pleasure', and commented that 'the pomp and grandeur of the most august city in the world changed face in a moment, and gave much occasion of discourse, and thoughts of heart, what all this would end in . . .'[29]

There was good cause for apprehension, because the 'generality of the corporations' were 'poor decayed places, and so not able as the City of London to contest their charters'. Once the City had been defeated, as Lord Halifax predicted, 'every other corporation would be obliged to truckle'.[30] So they were. Of the 240 other corporations served or threatened with writs of *Quo Warranto* not one defended its case to final judgement. These hapless victims included, naturally enough, the Livery Companies, who received their writs in April 1684. The legal panic which ensued varied from Company to Company, but in all cases the result was the same: a supplication for royal pardon, surrender of the charter and the acceptance of a regrant. Some Companies could not refrain from accompanying their surrenders with expressions of obsequious humility. The Merchant Taylors, for example, resolved to present an address of thanks to the King for his 'gracious' charter. When Jeffreys attended on the Company to dissuade it from setting such an embarrassing precedent for its fellows to follow, the Assistants decided to present him with plate worth £100 (to which each of them was to contribute) in view of 'the great and extraordinary honour his lordship had been pleased to confer on the court that day'.[31] The Drapers went almost as far by inviting the Chief Justice to a Stewards' dinner and making him a guest at all such future occasions. Their only apparent excuse was that Jeffreys was a tenant and honorary freeman of the Company.

A partial explanation for the sycophancy may be found in the Companies' relief when they came to examine their regranted charters. The changes, even in the charters enrolled after Charles's death, were few in number and adhered faithfully to the King's earlier assurance that he was concerned only to 'regulate the governing part' of the Companies and to 'have in himself a moving power of any officer' for what was termed 'misgovernment'.[32] In this Charles was doubtless sincere, and in his dealings with both the City and the Companies he kept his interference within bounds. But such a policy was pregnant with dangers for the well-being of the City, especially when administered by Charles's less confident successor. James, it is true, saw the City only as a political institution and concentrated on securing the return of loyal M.P.s through the selection of suitable Aldermen and Liverymen. Wholesale purges followed the tergiversations in his attempts to win parliamentary approval for the repeal of the penal laws against Catholics.

But 'what all this would end in' nobody could tell. The government of the City by royal commission might well have become a permanent convenience if it had continued for many years. Had it done so, the already precarious position of the Corporation and the Companies would surely have been irrevocably undermined. As it was, the imminence of invasion prompted James hastily to restore the *status quo ante* of 1683 by royal proclamation in October 1688. By this time, of course, his cause was lost and in the aftermath of the Revolution the City was assured (as we have seen) of affectionate consideration from Parliament. Legislation was secured in May 1690 which declared the *Quo Warranto* judgement 'illegal and arbitrary' and provided that henceforward the City's charter should never be forfeited for any cause whatsoever.

Within this accolade from Parliament, the Corporation, and the Companies, could proceed with confidence. They could also take comfort from what proved to be the most enduring legacy of the Revolution: an acute sense of the sanctity of the constitution. For the following century and a half Governments would tamper with chartered privileges at their peril. A howl of parliamentary outrage accompanied any attempt, however well-intentioned, to interfere with corporations. The only such assault with which the City had to deal came in 1725, when Sir Robert Walpole tried to settle the constitutional wrangles which had bedevilled the City's elections in the early part of the century. Even these sensible and largely equitable provisions met with a storm of protest and it was only after a severe mauling in both the press and the Commons that an amended bill reached the statute book. Even then the Act was not allowed to remain intact, for in 1746 its most notorious clause, 'confirming' the Aldermen's right to veto proceedings in Common Council, was repealed. With that the interference with the City's charters ceased. Even the Corporation's fierce opposition to successive Administrations did not lead to any curtailment of its liberties and privileges. Ministers considered it more expedient to withstand the personal onslaughts of City demagogues, such as William Beckford and John Wilkes, and the bombardment of surly addresses from Guildhall, than to incur the wrath of backbench M.P.s for attacking the foremost Corporation in the land.

Such sentiments, of course, did not last for ever, and as the decades passed by, and self-confidence ebbed, men began to question the principles on which the sacred consitution was based. The excesses of the French

Revolution, it is true, retarded the trend, but the impetus was soon regained in the early nineteenth century. Catholic emancipation in 1829 marked the first major victory for the forces of change, and parliamentary reform followed in 1832. Then the radicals turned their attentions towards the municipal corporations and once again, after a century-and-a-half of calm, the City and the Livery Companies had cause to fear for their safety.

CHAPTER II

MUNICIPAL CORPORATIONS REFORM (1835–53)

The non-elective Municipal Corporations
The 1830s were years of self-criticism and change. As many contemporaries had feared (or hoped), the successful assaults on the vaunted constitution in 1829 and 1832 seemed to open the floodgates of reform. With a Whig ministry at the helm for almost the entire decade, few aspects of government or society escaped critical attention. Under pressure from the intellectuals and radicals and acutely aware of an increasingly vociferous and organized 'public opinion', the politicians scrutinised the poor law, public health, factory conditions, prisons, the police, the legal system, and even the established church. Nor was local government overlooked. The anomalies and iniquities of parish vestries had long been a cause of disquiet or anger and in 1831 provision was made for ratepayer elections. The corporations were the next obvious target, particularly after the Reform Act of 1832. The new parliamentary franchise for towns comprehended the £10 householders and it was plainly absurd for such men to be allowed to vote for their M.P.s and yet prevented from choosing their borough officials. Logic was reinforced by politics. The reformers were determined to ensure that the gains of 1832 were not jeopardised by the electoral influence which many corporations were still able to exercise in the Tory interest. In more general terms, the corporations represented a challenge and an affront to democratic sensibilities. As Sidney and Beatrice Webb put it in their celebrated study of *English Local Government:*[1]

> . . . *it was almost irrelevant (to the radicals) to inquire whether Municipal Corporations provided an efficient or an inefficient Magistracy; whether they spent their own funds for the public good or embezzled trust estates for their personal ends; whether, in short, they constituted a good or a bad government of the Boroughs. By their very nature, the non-elective Municipal Corporations were in the same political category as Hereditary Monarchy, the House of Lords, the Established Church, a Restricted Suffrage, and Life Office.*

It was, in fact, in February 1833, during the first session of the reformed and overwhelmingly Whiggish Parliament, that Lord Grey's ministry proposed the establishment of a Select Committee to consider the question of the municipal corporations. The deputed M.P.s decided that the investigation could only be satisfactorily conducted by a Royal Commission, and this was duly appointed in July to 'inquire into the existing state of the

Municipal Corporations in England and Wales and to collect information respecting the defects in their constitution'.[2] The Government appointed as commissioners a group of clever young men, mostly barristers, who were known to be committed to reform. Their chairman was an M.P., John Blackburne, but their driving force was the formidable Joseph Parkes who acted as secretary to the Commission and effectively controlled its proceedings. Parkes was resolved to effect what he sometimes chose to term 'the dissolution of the Municipal Monasteries'[3] and to shatter the Toryism of the old corporations. When the Commissioners began to report their findings towards the end of 1834 Parkes had little difficulty in framing (with Blackburne) a powerful indictment of corporate affairs, and by March 1835 the Commission's conclusions calling for a 'thorough reform'[4] were complete. The report was warmly received by Lord Melbourne's administration, perhaps because it was seen as the basis for legislation which would please the radicals on whom the Whigs relied to protect a shaky position in Parliament. A draft statute was swiftly prepared (with Parkes's assistance) and presented to the House in June 1835. It provided for an entirely new and uniform style of town government based on regular elections and a ratepayer franchise. Aldermen were abolished and freemen doomed.

No less than 183 corporations were earmarked for this democratic overhaul but, strange to tell, the City of London was not among them. The reasons for this remarkable omission have to be retraced to 1833 when the Commission began its work. Parkes was anxious to proceed with some speed and to avoid the quicksands of historical research in borough archives. He saw no particular virtue in making a complete survey of all the country's corporations or cataloguing all their defects. Once most of the boroughs had been reformed on democratic principles the others would follow. For the most part his scheme worked admirably, but there were some problems. One difficulty concerned the City and its Livery Companies whose voluminous records, quite apart from their power and influence, represented a daunting obstacle to the impatient reformers. Another problem took a human form in the person of Sir Francis Palgrave. Although he possessed impeccable Whig credentials by virtue of his contacts with Holland House (where the heritage of Charles James Fox was reverently preserved by his nephew) and despite his commitment to corporation reform (as evidenced by a pamphlet on the subject in 1833), Palgrave was regarded with suspicion by his colleagues on the Commission. His expertise as an historian (which resulted in a succession of scholarly works on the Middle Ages, as well as his appointment as Deputy Keeper of the Public Records), made it unlikely that he would proceed as quickly as the other less academic and less conscientious Commissioners.

Parkes, therefore, decided on a disarmingly simple strategem – setting Palgrave to work on London. In a letter of September 1835 Parkes made mention of the difficulties posed by this 'damned antiquary', this ' "Holland Householder" who want to move centuries retrospectively', and described the solution: 'we have put him in a trap, and restricted his voracity and set him on the City records'.[5] The device worked perfectly. When Parkes and Blackburne came to prepare their report Palgrave was still hard at work. They ignored his protests at their hasty and partisan conclusions and published their findings with no more than occasional references to London, explaining a little disingenuously that 'the importance of that city is so great and its institutions are so peculiar, that it will be necessary to make them the subject of a special Supplementary Report.'[6]

Two months later when the Commission's conclusions (and its proceedings) came before Parliament 'London' had still to appear. On 1 June Blackburne told M.P.s that 'the report for London was not yet quite ready'.[7] A few days later still the Government presented its proposals to the House and, not surprisingly, the City was not included. According to *Hansard*, Lord John Russell (Melbourne's Home Secretary) 'was understood to say' that a separate measure would be introduced for London.[8] Parliament then proceeded to debate the bill. Little opposition was aroused in the Commons where the leader of the Tories, Sir Robert Peel, accepted the need for reform, but in the Lords a bitter assault was mounted by the die-hards, who brought their House to the brink of a constitutional crisis. At length, however, they rested content with a number of amendments and the Act was allowed to pass in September 1835. Despite the changes (which included a qualified reprieve for both Aldermen and freemen), the Act could be regarded as a considerable triumph for the reformers, since it facilitated the establishment of elective and accountable government in a large number of the country's towns.

A London Corporation bill

Whether London would be added to the list remained to be seen. Parkes certainly appears to have imagined that it would be. In a letter of January 1836 he looked forward to a successful appeal to the country after a dissolution at Easter 'when the Lords maul or reject the Irish Corporation bill or a London Corporation bill'.[9]

Of course, the nature, indeed the appearance of that bill depended on the outcome of Palgrave's still unfinished deliberations. There were, in fact, three other Commissioners who worked on London: J.E. Drinkwater Bethune, a future legislator and educationalist in India; T.F. Ellis, lawyer and close friend of the historian Macaulay; and D. Jardine, the author of various works on law and history. They may well have made their own independent contributions to the report (Drinkwater Bethune, for instance, is known to have studied the Companies's finances), but nothing controverts the impression that Palgrave was *primus inter pares*. It can certainly be shown that it was Palgrave who did most of the preparatory research. As he told Sir Robert Peel in November 1844 (among some

'Observations on the mode of collecting documentary evidence for the ease of governments'):[10]

Previously to the viva voce *examination, he employed himself in collecting the documentary evidence relating to the City and the Companies, arranging the information under the heads of the several officers, courts, etc., as they now stand in the Report, Aldermen, Common Council, etc. And the writer had the satisfaction of being informed by the other Commissioners that this mode of proceeding expedited and facilitated the enquiry: and that it also drew their attention to many points which would otherwise have been overlooked.*

No less than ten volumes of transcripts survive to this day in the Guildhall Library as testimony to Palgrave's conscientious, or perhaps (as Parkes viewed it) his antiquarian zeal. The pages are peppered with Palgrave's annotations. One example will give an idea of his care. When the learned transcription of an ancient text broke off abruptly Palgrave added: 'not legible from the folding up of the charter, but can be completed from the Tower if required. F.P.'[11] His shelves were full of tracts and treatises on the City and the Companies, as the posthumous sale of his magnificent library revealed. The catalogue mentions not only draft versions of the London report but also a daunting mass of background material.

Armed with this knowledge the Commissioners descended on the City during the years 1833-5 and proceeded with their investigation. The Corporation rendered them all reasonable assistance, allowing all save its law officers to give evidence, providing full answers to enquiries, and granting unrestricted access to its records. The Companies were somewhat less accommodating: many protested at the 'illegality' of the Commission, some offered only a carefully edited account of their corporate (especially their financial) affairs, and a few refused to co-operate at all. The Merchant Taylors took courage from a legal opinion (which compared the investigation unfavourably with the *Quo Warrantos* of Charles II) and promised 'unqualified resistance',[12] while the Ironmongers withheld information, at least for a time, on the less than convincing grounds that they had 'no Municipal duties to perform' nor enjoyed 'any Municipal privileges'.[13] In such cases, and others, the Commissioners listened to the views of outsiders. Disgruntled citizens queued up with their complaints. Two members of the reticent Plaisterers' Company spoke of the studied omission of certain Liverymen from the feast on Lord Mayor's day each year, while a Fishmonger claimed that when his grandfather had expressed a wish to purchase the Company's freedom, 'he was at first told that he might as well expect to get into Heaven as into the Fishmongers' Company, if he was not a Dissenter. When, however, it was found that he was a Quaker, he was admitted.'[14] Ironically, it was not an outsider, but the Town Clerk, who furnished one of the most damning instances of Company misconduct. This concerned a tradesman:[15]

> ... *who, having been admitted a Wheelwright, set up shop as a cheesemonger; and as in this occupation he sold butter and eggs, he was summoned by the Poulterers to become a freeman of their Company, with which he complied: he then added sucking pigs and small pork to his stock, and the Butchers required him to become a member of their Company, and he complied also with this summons: he then having left off business was summoned by the Poulterers to take their Livery, which he refused, he appearing on the City's books as a citizen and Wheelwright. An action was commenced against him, but upon the suggestion of the Court of Aldermen the action was discontinued.*

This passage was cited time and again in attacks on the City in the following years.

The Commissioners finished their work and completed a draft report by December 1835, but extensive revisions (whose character is unclear) were necessary before the final text appeared in 1837. As might have been expected from a team headed by Sir Francis Palgrave, it was a judicious and comprehensive document. There was no uncritical condemnation. In fact, the Commissioners had been impressed by the quality of City government. Some years later Palgrave told a former Lord Mayor, the staunchly Conservative Sir Peter Laurie: 'I do not wish to pay the Corporation any needless compliments, but when we were employed upon the Commission, we all of us, men of very different opinions and views, agreed in thinking that your affairs were managed with great good sense and discretion.'[16] This conclusion that the City was 'much above the average of any local administration with which we were acquainted' explains the note of caution which runs throughout the report. At the outset it was stressed that they felt 'bound to point out whatever appears to us to produce evil effects in the Corporation, even in cases where it may appear doubtful whether the evil can be removed without introducing another or destroying some advantage.' They did not consider it within their province 'to estimate the result which, in the event of alteration, might be produced by conflicting advantages and disadvantages.'[17] Nonetheless, if chary of prescribing a cure, they had no hesitation in supplying a full and unflinching diagnosis of the patient's ailments. The corruption of the City's body politic was laid bare: the freedom was anachronistic, the Livery franchise absurd, the Court of Aldermen oligarchic, and the ward-system inequitable. As for the Companies, the vast majority of them were at best mere charitable trusts and at worst self-regarding clubs. Between the lines the message was clear. Parliament was expected to act; some kind of reform was essential. At one point the inference was made explicit. After commenting on the 'very liberal' salaries and allowances paid to Corporation officials, the Commissioners refrained from suggesting reductions on the grounds that the question was one which could 'safely be left to a civic legislature fairly chosen'.[18]

Our corrupt, rotting, robbing, infamous Corporation of London

In the light of such evidence it comes as a surprise to discover that the report was greeted with a resounding silence at Westminster. The contrast between the controversy aroused by the Commission's main report in 1835 and the neglect of its supplement in 1837 could not be more marked. How can it be explained? It would certainly be wrong to imagine that the radicals lost interest in London once a general measure of corporate reform had been achieved. One man at least kept the question very much alive.

Francis Place was a Charing Cross tailor who devoted much of his life to radical reform. He was maddened by the inequalities and anomalies of City government and was determined that they should not escape the attentions of the Corporation Commissioners. In November 1833, at the beginning of the enquiry, he wrote to Parkes about 'our corrupt, rotting, robbing, infamous Corporation of London' and about the Court of Aldermen, 'old men – no, old women, gossiping, guzzling, drinking, cheating, old chandlers-shop women, elected for life.' He outlined his proposals for a new, democratic City: twenty-one Common Councilmen elected by ballot for twenty-one wards; small committees drawing payments for service and under strict supervision; seven Aldermen receiving a small salary; and a Mayor with an allowance of no more than £1,000 a year ('and call him Lord if you like it' but 'no shows, no parade, no feasts, no fooleries'). In the preceding year he had made his celebrated denunciation of 'the whole of the City government' as 'a burlesque on the human understanding more contemptible than the most paltry farce played in a booth at Bartholomew's Fair' . . . and had told a Common Councillor friend that he regarded the Corporation's property as 'public property applicable only to public uses'.[19] (The once-famous Bartholomew Fair at Smithfield had long been recognized as a degenerate nuisance. Between 1830 and 1850, by means of a 'beneficent and disinterested extortion', the Corporation drove the showmen out and put the Fair quietly to sleep.)

When the opportunity for reform arrived Place acted with eager determination. The entry in his diary for December 1835 reads: 'Occupied in reading and commenting on Municipal Corporation Commissioners' inquiry respecting London, with a view to obtaining further particulars, and framing a bill for the City of London'; and for January 1836: 'Continue reading, inquiring, and writing in conjunction with Joseph Fletcher on London Corporation and the report of the Commissioners (the proofs only)'.[20] Fletcher was an ideal partner in the enterprise. He had served as Parkes's assistant secretary on the Commission and later contributed a series of detailed and animated papers on London's social and administrative problems to the Statistical Society. He and Place proceeded so well with their work that early in January Parkes (as noted earlier) was contemplating an Easter dissolution over 'a London Corporation bill'.

Yet in the event nothing transpired. Despite the agitation of the radicals and despite the publication of Palgrave's critical, if cautious, report, the Government allowed the issue to sink without trace. This may perhaps be attributed in part to an absence of those political pressures which had forced the ministry's hand in 1835. The need to appease the radicals does not seem to have been so acute. Melbourne could allow his easy-going lethargy full rein. In the case of the City he may well have felt what he expressed on a similar occasion when a reform of the Duchy of Cornwall was proposed: 'Whenever you meddle with these ancient rights and jurisdictions it appears to me that for the sake of remedying comparatively insignificant abuses you create new ones and always produce considerable discontent.'[21] Melbourne must have been fortified in his complacent resolve by the reflection that there was no public clamour for change. The City and its Companies may have offended the sensibilities of the radicals and the rational good sense of the Commissioners, but they could not be said to have attracted a general odium. The number of complaints about misconduct raised in 1833–5 was less than impressive and in many instances there was more than a hint of personal pique. They certainly constituted no undeniable case for reform. In fact, the City of London was generally excepted from the blackest condemnations of the radicals. Place may have blustered with colourful vitriol, but others looked with favour on the Corporation's independent politics based on a wide franchise. Indeed the Commissioners of 1835 supported their case for open and elective government by reference to the efficiency of the City Corporation!

One further consideration may well have encouraged Melbourne and his advisers to leave well alone. Palgrave's report made it plain that there was no easy solution to the problem. To follow the course adopted elsewhere, and enlarge the City's powers so as to embrace the entire metropolis, might be justifiable in theory, but in practice could be thought to involve a change of such magnitude as to convert what was otherwise 'only a practical difficulty into an objection of principle'. On the other hand to divide up the rest of the capital into separate communities would, 'in getting rid of an anomaly, tend to multiply and perpetuate an evil'.[22] These were portentous remarks, heavy with significance for the future. Another harbinger of future arguments emerged when the Commissioners addressed themselves to the delicate question of power. If a huge new authority was to be created for London as a whole, who was to control it? As the report put it in its measured phrases, peculiar problems attended 'a town which is the seat of the legislature and supreme executive power of the state, with respect to the proper division of municipal authority between the officers of Government and a municipal body which might be established in the metropolis . . .'[23] These were difficulties which were to perplex successive generations of politicians and it is little wonder that Melbourne decided not to grasp the nettle.

Evils and abuses, rights and privileges

So it was that, for a variety of reasons, the City emerged unscathed from the dangers of 1837. For the immediate future the Corporation and the Companies were safe, but in the longer term there was little cause for complacency. The writing was on the wall. The Corporation would have to reform itself if it were to avoid further inquisitorial visitations from Westminster. Indeed radicals claimed, though without explicit evidence, that Russell had threatened Guildhall with a separate measure of municipal reform should it fail to put its house in order. Considerable significance, therefore, attaches to the changes in the City's constitution and administration which followed the perilous events of 1837.

The square mile was certainly not devoid of liberal instincts. For some while before 1833 there had been a vociferous 'out-of-doors' campaign for reform of both the City Corporation and the Livery Companies; and when the Royal Commission was appointed there were offers of 'every possible' assistance and revelations of 'evils and abuses' to be remedied.[24] These views were also represented in Common Council where a sizeable majority acknowledged at least the expediency of co-operating with the Commission and proposing changes before the Government or Parliament did it for them. Unfortunately, the plans invariably involved curtailing the oligarchic privileges of the Upper Court and the Aldermen reacted with almost manic determination. They managed not only to prevent the City from speaking with one voice, but through the malicious offices of successive Lord Mayors, especially the cantankerous and eccentric Henry Winchester, they undermined almost all Common Council's independent initiatives.

Only a few piecemeal changes were effected. In 1835 came the first in a series of reductions in the size of the freedom fine, while at the same time Common Council resolved that it was no longer necessary for a freeman of the City to belong to a Company. In 1840 the Common Councilmen were reduced in number from 240 to 206 and allocated to the wards in a more equitable manner. Then in 1843 there began a determined attempt to widen the franchise. There were many in the Corporation who wanted to allow rate-paying non-freemen to vote for ward and civic officials, as well as to place some restrictions on the Livery franchise in Common Hall. Proposals of this kind were raised on a number of occasions during the following years, but they encountered serious difficulties. There were objections, predictably enough, from the Aldermen, partly no doubt because of their incorrigible conservatism, though professedly because they doubted whether Common Council had the legal capacity to make changes of this nature (hence the removal of the Company qualification in 1835 by resolution rather than Act of Common Council). The alternative, of course, was to apply to Parliament for legislation to implement the desired reforms (and in particular to repeal the Act of 1725 which had made final and comprehensive provision for City elections). But this too presented dangers, as Councilmen as well as Aldermen were only too well aware. On the one hand, the Corporation's powers would no longer be based on mere longevity or prescription but on the much more vulnerable footing of statute law. As Palgrave and other experts told the Corporation, this would 'destroy the very foundation of your privileges.' On the other hand, an application to Parliament gave the City's enemies a golden opportunity to wreak their democratic havoc. Palgrave pointed out that 'when a bill is once launched in Parliament it will be quite out of your power. Parliament will legislate as it thinks best, and I can see no reason whatever why it should stop short at reducing the City to the shadow of existence of all the other municipal corporations in the Kingdom.'[25]

These were powerful arguments which were overcome only when the City realised that its foundations were crumbling. Unless the restrictions of the anachronistic freedom were removed, it was argued, the Corporation would become an introspective and clubbish clique, an easy target for the reformers. Yet when its diffidence was finally put to one side, the City had to contend with fierce opposition from the Livery Companies who were alarmed at the assault on their voting privileges. Their strident hostility contrived to defeat a series of proposals for introducing a ratepaying electorate in this and the following decade. All the Corporation was able to achieve took the modest form of an Act of Parliament in 1849 which re-defined the franchise for ward elections and imposed the same qualification (occupying property rated at £10 p.a. or more) on candidates for Common Council.

Some observers no doubt recognized the delicacy of the City's position, but others were not so kind. One critic regarded the Guildhall liberals as merely the honourable exceptions to the general rule of corrupt self-interest: 'The salt of the Corporation, they preserve it from external signs of the corruption which, as they know with sorrow, is all the while consuming its vitals. Were it not for their vivifying presence, the rotten carcass would before now have been consigned to quicklime, amidst a universal holding of noses'.[26] Most critics did not even go this far and dismissed the reforms as grudging and superficial concessions, exacted rather than granted. This, of course, was a perfectly plausible interpretation of changes designed to bring an ancient institution up-to-date. 'Increasing the size of the constituency' could easily be denounced as meddlesome and malicious, especially since it entailed (after the failure of the campaign for a ratepaying franchise) an attempt to enforce the freedom not only on retailers but on wholesalers too. The critics' views gained further credence from the graceless, stumbling way in which the changes were made; and there were always diehards prepared to do their best to confirm the impression. In a tract published in 1858 with the uncompromising title, *The Corporation of London: its Rights and Privileges*, Alderman W.F. Allen described the revenue lost by the reduction of the freedom fine in 1835 and thereafter as a sacrifice 'offered on the altar of public opinion'.[27]

The Corporation of London and Municipal Reform
So despite the reforms there was plenty of scope for crusaders and busy-bodies, and after a brief interlude which followed the set-back of 1837 the agitation continued. Not that all the Corporation's assailants were intent on its destruction. Some of the most influential calls for change came from Joshua Toulmin Smith, who wanted to foster the spirit of local self-government in the metropolis. In the City this meant championing the rights of mere 'inhabitants' against the exclusive privileges of the freemen. This romantic vision, buttressed by industrious historical research and given practical effect by canvassing in the ward-motes of Farringdon With-out, may have seemed mischievous to the most obdurate zealots at Guild-hall, but others would have recognized that Smith was trying to do no more than the City had been struggling to achieve in recent years, *viz*. to revive the square mile as a community. They may also have glimpsed in Smith's utopia a means of salvation for the future. A metropolis divided into a number of local self-governing communities would probably find a home at its centre for the City Corporation.

Less comfort was afforded by the attacks which appeared in the *Westminster Review*, the erstwhile mouthpiece of the Utilitarians, now in the 1840s in the hands of W.E. Hickson, who had retired from his boot- and shoe-making in Smithfield to devote himself to more cerebral matters. A long-time campaigner for corporate reform, Hickson was infuriated by the parlous state of London's government. In 1843 he was presented with an opportunity to put his views into print. On 2 March Lord Brougham, the former Whig Lord Chancellor who had done so much to defend the Municipal Corporations bill from the assaults of his fellow peers in 1835, made a resounding attack on the City Corporation's conduct, particularly its administration of justice. The evidence of extravagance and favouritism was such (in Brougham's opinion) as to make it 'utterly impossible that many months should elapse before municipal reform shall be extended to the City of London.'[28] He moved that an address be presented to the Queen asking her to consider Palgrave's report with a view to legislation. It was only with some difficulty that the current Lord Chancellor, Lyndhurst (Brougham's chief antagonist in 1835), persuaded his rival to withdraw his motion, on the understanding that if Brougham were to incorporate his proposals in a bill the measure would meet with the Government's 'most attentive consideration'. There the matter rested. Brougham ignored the

BROUGHAM AND THE CIVIC GIANTS.

"A few nights ago he made dreadful sparring with his old civic friends, the Guildhall giants."—*Vide page* 116.

offer, and though he took up his theme on at least three subsequent occasions (at the Mansion House itself later in 1843 and in the Lords again in 1845 and 1846), nothing came of his oratory. It would be wrong, however, to imagine that his words had no impact at all. Irrevocably estranged from the Whig party and intermittently insane he may have been in this the twilight of his life, but he was still capable of causing a stir outside Parliament.

It was almost certainly the interest generated by Brougham's initial speech which prompted Hickson, two months later, to contribute an article on 'The Corporation of London and Municipal Reform' to his *Review*. With both statistics and eloquence at his disposal Hickson presented a powerful case for change. Utility, not surprisingly, was the yardstick. It was time, he declared, to consider 'for what good object (if any) (the Corporation) exists; whether, should its utility be proved, its usefulness cannot be increased; or, if this be impracticable, whether the Corporation might not be dispensed with altogether, and be replaced by institutions less expensive, perhaps, yet more comprehensive in their functions, and better deserving the confidence of the public'.[29] A highlight of the ensuing analysis occurred during a withering assault on the Corporation's self-importance. A fictional dialogue on the subject of the Lord Mayor has a peculiarly modern flavour. Puzzled foreigners were said to ask:[30]

'Who is the Lord Mayor? I read in your journals that he lately gave a dinner at which nearly all the Cabinet Ministers were present, with the Governor of the Bank of England, and the Chairman of the East India Company; is it that he is a man so remarkable for talent or superior intelligence that your great men are proud of his society?'
'Why — not exactly'.
'Is it from respect to the interests of commerce? The Lord Mayor is perhaps the first of your London merchants?'
'There are greater'.
'Is it then because of his position; and certainly it is a noble one — the representative of London — the metropolis of the world; a population of two millions'.
'Of whom not more than one fifteenth portion are under his control'.
'But did I not read somewhere that there were more than a hundred parishes in the City?'
'All of them united not so large as the one parish of Marylebone, the vestry of which has more power over the church, the poor, and the ordinary business of local government than all the officers of the London Corporation! The respect of which you speak is paid only to a dream of the past, and to custom, the chains of which bind even a strong mind, till they are broken by a stronger'.
'And this chief of a subordinate department, who invites our ambassador to dine; whose accession to office, as I have heard, is honoured by a state

procession; whose expenses for any one year must exceed the revenues of a
German prince — this Lord Mayor — '
'Is only the Alderman in rotation, the worthy representative of perhaps
eighty resident freemen in the Ward of Bridge'.

To this last remark is attached a footnote disclaiming any reference to the present Lord Mayor, who happened to represent the relatively populous ward of Aldgate; but elsewhere Hickson's charges were not hypothetical and they provoked a thoroughly human response. Charles Pearson was a former Common Councilman who had instigated or supported many of the liberal reforms of earlier years. (One of his achievements had been the removal of the words on the Monument which attributed the Fire to Roman Catholic 'frenzy'.) Now as City Solicitor he stood accused of pocketing lavish allowances and conniving at the mismanagement around him. He was stung into retaliation and on three December days at the London Tavern he conducted his own and (to a lesser extent) the Corporation's defence. Among an audience said (by Pearson) to have been three or four hundred strong, sat Hickson, mutely suffering (as he put it) 'the punishment of listening to a personal philippic of twelve hours' duration'.[31] In his published version of proceedings Pearson claimed a complete vindication, but it was a somewhat brittle triumph. Pearson's personal integrity was not really in question for, as acquaintances pointed out, Hickson was no more thinking of the Solicitor personally than the Turkish huckster thought of Mohammed when calling out 'in the name of the Prophet, figs'.[32] Hickson's criticisms of the system tended to be lost in the self-vindication. Nor did Pearson's point that the Corporation had done much to improve itself in recent years strike at the heart of the issue. The City might not be a wholly reprehensible institution but was it the best form of local government?

The apparently dumbfounded reviewer soon recovered his voice. Two more papers on the subject of 'City Administration' appeared in the *Westminster Review* for 1844 and 1845. They were followed by William Carpenter's *The Corporation of London as it is and as it should be* (1847), which was designed as 'a sort of text book for Corporation reformers'. His work owed much to Hickson, though the tone was more aggressive. His application of the test of utility serves as an example: 'It is not that the Corporation is of less utility than it might be – it is not that it is of no perceptible utility at all; it is, that it does positive mischief – that it is an ascertained nuisance; and that, therefore, it would be really better that it should be altogether swept away, than remain as it at present is'.[33] There is no need to follow the rest of the argument through its compound of polemic and detail, but there may be some point in rescuing one nugget of gold from the dross. Carpenter managed to unearth the following comment on the City's ceremonial from none other than Charles Pearson back in 1834:[34]

The time has arrived when the civic exhibitions, with the Mayor as chief performer, can no longer be tolerated. I have, in disguise, mixed with the attendant crowd on a Lord Mayor's Day, and I declare that the whole parade is the subject of the most contemptuous sneering, even amongst children; and the apprentices, instead of being moved, as in the days of Whittington, with the spirit of competition and glory, at seeing the gilt coach, laugh aloud, as it trundles along. This scorn and contempt are the result of the attempt to call back people to the recollections of their childhood. This is no time for puerilities. Pantomime has been driven even from its proper sphere, and surely the pantomime and clownish displays of civic barbarisms can no longer be cherished.

Such journalism may not have been very inspired but it did serve to keep the issue of London's government alive. This was most important because the City's best friend was anonymity. It was not well equipped to defend itself in the cold and logical terms of utility, and any controversy, however contrived, or spurious, which obliged it do so was a grave embarrassment.

This was true, not only of attacks in the press, but even more so of the periodic interventions of Government in metropolitan administration. On a number of occasions ministers felt it necessary to make provision for the needs of London's ever-growing population and each time the question of the Corporation's anomalous position was raised. Indeed the City went out of its way to attract attention by opposing all attempts to encroach on its privileged status. In 1839 an effort was made to amalgamate the City's police with Sir Robert Peel's newly established metropolitan force. Joseph Fletcher's remark that 'the proposal aroused into action every means of influence which the Corporation at large, and every class of it, possessed, to avert what they considered a fatal blow at its very existence' was an exaggeration, but a pardonable one.[35] The campaign included a petition to the Commons, an address to the Crown and nationwide lobbying. Melbourne relented and the City's police were left untouched. A similar exemption was secured in 1847–8 when Lord Morpeth and Edwin Chadwick wanted to include the City in their Public Health legislation. Ruthlessly exploiting the prevailing neurosis about 'centralization', the Corporation's supporters ransacked their minds for suitable battle-cries. One Alderman declared that 'if there is not a firm and determined stand made against the measure, our rights and privileges will be lost' and a Common Councilman was reported as describing the bill as 'one of the most atrocious measures that had ever been introduced into Parliament'.[36] Hysteria of this kind, though largely successful in this instance (for the City retained its own, albeit reconstituted, Commission of Sewers) was a two-edged weapon. It might intimidate some opponents, but it hardened the resolve of others. Still more importantly it clouded the vision. All interference, no matter how innocuous, was opposed with bitter determination; and this

THE DIRTY LONDON ALDERMAN.

What ! cry when I 'd wash you ! not wish to be clean !
There go, and be dirty—as always you 've been ;
It 's not worth my while to begin a dispute :
I 'll not take the trouble to wash such a brute.

So, so ! I have hurt you. 'Tis useless to cry,
'Twill only wash down all the dirt from your eye ;
But let kind Nurse MORPETH at once interfere—
You 'll be a good Alderman, won't you, my dear ?

lack of discrimination almost had disastrous consequences. For it seems to have been the Corporation's prolonged resistance to the removal of the live cattle market from Smithfield and its long-drawn-out suit in Chancery over the soil and bed of the Thames which finally snapped the Government's patience. These at any rate were the reasons which the City advanced for the appearance of the next serious threat to its existence – the Royal Commission of 1853–4.

CHAPTER III

LONDON CORPORATION REFORM (1853–54)

Defenders of the Filth

The political world of the 1850s was in the process of realignment. The traditional allegiances of Whig and Tory, which could be retraced in one form or another to Stuart times, no longer held sway. The Whigs, always an uneasy alliance of aristocrats, intellectuals and radicals, had lost direction and cohesion after the reforming successes of the 1830s; whilst the Tories, only recently reunited after the disasters of 1829–32, had been split asunder by Sir Robert Peel's repeal of the sacred Corn Laws in 1846. It took time for a Liberal party to emerge out of a union of Whigs, Peelites and 'liberals' and for the Tories to fashion a credible alternative under their new leaders Derby and Disraeli. For much of the middle part of the century the country had to endure a succession of short-lived alliances dominated as much by personality as by party or policy. The Aberdeen Coalition of 1852–5 was a typical example. Nominally under the control of the Earl of Aberdeen and politically a mixture of Whigs, Radicals and Peelites, its precarious existence depended almost entirely on the personal conduct of the two great 'Liberals' of the day, Lord Palmerston and Lord John Russell.

The City too watched the behaviour of the two men with close interest. Both were in positions of peculiar importance for the Corporation. Palmerston was Home Secretary, from whose ministry any plans to reform the Corporation were likely to emanate; while the former Prime Minister Russell was one of the City's own M.P.s and was expected to protect his constituency from the malevolent designs of his colleagues. How surprising, then, it was that on 8 April 1853, in reply to a question from Sir Benjamin Hall, Russell told the House of Commons that the Government intended shortly to appoint a Royal Commission to consider the reform of the Corporation with a view to legislation. Of course it is not impossible that Russell was merely acting as a spokesman for the cabinet. Nor is it inconceivable that the plans did indeed originate with the Home Office where, for a man who longed to be in charge of foreign affairs, Palmerston showed a surprising zest for the mundane details of prison reform, factory conditions, smoke abatement and public health. There are, however, one or two snippets of evidence which hint at Russell's personal responsibility for the announcement.

A fortnight before the first meeting of the Commission later in 1853 one of the Commissioners wrote to a friend that 'the principal object seems to be to throw the municipal franchise open to a larger number of persons'.[1]

This is a curious comment which is difficult to explain unless it is remembered that in these same months Russell was trying, once again, to widen the parliamentary franchise. One of his chief concerns was those boroughs where the electorate was small and unrepresentative. Could he have seen the call for an enquiry into the Corporation as an opportunity for effecting a reform which would complement his more fundamental scheme for an extension of the parliamentary franchise? The other reason for associating Russell with the proposal lies in the choice of Commissioners. One selection was unremarkable enough – Sir John Patteson, a King's Bench judge who had been forced to retire through ill-health the previous year. The other two are more interesting. Sir George Cornewall Lewis and Henry Labouchere were both out-of-office Whigs who had, and were to retain, close links with Russell. Lewis had held junior posts under Russell before losing his seat in 1852 and was destined to hold the highest offices in subsequent Liberal ministries, while Labouchere had already served with Russell at the Board of Trade. One further point can be mustered in favour of the hypothesis. If Russell was indeed contemplating a widening of the City's franchise, in no sense could he be regarded as betraying the trust of his constituents. The Corporation itself had been pressing for the abolition of the freedom qualification and the creation of a ratepaying electorate. As recently as March 1852 it had secured a second reading for a bill which would (or so it was claimed) have increased the number of voters in both wards and Common Hall from 6,000 or 7,000 to 20,000 and which drew support even from some rather mystified radicals whose only complaint was that the bill should have been a public not a private measure. Perhaps Russell agreed and decided that it was time for the Government to assist.

It is tempting to take this speculation one final stage further and ask whether Russell might not have seen the merits of a well-judged, modest reform of the Corporation which would thwart more radical attacks. For even if he had not been personally committed to reform elsewhere he could not have denied that the pressure for change in the City was becoming well-nigh irresistible. *The Times*, in particular, was maintaining a continual barrage of invective and sarcasm against Guildhall. It had been especially infuriated by the Corporation's obscurantist dilatoriness over sanitary improvements. With cholera raging in the capital and the newly appointed medical officer of health, Dr. John Simon, chafing at the bit, a so-called 'dirty party' (led by H. Lowman Taylor, 'Defender of the Filth')[2] had done its wilful best to keep public health administration as cheap and ineffective as possible. *The Times* had done everything it could to facilitate Simon's eventual triumph over his reactionary employers and bring his difficulties to the attention of the public. The memory of that struggle was still fresh in mind in 1854 and the Thunderer's anger unassuaged.

In a sense the paper was preaching to the converted. Quite apart from its notoriously close relations with Aberdeen and his Government (at least

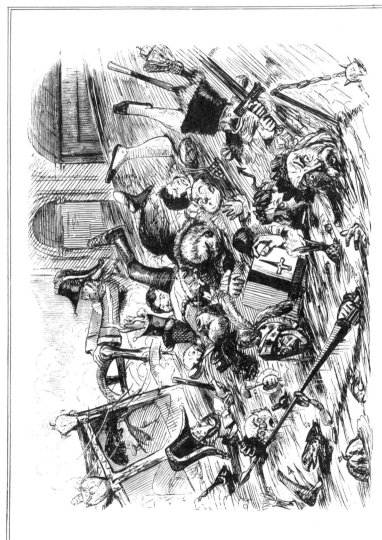

FLUSHING THE GREAT CITY SEWERS.

until the Crimean War broke out), it was urging a proposition whose truth was fast becoming self-evident – that something had to be done about the health of the metropolis. Even if M.P.s could remain unmoved by the ravages of King Cholera, they had only to take breath to realise that the Thames had become a festering sewer. The 'pestilential stench'[3] which afflicted Parliament each summer gave an immediacy to the problem of London's government which no amount of statistics, even mortality statistics could do. So when the City showed such obstinacy over the Government's claim to the soil and bed of the Thames and the clamour for the removal of Smithfield Market, politicians must have been incensed and ministers cannot have failed to take note. In this sense, therefore, City officials were right; it probably *was* these comparatively minor matters which brought the visitation of a Royal Commission down upon their heads. They failed, however, to recognize, or at least acknowledge, that there existed a more general demand for fundamental change in the structure of metropolitan government.

A Parliament of Shopkeepers
Such seems to have been the background, both personal and political, to Russell's statement in the Commons. Two months later, in June 1853, the Commissioners were appointed to inquire into the Corporation and 'consider whether any measures may be necessary to make better provision for the (City's) future government'.[4] What qualities did they bring to their task? Once again it is difficult to say much about Patteson. He remains lost behind a fog of platitudinous tributes to his legal acumen. His colleagues are less elusive. Labouchere was described by an opponent, the young Lord Stanley (son of the Conservative leader, the Earl of Derby), as 'an amiable, honest, and not incompetent Whig of the old school: speaks seldom when not in office, and suffers from bad health'.[5] About Lewis Stanley offered an equally frank assessment 'a sensible, laborious student, better versed in the affairs of the last century than of the present'.[6] Lack of evidence makes it difficult to assess the truth of the former verdict, but the latter was certainly not far from the mark. Stanley may have perversely underestimated Lewis's political ability, but he did highlight a most salient characteristic – Lewis's love for scholarship and letters. When he was displaced from his constituency in 1852 he became editor of the *Edinburgh Review* and contributed a number of his own articles to it. He also used the hiatus in his public career to pursue his work on ancient history and political theory. The correspondence published shortly after his death shows a man, if not quite living in the past, then at least taking periodic refuge in it.

The Commission, therefore, was composed of men who, though assuredly of the highest intellectual calibre and considerable weight, were likely to err on the side of caution – as *The Times* was later to put it, men

THE CITY NARCISSUS;

Or, The Alderman Enamoured of his Dirty Appearance.

'whose prejudices and opinions were far more likely to run in favour of maintaining than of destroying constituted authority'.[7] They held their first meeting towards the end of October and began to hear witnesses on 1 November. At the outset they decided to omit from their deliberations the Livery Companies, which they rather glibly asserted were 'not constituent portions of the Corporation'.[8] This relieved them of many of the difficulties which had confronted the Commissioners of 1837 to whose painstaking historical research they were anyway heavily indebted. But the task in 1853–4 was in one respect more difficult than that of 1833–7. Public opinion was now fully aroused. Critics were ready to come forward in droves to make their allegations and offer their panaceas. The Commissioners decided to hear these outsiders first and to hear the Corporation in its own defence later.

Four months of intensive questioning produced a mass of evidence which is now entombed in a fat and pristine volume. There is little point in cataloguing the repeated 'revelations' of corruption in City elections (most frequently in Common Hall) and the denunciations of the iniquities of the tolls, fees and fines which the Corporation imposed on its freemen and inhabitants. Some general themes, however, did emerge from the otherwise tendentious accusations, and these deserve consideration. First there was a widespread conviction that the Corporation had become separated from the world of commerce and finance. This view was most forcefully expressed by James Acland, founder of the newly established 'City of London Municipal Reform Association'. For the representative of some 1,200 disgruntled citizens, chiefly shopkeepers unable to pay the fees for the freedom, he made a somewhat unfortunate assertion on the question of the City's commercial connections:[9]

My impression is this. The corporators of London, Common Councilmen and Aldermen, are of the shopkeeping class; and entertaining the conviction, as I do, that counter transactions in small coins have no tendency to give a man an enlarged view, or habits of viewing in a large sense any interests which he may be delegated to promote, such men, I believe, have not the power of promoting them, and therefore they are not qualified for the offices they fill.

This may have been tactless and over-stated but it did not lack a kernel of truth. One did not have to agree that the Corporation was an 'anticommerical body' or that Common Council was 'a Parliament of shopkeepers'[10] to concede that men of the highest rank in finance and commerce were conspicuously absent from the City's councils. J.G. Hubbard (later Baron Addington), for example, was a merchant of twenty-five years standing in the City and Governor of the Bank of England, yet he professed to 'know nothing about the Corporation. I am not intimately acquainted with any member of the Corporation, except one Alderman, who has served the office of Lord Mayor and is also a member of the direction of the Bank of England, Alderman (William) Thompson. Besides him, I hardly know a single member of the Corporation'. Since he had never resided in the square mile 'I have not been situated as to learn anything' of the City's constitution, 'nor has anything occurred to interest me in it'.[11] Men like Hubbard refused to spare time to take part in the Corporation's life and squirmed at the prospect of submitting themselves to the civic ceremonial.

Another reiterated point concerned the way in which the City had contrived to escape the attentions of the legislators on successive occasions in the recent past. The Commissioners were treated to a welter of charges and countercharges concerning the elaborate and expensive opposition mounted to the attempts to merge the City with the Metropolitan police force in 1839 and, more recently, to remove Smithfield Market. There were heated debates too about manoeuvres to secure favourable coverage of the Corporation's views in the newspapers. Support for a short-lived *The Citizen* (owned and edited by Toulmin Smith) was followed by regular purchases of those issues of established papers which came up to requirements. For *The Times* at least this was paying for 'praise by the column'.[12] Needless to say *The Times* was not a recipient of these favours. Indeed the largesse was partly designed to counteract The Thunderer's unremitting hostility.

Help thyself, and Heaven will help thee

The City's opportunity to reply to these allegations came in the New Year. It had long since resolved to give the Commission all possible assistance and this 'co-operation' now took the form of a powerful defence of the Corporation's past conduct and present position. It began with a long statement read to the Commissioners on 11 January 1854 which attempted to refute some of the more serious charges. The Corporation was particularly anxious to set the record straight on the reimposition of the freedom, which was explained to have been the only means of extending the City electorate once the Livery Companies had defeated all attempts to introduce a ratepaying franchise. This and other expositions made the statement a powerful document; but the next stage in the defence was more powerful still.

The performance of the City's officials had always impressed commissioners of enquiry, as at least one reformer ruefully acknowledged. At the time of the first Commission, William Williams, formerly M.P. for Coventry and now for Lambeth, had already acquired some knowledge of the City's accounts during his auditorship in 1830 (and he joined Common Council shortly afterwards to gain more information). Yet when he and others presented their findings to Palgrave and his colleagues in 1833–4, 'the Commissioners made very light indeed of our evidence; and they were entirely led away by the evidence of the City officers, who knew everything and could put the best face upon everything'. The Corporation had invariably appointed clever men to its highest offices and had 'maintained the present state of things in my opinion a good deal from that circumstance. Whenever any inquiry takes place, those officers show great ability and adroitness'.[13]

This was certainly the case again in 1854. The Town Clerk (Merewether), Chamberlain (Key), Recorder (Wortley) and Solicitor (Charles Pearson) all acquitted themselves with assurance and expertise. Even Benjamin Scott, for long Chief Clerk in the Chamberlain's office, recently disappointed in his hopes for the Chamberlaincy itself in a controversial election and soon to spend four years in commercial practice before finally securing his coveted goal, stood up well to persistent interrogation.

It was, in truth, a relatively easy task to explain the Corporation's failure to effect a thorough self-reformation and its consequent need to maintain anachronistic regulations. The officers had more difficulty in refuting the charge that the City had used improper means to orchestrate public opinion and ward off legislative interference. The Remembrancer (Tyrrell), who dealt with parliamentary business, was obliged to reveal that £2,750 (in addition to the 'usual' legal charges of £3,169) had been spent in opposing the Smithfield Market bill. He was also required to comment on an ex-Common Councilman's account of the manoeuvres used to defeat the Police bill of 1839:[14]

. . . the Minister of the day, Lord Melbourne, brought in a bill to unite the City police to the Metropolitan police; it was objected to by the Corporation. They petitioned the House of Commons. They saw the Minister was determined. They then addressed the Crown, and a gracious answer was given; but they understood its nature. The Minister was still determined, and they then acted on the French maxim, 'Help thyself, and Heaven will help thee'. They immediately fixed their Town Clerk in New Palace Yard; they gave him a large body of assistants, and instructed him to communicate with every corporation in the United Kingdom. The consequence was, by the influence of those country corporations, the Minister found that his support fell like a rope of sand. He gave up his measure . . .

Tyrell thought the description 'overcharged' but did not attempt to deny its basic veracity.

A similar uneasiness characterised the attempts to confront the claim that the Corporation was being treated with disdain by the business community and was fast becoming the preserve of a clique of retailers. Some tried to deny the proposition outright and presented a mixture of statistics and eulogistic biographies to prove their case. Others however felt it necessary to explain the phenomenon. Town Clerk Merewether, for example, conceded that 'it did appear to me, when I first came into the City, an extraordinary thing that persons of great property, making large fortunes in the City, should live there, go to Temple Bar, shake the dust off their feet, and have no more to do with the City'.[15] On approaching several of the more important bankers he found that they professed to be principally afraid of nomination as Sheriff. Merewether assured them that recent abuses of the 'fining-off' system would not recur. He urged them to take up the freedom before it was enforced upon them, and they appeared ready to do so. The Corporation, however, had second thoughts about enforcing its bye-laws and Merewether felt himself unable to continue his solicitation. So ended his personal campaign to woo the financiers. The final word on the subject came from a Common Councilman who decided that Macaulay had struck at the heart of the matter. London's 'municipal honours and duties are abandoned to men who, though useful and highly respectable, seldom belong to the princely commercial houses of which the names are renowned throughout the world':[16]

The City is no longer regarded by the wealthiest traders with that attachment that every man naturally feels for his home. It is no longer associated in their minds with domestic affections and endearments. The fireside, the nursery, the social table, the quiet bed are not there. Lombard Street and Thread-needle Street are merely places where men toil and accumulate.

This account of argument and counter-argument might convey the impression that witnesses were myopically concerned only to denigrate the Corporation. This was not the case. Observers were well aware that the debate could no longer be confined to the constitution or the conduct of the City. Broader, metropolitan issues were at stake. When John Dillon, chairman of the committee of freemen-reformers which had presented its views to the first Commission, cast his mind back to the 1830s he admitted that:[17]

At that time I certainly took more interest than I have done since in the subject, as many of the grievances of which we then complained have been remedied. Besides that, I look at the subject now from a different point of view. Some very large and important questions have since arisen; the question of police and various sanitary questions have extended the enquiry; and if you were now to make the existing Corporation of the City of London as perfect as man could make it, you would be compelled to extend it beyond the present area, and beyond the present limits of the City of London.

The Commissioners agreed and frequently asked witnesses for their opinions on the future for London's government. They realised that their

Report on the Corporation would be worthless if it failed to take the metropolis into consideration.

This gigantic anomaly
The Commissioners finished hearing evidence on 23 February and spent the next two months drawing up their conclusions. What sort of an impression had they formed of the City Corporation? This can only be inferred from their final, composite statement, but we do possess the views of one of them at an early stage of the enquiry when the critics were in full cry. On 1 December 1853 Lewis wrote to his friend Sir Edmund Head (who was shortly to become Governor-General of Canada) that:[18]

It is evident to me that the City have continued their old system just a little too long, that public opinion among the great body of the community has got ahead of them, and that when the exposure has arrived they find themselves with scarcely a friend out of their own ranks. They are like Louis Philippe when the day of adversity and trial is come: they have nothing to look back upon but a long course of selfish and sordid conduct, and there are no acts which enlist any public sympathy in their favour.

Whether this emphatic judgement was modified over the following weeks or whether Lewis had to make concessions to his colleagues is difficult to say, but when the report arrived late in April it certainly did not fulfil the prophecies of doom and destruction widely canvassed in the press. The close attention given to the issue in the papers (partly, thought Lewis, for want of other news during the autumn parliamentary recess) had indeed aroused apocalyptic expectations:

This gigantic anomaly, the Corporation of London, is said, at length, to totter to its fall. A Royal Commission is even now consulting of its agony; sanguine prophets tell us it cannot survive the year; the last Lord Mayor's Show has been given; the stage coach is bespoke by Madame Tussaud; Gog and Magog doing duty as humble firewood, will frown no more over turtle and champagne.

So began the first part of 'The Decline and Fall of the Corporation of London' in *Fraser's Magazine* for January 1854.[19] Six months and six intalments later, with the conclusions of the Commissioners before him, the embarrassed author was doing his subtle best to explain his earlier prediction and justify his title, but with no great success.

For the truth was that the Commissioners' Report represented yet another reprieve for the City Corporation. It is true that wholesale changes were proposed for the City's ancient constitution. The Lord Mayor, for example, was to be elected from Common Councilmen or men qualified to be such, in order that men of 'commercial eminence' might be eligible and 'a greater degree of sympathy between the higher class of merchants of London and the Corporation' be thereby established.[20] Aldermen were to be subject to periodic re-election, their Court abolished and its functions transferred to Common Council. The wards were to be reduced in number to between twelve and sixteen and their area, population and representation (one Alderman and only five Councilmen) made as equal as possible. Ward elections were to be thrown open to all £10 ratepayers and Common Hall elections to cease.

These were indeed radical proposals which must have caused considerable consternation at Guildhall. Only the ratepaying franchise in the wards had figured in the Corporation's own plans for reform. Further shocks were provided by those provisions which dealt with more public matters. The Corporation may have welcomed the decision to remove the restrictions on trade imposed through the freedom and street tolls, and it may even have been prepared to accept the transfer of its control of the Conservancy of the Thames to a public body (only one of whose places was reserved for the City), but it viewed with indignation the renewed threat to the independence of its police force, with dismay the removal of its compulsory powers over the metage of produce (notably corn) brought into the Port of London (a prescriptive right which it regarded as part of its personal property), and with positive anger the loss of those coal dues on which its capacity to raise the vast sums needed to 'improve' the square mile depended.

Yet these changes, fundamental as they were, did at least leave the Corporation intact. Altered, even undermined, it may have been, but it lived on. The proposals were the price to be paid for salvation. This became abundantly clear at the end of the Report when the Commissioners addressed themselves to the question of London's future government. They were confronted with three familiar courses of action. The first was to abolish the Corporation altogether. This they rejected with little fuss. Indeed they went out of their way to state that:

... *although we have found much which in our judgement calls for amendment, yet we have discovered nothing which can affect injuriously the honour and integrity of the officers to whom the affairs of this great Corporation have been confided.*

And they went on to hope that the proposed changes in the City's constitution 'will place it on a more solid and enlarged basis; and that the Corporation will continue, under an amended system, to possess abundant means, not only for purposes of public usefulness, but also for the exercise of a decent hospitality and splendour'.[21] The second possibility was to make the City Corporation responsible for the whole of London. This was rejected on two grounds:[22]

WHY COALS ARE DEAR.

[PUNCH. No. 644.

. . . if an attempt was made to give a municipal organization to the entire metropolis, by a wider extension of the present boundaries of the City, the utility of the present Corporation, as an institution suited to its present limited area, would be destroyed; while, at the same time, a municipal administration of an excessive magnitude, and therefore ill adapted to the wants of the other parts of the metropolis, would be created.

The third and chosen course was predictable enough. The external boundaries of the City were to be left untouched and the rest of the capital divided into seven municipal districts (to coincide with the existing parliamentary boroughs of Finsbury, Marylebone, Tower Hamlets, Westminster, Lambeth, Southwark and Greenwich). These new councils, together with the City, would send representatives to a Metropolitan Board of Works which would superintend those 'public improvements' which London's ever-growing population (now estimated at 2.5 million) so badly needed.

Big Ben

Shortly before he signed the Report Lewis told Head that he thought the plan for 'dividing the entire metropolis into municipalities' would be 'attended with important results, if it is ever carried into effect'.[23] He was right to be cautious. Britain had just drifted into the Crimean War. For the rest of the year the Government, not to mention the jingoistic public, were engrossed in the grim heroics of Balaclava, Inkerman and the siege of Sebastopol. By comparison the Report on London presented a less than irresistible claim for attention. Not that ministers had forgotten entirely about the question. We know, for instance, that Palmerston, as Home Secretary, asked for the opinion of at least one expert, Lord Fortescue, former chairman of the Metropolitan Commission of Sewers, at this time; and the public was treated to a printed version of his views in May 1854. But even the most ardent reformer can hardly have expected a rapid response to the Commissioners' mass of evidence and far-reaching proposals. And by the time the Coalition collapsed at the end of January 1855 nothing had been done.

It was left to Palmerston's ministry of 1855–8 (in which Lewis, as Chancellor of the Exchequer, and Labouchere, as Secretary of State for the Colonies, both served) to grasp the nettle. On 6 March 1855 Labouchere asked the Home Secretary about the fate of the Report he had helped to compose. Sir George Grey replied that a bill based on the Commissioners' recommendations was in preparation, but that it was thought best for the House to consider first the bills which had been introduced by Sir Benjamin Hall for the whole metropolitan area. 'He hoped, however, to be able to bring in a bill for the reform of the Corporation in the course of the present session'.[24]

After considerable debate the plans for the metropolis bore fruit, though in a rather desiccated form. Instead of seven municipal councils the Metropolis Local Management Act introduced no less than thirty-eight local units – a curious mixture of revamped vestries and new district boards. These bodies, and the City too, were to send delegates to a Metropolitan Board of Works which was given vague supervisory powers over buildings, streets and sewers. The creator of this hamstrung, yet still highly suspect, forerunner of the L.C.C. was Sir Benjamin Hall (later Lord Llanover), M.P. for Marylebone. Now he is less reverently remembered by the nickname of the great bell installed in the clock tower of the rebuilt Houses of Parliament – 'Big Ben'.

These discussions tended to divert attention from the City, but on 19 June Sir John Shelley, the member for Westminster, enquired about the proposed Corporation bill. Grey replied that as far as its nature was concerned it was founded largely on the Report's suggestions though there were modifications on points of detail. He regretted, however, that the press of other business before the House made it unwise to introduce the bill, as he had hoped, in the present session, but he would do so early in the next. 'That, he thought, was the best course to ensure its passing'.[25]

A NEW CHIME FOR BOW BELLS.

DON'T TURN AGAIN, WHITTINGTON;
DON'T BE LORD MAYOR OF LONDON.

CHAPTER IV

THE LONDON CORPORATION BILLS (1854–63)

The April Fool's bill
On 1 April 1856 the long-awaited bill for the reform of the City of London finally transpired. In moving the first reading Grey went out of his way to show that the Government bore no ill-will towards the Corporation:[1]

On the contrary, we are sensible that from its great antiquity – from its connection with the metropolis of this country — from its historical associations — and from the services it has at various periods rendered to the cause of civil and religious liberty and of constitutional government, the City of London is entitled to every respect and consideration. The object of the present bill . . . is not in any degree to diminish the importance nor to impair the dignity of the Corporation, but by amending defects in its constitution and in the administration of its affairs, and by bringing it more into harmony with the spirit of recent municipal legislation, to increase its usefulness, to enhance its influence and efficiency, and to render it better adapted to fulfil all the legitimate purposes of its existence.

It is easy to dismiss these sentiments as parliamentary humbug and critics were not slow to throw these words back in Grey's face in the course of the ensuing rumpus; but they do seem to reflect a genuine spirit of consideration and care. The Commissioners' careful recommendations were scrupulously followed, as Grey had promised the previous year. And on two points the 'modifications' entailed compromises of some importance. In the first place, the coal dues were not to be transferred to the Board of Works but allowed to expire over some years and not until existing charges on them had been met. Secondly, and more significantly, there was to be no amalgamation of the City with the Metropolitan police – a cause, as we have seen, of unholy rows still fresh in memory.

In due course M.P.s would decide whether these were signs of good faith or mere tactical concessions. In the meantime the extra-parliamentary struggle would begin. Ominous rumbles were heard as soon as Grey sat down. Sir James Duke, the member for the City, corrected with icy politeness one or two points in the Home Secretary's speech and asked when the second reading could be expected. He hoped that the Corporation would have ample time to 'consider' the bill, a point which also exercised his colleague J. Masterman. The reformers also had their say, with ex-Common Councilman Williams offering an old citizen's thanks to the minister 'for having attended to the excellent suggestions of the Commissioners'.[2] After these harbingers of the coming storm, Grey fixed the second reading for the 21st of the same month. The bill was then read for the first time.

The focus of attention now switched to Guildhall. With what kind of opposition would the bill be confronted? For only an overwhelming show of hostility would make the ministers pause. Time was not really a problem. Three weeks was scarcely a generous allowance, but past experience ensured that the City's battery of courts and committees would work with speed and efficiency. It was rather a question of the degree of unanimity. The Aldermen, Common Councilmen and freemen would undoubtedly stand firm, but how would the Liverymen react? After all, relations between the Corporation and the Companies were less than harmonious. Common Council's persistent attempts to dismantle the freedom regulations and replace the Livery franchise with a ratepaying one had struck at the Companies' very foundations, and (as we have seen) met with determined and successful opposition. There was a very real danger that the Liverymen would leave the Corporation to face its fate alone. This was the road to mutual disaster, as Sir Francis Palgrave recognized in his letter to Alderman Sir Peter Laurie:[3]

I am, of course, fully aware that, legally speaking, the City and the Companies are, as corporations, independent of each other; yet in the opinion of the world you are identified; and although the City is not a penny the richer for the funds of the Companies, still, in the judgement of the public, you have the benefit of their opulence and respectability. During the inquiry I recollect hearing some of the Company officers say that they did not care for the City; and I could only feel that this unseasonable disunity of parties, who, in fact, form a federation, could only expose them to the common enemy.

As it transpired, the Liverymen did unite with their confederates in the Corporation. They had only to look at the clauses of the bill to realise that they could not stand aloof. Not only did Grey intend to implement the Corporation's longstanding proposals for unrestricted trade and a ratepaying ward electorate, but also to abolish the Livery franchise in Common Hall. How would those Companies who lacked prestige and wealth attract new members now? Some had little choice but to oppose the bill. Not that all did so; some followed the advice of a Warden of the Stationers (who themselves rejected the call for support), as expressed in a letter to *The Times*: 'the City Companies will find it much safer to let the Corporation undergo its sifting and reformation without interfering in the question . . .'[4] But twenty-nine out of sixty-nine, from the Mercers to the Spectacle Makers, decided to petition against the bill. When these were complemented by 2,130 signatures to a general Livery petition it could fairly be claimed that the Livery was aroused and the City united.

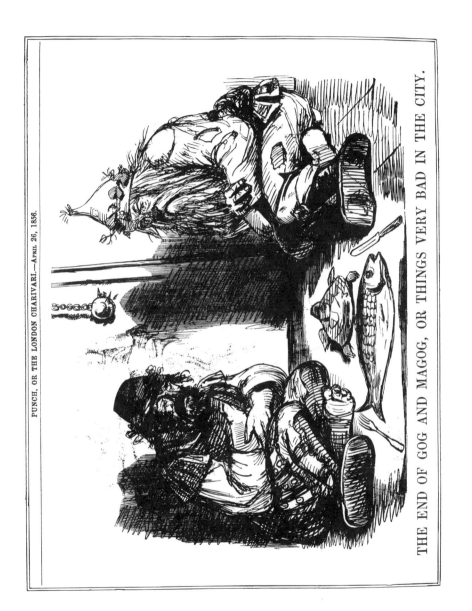

THE END OF GOG AND MAGOG, OR THINGS VERY BAD IN THE CITY.

The moderation of the border plunderer

The campaign began on 11 April with a special Court of Common Council. The mood of the meeting was soon apparent from the enthusiastic response to the speech of H.W. Vallance who denounced the proposed legislation as 'a bill of pains and penalties' and pronounced the abolition of the coal dues an assault on property rights. He was warmly supported by Deputy Pewtress who stressed the Corporation's recent reforms and Alderman Sidney who argued that the extension of the constituency, as embodied in the City's own bill of 1852, did all that was required. Parliament was told then, as the Government should be now, that 'after extending the municipality to every person interested in its good government, the Corporation should be left to manage their own affairs. (Loud cheers)'.[5] Motions urging that opposition to the bill be less than total or confined to certain clauses were lost by overwhelming margins. Instead resolutions proposed by Vallance were carried with acclamation. As published a day or two later (and subsequently presented to Parliament), these constituted little less than a declaration of war. There was a reckless absurdity about the assertions: 'the honours, privileges and properties of corporations ought to be as inviolable and secure under the protection of the law as the rights of peasant or peer, or even of the Crown itself'.[6] Reason and commonsense had departed the field.

Feverish irrationality also prevailed at a meeting of Common Hall on the 15th. Vallance's part was played on this occasion by J.C. Lawrence, son of an Alderman and soon to become an Alderman himself. Lawrence tore into this 'April fool's bill' with all the oratory at his command and he was dubbed 'The City Demosthenes'[7] for the following purple passage:

The bill has been called a moderate measure. That moderation was the moderation of the border plunderer, who took away as much as he could in one foray, leaving the remainder for a future incursion; it was the moderation of the pickpocket, who stole a man's purse and then thought him well off that he left him his hat and coat; it was the moderation of the housebreaker, who, after taking away plate and money, thought the owner of it had no reason to complain so long as his life was spared. (Cheers).

When one brave soul, Francis Bennoch, tried to speak up for the measure and mischievously reminded the Liverymen of the Corporation's bill of 1852, he found that his presence 'was by no means welcomed' (as the official report put it).[8] In other words, his speech was drowned in a chorus of hisses and hoots. Another set of resolutions opposing the abolition of the Livery's rights and the 'inconsiderate change' embodied in the bill (though recognizing the need for reform) was passed unanimously amid much cheering. And it was agreed to petition the House of Commons.

The Court of Aldermen held a week later differed from the other meetings only in style, not sentiment. The Aldermen were quite as determined as the Councilmen and Liverymen, indeed were more so since their office was to made subject to re-election and their Court abolished. But they decided that it was best to present a careful rehearsal of their views to members of both Houses of Parliament. They eschewed sweeping, eyecatching histrionics and made a rational appeal for fair play. The Commission, they urged, was no basis for legislation, being quite unlike a court of law. The Corporation had been given no opportunity to cross-examine its critics. A 'cold utilitarian test'[9] of the Aldermen's work as magistrates was inapplicable. And so on. It was a case which, if not quite ingenuous and scarcely irrefutable, was certainly persuasive enough to make M.P.s pause. (Provided, of course, that they read it. The outspoken Deputy Lowman Taylor predicted that 'not one out of fifty of the whole House of Commons will ever read that voluminous, tedious document.' Alderman Sidney, however, had reassuring evidence to the contrary.)[10]

Outside Guildhall there was opposition too. Most of the wards held meetings to discuss the bill. Not surprisingly, perhaps, ordinary inhabitants showed somewhat less unanimity than their elected representatives. In Cheap Ward, for example, a Mr. Connell regretted the opposition made by the Corporation and the Livery since 'the time for reform had come; and either the bill then proposed must pass, or another one of a similar character, much more extended in its application, would be forced upon them by the Imperial Legislature.'[11] But for the most part even such wise, cautionary counsel as this convinced only the few. The oratory of the diehards, especially Common Councilmen and Aldermen, generally carried the day. Most of the inhabitants of Bassishaw listened with approval to the strictures of Town Clerk Merewether and Councilman Fuller. Merewether (speaking, it was emphasised, in a personal not an official capacity) said that the Corporation had been vindicated by the Commission and he doubted the legality of an Act of Parliament which was contrary to justice; while Fuller attacked the new mode of electing the Lord Mayor, now vested in Common Council. 'Under such a state of things, would it be at all likely that such men as Rothschild and Baring would ever be elected?[12] The Councillors were sure to elect one of their own number.

Swayed by such arguments the ward duly petitioned against the bill, which was described, *inter alia*, as an attack on local independence and an impediment to further reform, as well as 'an arbitary and theoretical attempt to make the City of London conform with other municipalities without really accomplishing such object'[13] (apparently an allusion, not only to the Act of 1835, but also to the Commissioners' interest in Liverpool). Bassishaw's example serves for all, but two other wards deserve to be mentioned. In Walbrook one of the former 'dirty party' obscurantists, Alderman D.W. Wire, declared that the Corporation had done much to reform itself and would have done more had Parliament allowed it to do so (instancing, of course, the bill of 1852), while in Bread Street J. C. Lawrence lived up to his rhetorical reputation by pronouncing the bill 'unconstitutional and unjust, subversive of the rights of the people, and eminently prejudicial and injurious to the principle of local government'.[14] In all twenty-two wards passed resolutions against the bill, and almost all of them presented their views to Parliament.

A blot upon the municipal map of England

The Press too offered its opinion on an issue of such general interest. *The Times*, needless to say, welcomed the bill. Its only regret was that the provisions did not go further. The paper, in fact, hankered after a unified, metropolitan government based on an enlarged Corporation; but in the interim Grey's bill would suffice. 'If the reformers are content with it, and if the Conservatives, nowhere so numerous and so influential as in the City of London, are ready to compound for the measure, it will certainly remove some inconveniences and absurdities'.[15] When the City fought furiously against even this compromise settlement the paper thundered its rage. The Common Hall meeting provoked the following Leader:[16]

We deny not for a moment, that in the historic period of our annals the City of London did good service to the cause of liberty, and that the citizens of London in times long since gone past proved themselves worthy of their local opportunities. The great error in their present argument is that they deny London. London is not the trumpery city of three centuries back – grand enough, no doubt, in its day – but the capital of the world. These wise Liverymen, however, will have it that their parish, their Mansion House, their Aldgate pump, their Bow steeple are the be-all and end-all of London, with its 2,500,000 inhabitants. It is a mistake of which they must be convinced.

A few days later, when the bill was beginning to seem less certain of reaching the statute book, *The Times* adopted a more defensive, though no less indignant, tone. The framers of the bill, it remarked, 'do not propose to swamp the City in London; they do not ask for the entire destruction of the old arrangements; but simply for such concessions as may not leave the City any longer a blot upon the municipal map of England':[17]

We have not let loose the wild democracy of the metropolitan borough upon the civic dyarchy, but, in place of such an extreme measure, we ask for such a modicum of reform in the institutions of the City district as shall bring them somewhat more in harmony with the spirit of our own times.

Other papers were less dogmatic. The *Morning Advertiser*, though it admitted the need for change, dismissed the notion of 'a corporation for the *whole metropolis*' as its rival's old "castle in the air".' 'No Government . . . that we have lately had, or are likely to have, will gratify *The*

Times by trying so hazardous an experiment. In truth, the main object of all Governments seems to be, to save themselves trouble. The present bill is nothing more than might have been brought in in 1835'.[18] But the measure was so inadequate, such an 'absurd', 'bungling' mixture of liberalism and toryism,[19] that the *Advertiser* was not prepared to support it, even as a short-term compromise. The bill had no friends, and the Tories were quite right to oppose it (as they promised to do on second reading).

A leader in the *Morning Star* made much of one of the most vulnerable provisions – granting a much-diminished Common Council the right to elect City officers. The bill was 'a measure of disfranchisement, wholly opposed to the spirit of the age, and in its present shape it must not pass'.[20] Opposition was also expressed by the *Morning Herald*, noted for its Tory views. The City was not 'a nuisance to be abolished' but 'a noble institution, which merely requires some practical reforms'.[21] In another issue the paper remarked on the campaign of opposition in the City: 'the measure appears to be one which is wholly condemned by those for whose benefit it is propounded'.[22] From such editorials as these the City took considerable comfort, though whether they were sufficient in weight or number to counteract the overweening influence of *The Times* is rather doubtful.

The controversy also spawned a number of tracts and pamphlets. Some of these were freelance productions, ranging from the articles in *Fraser's Magazine* to an erudite piece by Serjeant Alexander Pulling (an expert on the Corporation's constitution) in the *Law Review*. Others came from Guildhall. The Corporation published various statements on the Commission and the bill, and also (it seems) commissioned George Norton, author of an authoritative textbook on the City's constitutional history, to write an 'Address to the Citizens of London' (which included a salutary reminder of the *Quo Warranto* case). Official sanction may also have been given to the letters which appeared in the *Morning Advertiser* under the name of 'Fitz Stow'. (John Stow (?1525–1605) has claims to be called London's first and greatest historian: his *Survey of London* remains indispensable.) One of the more entertaining passages concerned the difference between reforms from within and without.[23]

It is well for a man to set his house in order, but quite another to let a broker . . . in to scrub his floors, arrange his furniture, throw some fine old valued inheritances of plate, and antiquated, but still massive, and useful chairs and tables, out at windows, and, in lieu thereof, not only send in a quantity of equally showy and flimsy manufacture, but half a dozen strangers, in order to take care that all should be kept clean, and in a comme il faut *condition.*

The pages of the future historian
What meanwhile was happening to the bill itself? When 21 April arrived, Russell (out of office but still M.P. for the City) asked for information.

Grey replied that he hoped to bring in the bill at the end of the following week but that he could not be certain of being able to do so. This was the beginning of the end. More than one paper predicted the demise of the measure, and there was soon a marked slackening of public interest. The debate did not recapture attention until the second week of June when the Livery petition was presented to Parliament. A fortnight later Thomson Hankey, the Liberal M.P. for Peterborough, asked for news of the bill. Grey said that he had wanted to find time that week, but this seemed unlikely now. On the 26th Hankey repeated his question and received the widely anticipated reply – the bill was to be withdrawn. Grey expressed himself 'very unwilling to give up the hope of passing the bill during the present session' but pressure of other business made time very difficult to find, and certainly not enough to debate a bill 'upon which a difference of opinion must necessarily exist even among those who would agree to the second reading . . .' Grey also thought that 'various suggestions of importance' which he had recently received from persons friendly to the bill were 'entitled to much consideration'. So he believed it best to ask leave to withdraw the bill with the intention of introducing it early in the next session. He took the opportunity to state that 'though the suggestions which have been made are entitled to consideration, so far as the details are concerned, I cannot hold out any hope that the bill will be altered in its material features, founded as it is on the reports of two Commissions of Inquiry'.[24]

There seems little reason to doubt the essential truth of Grey's speech. The only other obvious explanation for the withdrawal – that the bill was likely to undermine the ministry's parliamentary position – does not seem plausible, unless Russell was thought capable of performing a *volte face* (if *volte face* it was) and creating a rumpus over his constituents' anger. But even the most optimistic of Oppositions would have found it hard to envisage Palmerston stumbling over such an issue. It appears much more realistic to accept Grey's explanation, without forgetting, of course, that the Government may not have given such a gratuitous reform all the help it required. The time which had to be devoted to the Crimean War and its aftermath, together with the prospect of a desperate opposition from the City, would have troubled the most zealous of reforming ministries. Some months later, when the dust had settled, *The Times* commented:[25]

The City has hitherto contrived to avoid the edge of the reformer's axe, not because its institutions did not stand in need of reform, not because they had not been condemned by public opinion, not because Parliament was unwilling to act in the case, but simply because other subjects with overpowering claims on the immediate attention of the Houses of Legislature and of the country followed each other in rapid succession.

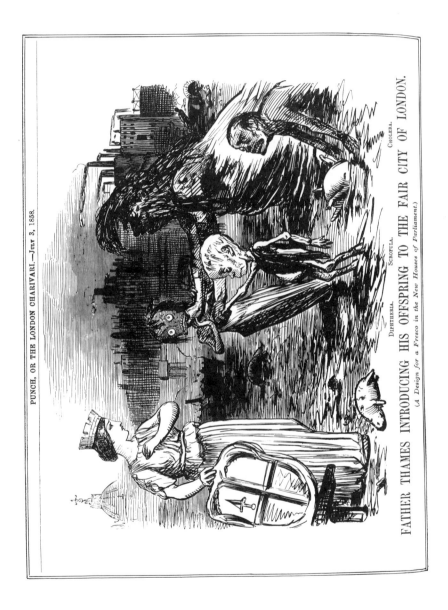

DIPHTHERIA.   SCROFULA.   CHOLERA.

FATHER THAMES INTRODUCING HIS OFFSPRING TO THE FAIR CITY OF LONDON.

(A Design for a Fresco in the New Houses of Parliament.)

There is no reason, either, to doubt Grey's determination to reintroduce his bill. The *Morning Advertiser*, it is true, had anticipated the loss of the bill back in April with the confident prediction that 'the Home Secretary's measure will soon be consigned to its grave, never more to be heard of, except in the columns of *Hansard*, or the pages of the future historian',[26] and later, amidst exuberant ridicule, comforted the citizens of London with the assurance that 'Sir George Grey will never again try his hand at City of London Corporation Reform'.[27] But subsequent events were to show that Grey was not to be defeated so easily. Reform had not been vanquished, only postponed. *The Times* remained sanguine, and accepted that reform would take time. 'When we look back on the many years during which we were occupied in carrying the mere outwork of Smithfield, we are not surprised that the main body of the place has not been captured in an hour.'[28] The siege would go on.

Before the next assault, however, the defenders of the Corporation's battered ramparts felt entitled to indulge in self-congratulation. At a special meeting of Common Hall on 28 October the Livery heard and approved a report on the proceedings in Parliament. Under the guidance of Lawrence and others they passed a series of exhortatory resolutions, including one to strengthen 'that harmony between the Livery and the executive requisite for the well-being of the City'.[29] But this euphoric defiance did not preclude wisdom and caution. A committee was appointed to watch the progress of any future bill; and more interestingly the Livery-men declared their desire to help other branches of the Corporation effect reforms. The garrison was not only ready and waiting, but also trying to lift the siege. (It can be no coincidence that it was in 1856 that the freedom requirement for retailing in the square mile was finally abolished.)

The City had decided to take the initiative. For some while it had been realised that there was much to be said for trying to modify the Commissioners' proposals in a spirit of co-operation and accommodation. Only disagreements on points of detail and tactics had defeated earlier attempts. Now it saw that the Government was in earnest and that it was only a matter of time before the bill was passed. It became apparent that Grey's measure, if suitably amended, could be an acceptable means of forestalling some more radical assault. To this end the Corporation drew up its own blueprint for change. By February 1857 this was ready for circulation to members of Common Council. It was etched in paler shades of Grey: twenty (not sixteen) wards; the Lord Mayor to be elected by Livery as well as municipal electors (and not the £10 ratepayers alone); 150 (not 80) Common Councilmen; a curtailment (not abolition) of the powers of the Court of Aldermen; Aldermen removable (not re-eligible); and so on. A deputation discussed the resolutions with Grey himself, but secured nothing more than a promise of careful consideration. A second visit in November was no more enlightening, with Grey merely telling the committee what he had told an M.P. in August, that he intended to introduce a bill as soon as possible. When the statement was repeated in the House on 11 December, Common Council decided to present its own views to Parliament in the shape of an alternative, private bill.

The old Quo Warranto *spirit*

Both measures came before the Commons early in February 1858. On the 4th Grey unveiled his second attempt at 'the better regulation of the Corporation of the City of London'.[30] In many respects the bill was the same as its predecessor, but there were some notable changes. The number of Common Councilmen was increased to 96 (i.e. six not five for each ward), Aldermen were to enjoy tenure for life (though they could be removed on a petition from a majority of their constituents); and, perhaps the most significant concession of all, the coal dues were to be left untouched. These second thoughts went some way towards meeting the City's objections, and Grey was justified in speaking of the 'closer agreement' between the two sides. He acknowledged that there would still be differences on some questions – especially the qualification for Lord Mayor (who could now be drawn from all those capable of becoming a Common Councilman and not simply from Aldermen who had served as Sheriff) and the mode of his election – but he had reason to hope from his discussions with the Corporation that 'there would be no objection to the principle of the bill' and that 'the details of the measure would be fairly and temperately discussed in committee'.[31] His optimism seemed to be borne out by the response of Alderman William Cubitt (one of the celebrated building brothers), who expressed his satisfaction with much of the Home Secretary's statement, though he dissented on certain details, namely the exclusion of the Lord Mayor and Aldermen from the Central Criminal Court and (as anticipated) the changes in the election of the Lord Mayor. Lord John Russell went so far as to express his 'great pleasure'[32] at Grey's change of plan, and particularly commended the return of life tenure for Aldermen and the omission of the coal dues provision. He regretted only that the bill persisted in removing the election of the Lord Mayor from Common Hall. He feared that he would have to oppose that clause, but that clause only, in committee. The other reactions are of less interest. Our old acquaintance W. Williams advocated the extension of the Corporation so as to include the whole metropolis. An Irish M.P. asked that the bill provide for the appropriation of the estates in Ireland granted to the City and Companies in the 17th century and supervised by the Irish Society. And two Westminster M.P.s, Sir John Shelley and Sir De Lacy Evans (who had both earlier asked questions in the House on Grey's plans for his bill) pressed Grey to amalgamate the City police with the Metropolitan force. They asked in vain.

The next few days saw first the introduction of the City's own measure, and then the second reading of the Government's bill which was referred to a Select Committee. The Corporation duly petitioned with its predictable list of complaints: the reductions in the number of wards and Councilmen were too large; disenfranchising the Livery was unwise; abolishing the Court of Aldermen was unnecessary . . . And all was prepared for that 'fair and temperate discussion' in committee. Then on 19 February the Government was quite unexpectedly defeated and Palmerston resigned.

It is testimony perhaps to the mildness of Grey's proposals that the incoming Tories, no friends of gratuitous reform, lost little time in adopting the bill as their own. Attention now turned to the deliberations of the Select Committee. The City was plainly hoping for substantial concessions, but it was to be disappointed. Only one revision of importance was secured. At Cubitt's insistence the choice of Lord Mayor was to remain confined to the Aldermen. All other important amendments, including Russell's attempt to preserve the Livery's right to vote for the Lord Mayor, were watered down or defeated.

The Corporation was provoked into vehement opposition. It protested that it had been given a quite inadequate hearing before the Select Committee, and that it was to be deprived of some of its property – the metage dues – without being able to defend itself. Petitions were also presented by other interested parties, *viz*. seventeen Livery Companies (though not all with official sanction) and no less than 5,110 ward inhabitants, worried by the effect abolishing the metage dues would have on the security of property and (doubtless much more importantly) on the level of their rates. The same high feelings were evident when the Commons came to consider the Select Committee's report on 24 June. The cry of 'the rights of property' was taken up by the lawyer John Rolt who rejected suggestions that it was merely a 'stale pretext' and demanded that the Corporation be heard fairly on the confiscatory clauses. The fact that the contentious tolls and dues had been restored to the City in 1689 occasioned an appeal to Whig sentiment. 'I cannot think that the Parliament of Victoria will destroy and take away without compensation these rights which the first Parliament of William and Mary, in vindication of the rights of the people and of property, restored to the City of London'.[33] His words were supported by one of the City M.P.s, R. W. Crawford, who, after stressing his desire to see anomalies removed and the Corporation 'placed on a footing more consonant to the spirit of modern times', complained bitterly about the Committee's conduct.[34] The next speaker was Grey, now of course in Opposition. He was in caustic mood. As for recommitting the bill he agreed that 'on the 24th of June – and especially in the present state of the Thames, of which the City had been so long (until 1857) the conservators – much might be said for delay . . .'[35] But delay would serve not to make the bill better, only more agreeable to the City. If the bill were put off, he felt he would be free to support a more radical measure. This ominous warning was echoed by the new Home Secretary, Spencer Walpole. He resisted the call for reconsideration and warned M.P.s that 'if this bill were not passed, there might be a pressure brought upon them which might perhaps lead to the introduction of a measure less favourable to the Corporation of London than that now before them.'[36] The threat was made still more explicit by Sir Benjamin Hall who felt 'quite sure that if the opposition was persisted in, the Corporation would regret that they had not accepted the present bill, which, after all, was a poor measure of a much-needed reform'.[37]

The other speeches can be briefly summarised. W. Williams made his usual contribution. Blithely unconcerned that he was by now completely out of touch with the subject – he told the Commissioners of 1854 that he had retired from business and left the City some seventeen years earlier and had 'very little knowledge of their proceedings since'[38] – he had his say. He made yet another reference to the Corporation's accounts for 1833 (which he had proudly laid bare for public scrutiny) to reiterate a well-worn assertion of the reformers, that the City's officials were paid more than cabinet ministers. On the other side of the argument appeared the novelist Samuel Warren, M.P. for Midhurst. Despite the stench from 'the sewer which runs by our walls', he managed, unlike Grey, to find some words of comfort for the river's former conservators. 'The Corporation of London has deserved far too well of this House, and of this country, to admit of being treated in the old *Quo Warranto* spirit of the lawless days of King Charles the Second'.[39]

This bantling of Sir George Cornewall Lewis

At length the debate was adjourned without a vote, and the prospects for the bill suddenly looked bleak. When Walpole privately admitted to the City M.P.s that it might become necessary to withdraw the measure, the Corporation (though not the Livery who had everything to lose and nothing to gain by the bill) tried desperately to dissuade him. M.P.s Duke and Cubitt were instructed to tell the minister of the Corporation's willingness to accede to a 'reasonable arrangement',[40] though it is plain that either the 'confiscatory clauses' had to be expunged or compensation given. It soon became evident, however, that the time for 'fair and temperate' discussion had passed. On 29 June the former Commissioner Henry Labouchere asked the Home Secretary about his plans. Walpole replied that he saw hardly any prospect of the bill passing now with the session so far advanced and reiterated his regret at the opposition mounted on the 24th. He also revealed that he had received a request from Common Council that the bill be proceeded with, and another from the Livery that it might not. It did not really require a further enquiry from Labouchere two days later to establish that the bill was dead. The Corporation was left to contemplate anxiously the consequences of its opposition. Had it gone too far and lost the chance of a moderate settlement? Would the next bill (which at least one Alderman said would decide the fate of the Corporation) be a more radical measure, as both Grey and Walpole predicted? (A 'regular pincher' was in prospect, it was claimed.[41]) The Corporation awaited the Government's next announcement with some trepidation.

It came in February 1859 when the Home Secretary reaffirmed his intention of legislating for the City but counselled patience. Other business, especially the parliamentary reform bill then pending, would have to take priority. At the end of March Walpole's successor at the Home Office, Sotherton Estcourt, gave further information. The bill was founded on the recommendations of the Select Committee and consisted of two parts, one municipal, the other 'national', in scope. Only the former would be proceeded with at this stage, and Estcourt hoped it would be ready before Easter.

Then the volatility of mid-nineteenth century politics took a hand once more. In the face of a Liberal reunification and an inconclusive general election, Derby's Conservatives were obliged to resign in June and Palmerston assumed power for the last time. The new Home Secretary was none other than the former Commissioner, G.C. Lewis. In view of his own recommendations in 1854 and his colleague Grey's undoubted indignation at the City's behaviour, some growl of authority might have been expected from Lewis's statement of 8 July. Instead it took the form of a whimpering surrender. The bill, Lewis declared, was based on the Select Committee's proposals (themselves a far cry from the Report of 1854), except in one respect. The 'financial part of the question' had been omitted altogether. In other words, the provisions dealing with the coal *and* metage dues were to be dropped or rather 'reserved for future consideration'. All significance the bill might have had for the metropolis as a whole was lost. No part of the Corporation's vaunted revenues was to be available for extra-mural use. Instead the bill concerned itself entirely with amending the City's constitution. Whether the ministry would find the time or the will to tackle the wider issue of metropolitan government and its finance remained to be seen. In the meantime the Corporation was delighted and the reformers appalled.

All the metropolitan M.P.s could do was indulge in their own prevarication. On three occasions in July Sir John Shelley (Westminster) urged the Home Secretary not to 'thrust the bill down the throats of hon. members at the close of the session'.[42] Such a complicated measure to which there was much opposition was best postponed. It would be better to bring in *both* bills – i.e. for the financing of the Corporation as well – early in the next session. A. S. Ayrton (Tower Hamlets) agreed and disparaged the bill as a legacy of the previous defeated administration. W. Williams was more candid and declared that he would not mind if the bill were lost.

His wish was granted. On 27 July Lewis's under-secretary moved that the second reading be postponed, and it was the Corporation's turn to expostulate. The City had plainly decided that, though there were still clauses to which it objected (and which it would try to remove at a later stage), the bill was worthy of support. The ministry's pusillanimity was profoundly disappointing. 'Nothing', said Sir James Duke (London), 'could be more lamentable than to see a feeble Government abandoning a good measure in order to please a section of its supporters'.[43] For once Williams spoke with some acuity when he commented that the reason why Duke 'felt satisfied with the measure was clear – it was not one of reform at all'.[44] To another radical, writing some years later, this 'bantling of Sir George Cornewall Lewis was a bill of very little value'.[45]

A power of resistance
The unwanted child made another appearance six months later in January 1860. Its features were unaltered and its reception much the same. Ayrton, fast becoming the *enfant terrible* of metropolitan reform, denounced it once again as a feeble bill and hoped the House would either send it into committee for improvement or refuse to proceed with it altogether. Williams pronounced it a thoroughly objectionable measure. Their attack was resumed in April when it came up for second reading. Ayrton began by re-asserting his determination to have the whole question of metropolitan administration discussed in depth by a Select Committee. As for the present bill, he thought there was no point in reforming the Corporation; it would be more sensible to exploit the potential of the Metropolitan Board of Works. 'Would it not be better now to utilize the new corporation they had established, than to endeavour to resuscitate the old one which was dying?'[46] Williams was equally scathing about Lewis's milk-and-water concoction, but could not be quite so detached in his contempt for the City. 'It was more extravagant, wasteful and corrupt than any Government which had ever existed in the world, municipal or national'.[47] Lewis managed to ease the bill through its second reading but it was clear that trouble lay ahead. Lewis and his colleagues realised that they were in danger of losing the support of an important group of radicals and liberals, and all for the sake of a bill which did nothing more than adjust the internal workings of an anachronistic corporation. On 19 July Lewis withdrew the bill.

The New Year's session in 1861 brought with it the traditional question – this time asked by Edwin James (Marylebone) – about the Home Secretary's intentions. It provoked for once an unfamiliar answer: 'it is not my intention at present to introduce any bill on the subject of the Corporation'.[48] All Lewis had in mind was a bill (as promised) to deal with 'the financial part of the question'. This entailed extending the coal and wine dues for ten years and committing them to public works. Lewis, however, was anxious not to revive the opposition of 1858 and left the City with the levy of 4d per chaldron which it regarded as its personal property. The disgust of Ayrton and his friends, expressed in a set of angry amendments, came to nothing.

But the radicals derived some consolation from an opportunity to air their views on more general metropolitan matters. At Ayrton's request a Select Committee was appointed to inquire into the 'local taxation and government of the metropolis, and the local administration of justice therein'.[49] With Ayrton in the chair, the Committee conducted a wide-ranging discussion of the perennial problems. The City, it need hardly be remarked, came under close scrutiny, and its officials (particularly the sorely tried Chamberlain, Benjamin Scott) were yet again subjected to rigorous examination. At one stage it looked as if the Committee would strike a serious blow at the Corporation's autonomy. The draft report included the suggestion that the City be extended to embrace the whole metropolitan area. (The alternative, increasing the power of the Metropolitan Board of Works, was considered less satisfactory.) But by a vote of 7:5 (with Lewis, Lord Mayor Cubitt and Alderman Copeland siding with the majority) a much less specific resolution was adopted:[50]

Various schemes for the improvement on a comprehensive scale of the municipal and local government of the metropolis have been suggested in the evidence taken by your committee. But your committee conceive that the discussion of these plans, involving imperial as well as local interests of such vast magnitude, should form the subject of future inquiry, and they therefore wish to express no opinion as to their respective merits.

When or indeed whether that 'future inquiry' would take place was far from clear, because the Committee's report sank like a stone. It is difficult to resist the conclusion that the Government had long ago decided to leave the divisive issue well alone and only appointed the Select Committee to allow the reformers to let off steam.

Certainly the following years were marked by an eerie silence on the question. It was broken only in 1863 when crowds greeting Princess Alexandra got out of control and several people were crushed to death. The subsequent outcry afforded the Government an opportunity to secure the long-awaited amalgamation of the City and Metropolitan police. In introducing the necessary bill Grey (Home Secretary once again) made a personal reflection which doubtless explains his colleagues' inactivity. 'Whenever I touched any question which affected (the City's) alleged rights and privileges, a power of resistance was shown which it is difficult to admire too highly'.[51] He was to be given further cause for admiration because the bill was defeated on a technicality, *viz*. failure to give sufficient notice of an amendment to a private Act. With this Parthian shot the City slipped away from the field to enjoy a brief respite and prepare itself for future battles.

THE CITY POLICE.

Magog. "I SAY, BROTHER GOG, THEY SEEM TO THINK WE AIN'T NO SORT O' USE."

CHAPTER V

METROPOLITAN REFORM (1863–80)

Talking slipslop to a defunct Lady Mayoress
In the latter part of the nineteenth century British politics began to assume a modern form. Two parties, Liberal and Conservative, and two great leaders, Gladstone and Disraeli, emerged from the mid-century confusion. Ministries tended to be better disciplined, more coherent and more durable than their predecessors. Genuine differences of policy emerged and alternative programmes were devised. Electors were given a choice of party not M.P.; and, though they might see politics in terms of the personalities of Gladstone and Disraeli, they appreciated that the vivid clash between the two men symbolised rather than transcended ideological differences.

These developments had important implications for the City in its struggle for survival. They made its position both less and more secure. Less secure, because a ministry determined to effect a thorough reform of London's government would have the time and strength to implement its proposals; but more so, because the question could easily become part of party warfare and the City might find its cause championed by a cautious Government or a concerted Opposition.

In due course such a pattern became clear, with naturally the Conservatives, warmly attached to the virtues of tradition, localism and self-government, defending the Corporation, and the Liberals, anxious for reform and impatient with anomalies, leading the assault. To begin with, however, neither party was prepared to tackle the question. The Liberals were given the first opportunity during their long tenure of power from 1868–74. They did nothing. Gladstone, it is true, spoke more than once of the need to effect some kind of reform of local government in the metropolis and his Home Secretary, H.A. Bruce, repeatedly stressed the ministry's intention to legislate on the matter when circumstances permitted. But despite some backroom preparations no action followed these fair words before the election of 1874 installed the Conservatives for a six-year terms. (It was later claimed that Robert Lowe, Home Secretary 1873–4, promised legislation on the question and that only the election defeat forestalled his plans.)

In his earlier more vigorous days Disraeli had been prepared at least to contemplate an initiative on the 'London' problem. In August 1866 he was persuaded by his erstwhile personal secretary, the self-seeking Ralph Earle, to press Gathorne-Hardy, Earle's new superior as President of the Poor Law Board, to take up the task of simplifying and unifying metropolitan government. But when Hardy rebutted the approach by timidly pro-

LONDON'S NIGHTMARE.

nouncing the question 'very puzzling' and lamely deciding that 'a number of municipalities would hardly vary from the vestries which are the local governments in many cases justly complained of',[1] Disraeli declined to repeat the attempt. Neither then nor later. By the time he was able to work with a secure Conservative majority in Parliament he had lost all interest in the minutiae of domestic legislation. The broad brush-strokes of foreign policy may have excited him, but not the administrative arrangements of London. Nevertheless he was too astute to allow his lieutenants an entirely free hand in such matters. Certain reforms were prescribed as incompatible with the principles of the party. So when the Home Secretary, R.A. Cross, wrote to him with a proposal for the metropolis, Disraeli replied:[2]

I am quite decided never to embark on a scheme for the government of London. I would rather at present, under any circumstances, leave the matter alone. We came in on the principle of not harrassing the country and I shrink from prematurely embarking on such questions . . .

Not that the Prime Minister had any particular affection for the Corporation itself. The zealots who made so much of Disraeli's periodic flamboyant tributes to the City as the embodiment of tradition and freedom would have been shocked to read the private description of one such occasion. Lady Bradford, the rather embarrassed recipient of a deluge of effusive letters in Disraeli's declining years, was treated to a description of a speech on the Eastern Question in 1876 at the Lord Mayor's banquet when he had to endure 'a heated hall full of gas and Aldermen and trumpeters' as well as the discomfiture of 'sitting for hours talking slipslop to a defunct Lady Mayoress.'[3] Such irreverence, however, did not preclude a healthy respect for the City's powers of survival. Another letter to Lady Bradford contained the following expansive pronouncement:[4]

When I entered political life [in the 1830s] there were three Great Powers in danger – the Grand Signior of the Ottomans, the Pope of Rome, and the Lord Mayor of London. The last will survive a long time: but the fall of France has destroyed the Pope, and will, ultimately, drive the Turk from Europe . . .

The Conservatives of 1874–80 never threatened to upset their leader's prophecy.

Tenification

In default of effective action from the two main parties, it was left to individual reformers and M.P.s to cure the ills of London's government. The first and most important of these initiatives came from James Beal and the Metropolitan Municipalities Association. Beal, a land agent and

ONE IN THE "CORPORATION."

"TAKE THAT IN YOUR CHARITY-BASKET, YOU 'FATTED, GORGED, NOT TO SAY BLOATED,' OLD GRABBER!"

[*See* MR. GLADSTONE'S *speech à propos of* Emanuel Hospital *and the City Aldermen.*

auctioneer of Piccadilly, was a member of the vestry of St. James's, West-minster. His work in co-ordinating support for a metropolitan Supply of Gas Act had convinced him of the need for a systematic reform of London's local affairs; and he launched himself into more than thirty years of agitation. His 'indefatigable perseverance and tireless energy'[5] earned him applause as the founder of London reform and vilification as the ring-leader of a radical faction.

Beal was an experienced practical man who was aware that only by compromise and concession would he succeed where so many others had failed. One scheme, and one scheme alone, had a chance of success in the 1860s, *viz.* the formation of a number of independent municipalities loosely linked by a supervisory central body. (This was effectively the plan suggested by the Commissioners in 1854 and partially implemented through the creation of the Metropolitan Board of Works.) Beal was acutely conscious that no Government would accept an over-mighty, unified metropolitan authority on its doorstep. He was equally aware of the vested interests of the City Corporation. Past events made clear that it was essential to placate the City fathers. They too would have no truck with centralization.

Beal did all he could to allay such suspicions. The very title of his Met-ropolitan Municipalities Association made plain his attachment to the cause of moderation. He was particularly anxious to stress his respect for the City; and he tried to be elusive as possible on the precise nature of his proposals, especially on points which affected the Corporation. When pressed for details he emphasised the exemptions and exceptions which the City would enjoy.

Mere expediency? It is hard to tell. Certainly when he addressed some fellow vestrymen in 1867 Beal reiterated the importance of winning the support of the City. Another set of proposals were criticised for ignoring the City of London and thereby inviting 'attacks from the powerful Corpor-ation which will render it impossible' that unless heavily amended they 'can ever become law'. The vestrymen should make no such mistake. 'If [the City] becomes our ally, we act with its force, we demand with its power, and our triumph is near'.[6] However, these may have been simply words of the moment, designed to win acceptance for unpalatable tactics.

Beal's proposals came in two packages. The first provided for the crea-tion of a number of municipalities, generally coterminous with the existing parliamentary boroughs. For obvious reasons this was nicknamed 'tenifica-tion', though the figure varied a little from scheme to scheme. (Since 1854 when there had been seven extra-mural constituencies (above page 49), Hackney and Chelsea had been created following the Second Reform Act of 1867.) The City, of course, was preserved and, though it was to be obliged to submit to the same constitution as the other corporations, some effort was made to protect vested interests. Existing freemen and Liverymen, for example, were to retain their votes. Reformers might see the restyled City as merely a local council; but diehard citizens could convince themselves that it remained the ancient Corporation of London. There was room for compromise, or at any rate mutual self-deception.

The second part of the plan was more controversial. At first glance the new central Municipal Council seemed to be nothing more sinister than a revamped Metropolitan Board of Works, supervising mundane matters of metropolitan concern in which the City had little interest. Closer inspection however revealed that the Council would impinge upon some of the old Corporation's most cherished privileges. The courts of justice, the gaols, asylums and (deepest cut of all) the police, were all included in the 'county' powers transferred to the new authority (thereby effectively abolishing the Court of Aldermen). There were even plans, though admittedly not in every scheme, to appropriate the City's property. Compensation for these changes was meagre: the City was allotted a disproportionately large number of councillors in the new Council; all existing Aldermen were allowed a seat; and the Lord Mayor (now designated Warden) was to be *ex-officio* deputy Lord Mayor.

An unconstituted aggregation of disunited people

In the City's eyes this was quite unacceptable; but for Beal his proposals represented an irreducible minimum, the very least that was required to effect a worthwhile reform. When his initial set of plans came to nothing he became not more accommodating but less so. His later proposals are characterised by a new emphasis on unity and efficiency. A single Municipality of London was to be created and the metropolis divided into districts and wards. This was indeed a bitter pill which the City was unlikely to swallow without a great deal of persuasion. Citizens might think that their Corporation was about to be destroyed, but Beal told them that it was to be 'absorbed', 'merged' or 'expanded'. His rhetoric knew no bounds when inspired by desperation or anger. Readers of *The Times* in October 1874 were told how the reformers began to pose the following question:[7]

'Shall the Metropolis swallow up the City, or shall the City be wedded to the Metropolis?' Either would do, but the result would be a trifle different. If the metropolis absorbed the 723 acres into its 70,000, the great historic traditions would be lost; if the City was to be amplified, the roof of Guildhall lifted over the metropolis, its wealth, its prestige, its municipal experience, the glory it sheds on our municipal life, would become the property of the developed municipality. Apart from the City proper, London has no past; it is 'an unconstituted aggregation of disunited people'. But allied with the City, it would have its place in English history, and be raised to its level, if not a little higher!'

The peroration was even more beguiling:

> . . . we accept the City as our model, value it for its past glorious history, seek to perpetuate on a wider scale its munificence and Imperial action, desire to see it fulfil the past promises of its citizens, gather the district beyond its walls into its scheme of municipal life, clothe us with its dignity, and enable this 'province of houses' to speak as one with it; to join with it in having kings and sultans for its guests, in distributing honour to worthy citizens, in symbolizing the loyalty of the nation, and in sharing in these things, to elevate one of the oldest municipal institutions on earth to its rightful place as the greatest municipality in the world.

Such millenarian enthusiasm, of course, had been the stock-in-trade of municipal reformers since the 1830s. Beal differed from his predecessors by adding practical action to words. In 1865 he served on the election committee which had secured the return of the political theorist and reformer, John Stuart Mill, as M.P. for Westminster. Mill had long been troubled by the disunity of London's government. His *Considerations on Representative Government* (1861) had included the following passage:[8]

> The subdivision of London into six or seven independent districts, each with its separate arrangements for local business (several of them without unity of administration even within themselves) prevents the possibility of consecutive or well regulated co-operation for common objects, precludes any uniform principle for the discharge of local duties, compels the general government to take things upon itself which would be best left to local authorities if there were any whose authority extended to the entire metropolis; and answers no purpose but to keep up the fantastical trappings of that union of modern jobbery and antiquated foppery, the Corporation of the City of London.

It was therefore with an intellectual as well as a personal commitment that Mill agreed to further Beal's cause in Parliament. In 1866–7 he expounded the Metropolitan Municipalities Association's case during his service on a Select Committee, and in the two following years he presented Beal's bills to the House of Commons. There was no chance of success, but it was hoped that public debate would force the Government's hand.

Mill's advocacy leant great weight to the reformer's cause. Respectability too, for he was at pains to disarm potential enemies. As his private correspondence with Beal reveals he was well aware of the vested interests which stood in the way. Despite his contempt for that 'union of modern jobbery and antiquated foppery', he tried earnestly to placate the City. When one of the bills was denounced as an attempt to 'overthrow the

"THE VOICE OF THE TURTLE."

Gog. "WHAT'S ALL THIS HERE ABOUT, BROTHER MAGOG?"

Magog. "THEY WANTS TO ENLARGE THE 'CORPORATION,' BROTHER GOG!"

Turtle. "ENLARGE THE CORPORATION?—HA! HA! THEY CAN'T DO THAT WITHOUT ME!"

oldest and most famous local government in the world',[9] Mill quietly replied that he believed the City would approve of the measure once its provisions became known. Even when he introduced the controversial proposal for establishing a Municipality of London and endowing it with the old Corporation's property, he still expressed his optimism that the City would concur. Like Beal, Mill was prepared to deceive himself, or others, in the Cause.

Mill's endeavours had produced no tangible result by the time he was defeated in the general election of 1868. His followers, however, remained to continue the work. Charles Buxton, Liberal M.P. for East Surrey. undertook to introduce another M.M.A. measure in 1869. He too felt it important to deal candidly with the problem of the City. It was quite wrong simply to ignore the City, as another plan had done, and start as if with *tabula rasa*. It was both imprudent and unreasonable 'to sweep away a system so ancient, so venerable, so powerful as that'. The present proposals made no such mistake. Apart from the fact that the Lord Mayor would become the deputy Lord Mayor of the new metropolitan council, 'the City would retain its privileges, its precedents, its property, and its organization unaltered, and it would stand at the head of the other corporations which it was proposed to create'.[10] Even these honey-sweet words, however, failed to persuade the Government to legislate and in the following year Buxton was back with another panacea for London's ills. The patient this time was to be given a rather stronger dose. The central corporation was no longer to be a refurbished Metropolitan Board of Works but an 'elevated and expanded'[11] City Corporation. The new governing body was to be endowed with all the functions, property and prestige of the former one. Nonetheless, Buxton assured M.P.s, there were those in the City who accepted the need for such a change. Again this elicited professions of interest and concern on the part of the Government, but no legislation. However much they may have approved of the reforms in abstract, ministers were obviously not convinced that opposition, especially from the City, would easily be overcome.

For the introduction of his still more radical proposals of 1874 Beal had to turn to a new sponsor. Buxton died in 1871 and another friend, Thomas Hughes (the author of *The Anarchy of London* as well as *Tom Brown's Schooldays*) had not been returned to the new Parliament. After a deputation from the M.M.A. had unsuccessfully pressed the plans upon Home Secretary Cross, Lord Elcho, the future Earl of Wemyss, was approached. Elcho agreed to act but insisted on some amendments to the plan for a centralised municipality. The Secretary of State was to be given control over certain appointments and, more interestingly from our point of view, the City's property was not to be transferred without its consent. Needless to say, even these and other tactful changes failed to save the bill.

There was plainly little hope of Parliament acceding to any legislation that the M.M.A. might propose. It was therefore decided to drop the tactic of bills and move 'resolutions' instead. In 1876 Elcho asked the Government and the House to declare their support for reform on the principle of a single municipal administration for the whole metropolis. He professed himself satisfied with Cross's sympathetic, but clearly non-committal, reply and withdrew his resolutions. (In later years Elcho (by then Lord Wemyss) repudiated the centralizing plans of his former associates and formed both a short-lived London Ratepayers' Defence League and the more important Liberty and Property Defence League.) In 1878 the M.M.A.'s spokesman was Sir Ughtred Kay-Shuttleworth, who placed another set of resolutions before the Commons. But even the anodyne proposition that 'the present state of local government in London is unsatisfactory and calls for reform'[12] failed to impress; and the other proposals, calling for a central municipality to be created by extending and remodelling the City Corporation, were lost by default. This dispiriting episode proved to be the M.M.A.'s last assault on the legislature and it soon ceased to be an effective force in the reform agitation.

A Municipal Council of London
Beal and his Association dominated the 'movement' in these years but they were by no means the only campaigners. Certain other names deserve to be noticed. A.S. Ayrton was still active, and in February 1866 he managed to obtain the appointment of another Select Committee 'to inquire into the local government and local taxation of the metropolis'.[13] When the report appeared in 1867 it showed many signs of the chairman's influence. Ayrton had always regarded the City with a mixture of anger and disdain and it can have caused little surprise that the Committee's recommendations made absolutely no reference to the existing Corporation. The metropolis was to be given a refurbished and more powerful Metropolitan Board of Works in the guise of a 'Municipal Council of London'[14] and there was to be a network of districts and wards of a size to be determined by the Government but plainly smaller than the corporations advocated by the M.M.A. While there would be a place for the City among the ten or so 'municipalities', it was by no means clear how, or indeed whether, it could survive in the Committee's new arrangements. Hence presumably the resounding silence on the point.

Ayrton had as little success with the report as he had done in 1861 but he was not entirely without support in the House. He had a willing adjutant in G.C. Bentinck, a fellow member of the 1867 Committee, who took it upon himself to sustain the Ayrton programme and to wreck the M.M.A.'s alternative proposals.

Mention must also be made of the activities of another M.P., the lawyer John Locke. He persistently, even tediously, urged the merits of extending the Corporation over the whole metropolis. All that had to be done was to create a set of new extra-mural wards, as the City should have done, but had declined to do, with Southwark (Locke's own constituency) back in the sixteenth century. Locke's cherished 'ward-accumulation' scheme (likened by Buxton to a bee adding 'new cells to a honeycomb')[15] was a recurring feature of deliberations in the Commons and the Select Committee but it was riddled with difficulties and was never regarded as a practical possibility.

One final name should be included, if only for the sake of old times. W.E. Hickson appeared before the Select Committee in 1866 with his radicalism undiluted. He said he wanted to 'extend and absorb'[16] the Corporation in a central metropolitan authority. This entailed applying the City's powers and constitution to the whole London area and using its property for metropolitan purposes.

Like some plump, well-favoured bird

Such were the proponents of reform. It is time now to turn to the City itself. What was its attitude? This was plainly of the utmost importance as the reformers were well aware. It was regularly claimed that certain plans had the approval of Guildhall while others would never be accepted. How accurate were these claims? Did any plan have a chance of City support or was there a total opposition to change of any kind? One M.P. at least believed that 'the root of all the opposition to municipal reform lay in the City itself. No plan had yet been brought forward for the benefit of the whole metropolis, which had not met with opposition in that quarter, led by some frantic or frenzied Alderman.'[17]

The Corporation would certainly have nothing to do with Ayrton's plan to strengthen the M.B.W. The City M.P. on the Select Committee, Alderman William Lawrence, fought hard against it. He even combined with J.S. Mill in support of the alternative scheme of separate municipalities. Common Council was similarly displeased by the Committee's conclusions. It unanimously adopted its Local Government and Taxation committee's report that the recommendations would have the effect of 'undermining municipal and representative government in the metropolis and elsewhere throughout the kingdom; and that to reconstruct the local government of London on such a principle would not only be inexpedient and unjust as regards the ancient City of London, but would disappoint the expectations of the other districts of the metropolis, who naturally look for free municipal institutions similar to those given to [other] towns . . .'[18] One report of the Court's proceedings notes that when Ayrton's name was mentioned there were hisses of disapproval.

There was a good deal more support for the proposals advanced by Beal and his M.M.A. As we have seen, great care had been taken to charm all potential opponents, and:[19]

. . . even the Corporation, it was said, were won over, or if they did not support, at least would not oppose; but would allow themselves to be swal-

lowed up — charters, revenues, privileges and all — like some plump, well-favoured bird, fascinated by the eye of the basilisk, and tumbling unresistingly into the mouth of the attractive devourer.

The Standard, in a leader article of 1867, was exaggerating, but only a little. There were many citizens who realised that the establishment of municipal corporations in the metropolis offered the City its best chance of survival. When Deputy Lowman Taylor counselled caution during a discussion of a letter from the M.M.A. asking for assistance, Councilman James Medwin countered with vigour:[20]

. . . he did not agree with the policy suggested by Mr. Taylor, of standing still and allowing every alteration to be dictated from Spring Gardens [the home of the M.B.W.]. (Hear, hear.) A most important movement was taking place in the large parishes and districts outside the City, and a great desire was entertained in those districts to obtain the power of self-government, and it appeared to him that it was the duty of this Corporation to aid them in effecting that object.

Medwin may not have been entirely representative since he was a member of Beal's own vestry of St. James's, Westminster, and he felt strongly enough to present his views to the Select Committee of 1866–7. But he was not alone. Chamberlain Scott too pronounced in favour of separate municipalities and declared the bill presented by Beal to the Committee in 1866 to be 'the best digested and completest attempt at a solution of the metropolitan problem which has as yet appeared'.[21] Part of its attraction was doubtless the clause which specifically stated that 'Nothing in this Act contained shall affect the City of London, or the powers, privileges or jurisdiction of any of its officers'.[22]

When pressed other Councilmen and officials expressed themselves in similar, if less specific and forthright terms; but there was no official pronouncement until 1870 when Common Council decided to adopt the principle that the best form of government for the metropolis would be the establishment of municipalities in the different parliamentary boroughs. This was an important declaration since it constituted the City's first positive contribution to the metropolitan debate; but it was also a limited and cautious one. Common Council refused to endorse the M.M.A.'s programme as a whole: the letter of 1867 was merely acknowledged and Beal was roundly rebuked for claiming that the City supported the proposed legislation of that year. The precise nature of the new arrangements, particularly the powers of the central authority, gave rise to considerable doubt and concern. Under no circumstances, for example, would the City consent to lose control of its independent police force. There were also doubts about the good intentions of Beal and his friends. It appears that a number of Common Councilmen joined the M.M.A. at its inception, but at least one of them left when he discovered that it went further than he had thought. The City found more comfortable associates in a body called the Municipal Corporations Association, which had set itself the irreproachable task of protecting the principle of local self-government and opposing centralization.

A sham from beginning to end

It need hardly be added that when Beal began to abandon his two-tier system for a more unified arrangement the City lost all interest. An indignant 'Analysis' of the 1870 bills by the Corporation's parliamentary agent, the Remembrancer, left M.P.s in no doubt as to Guildhall's uncompromising opposition to a central municipality. For the City 'extending' its powers and privileges meant abolishing them; 'transferring' its property meant confiscating it. The same message was conveyed personally to the Home Secretary. The chairman of the Local Government and Taxation committee told Bruce that he was sure that the bill would meet with the most determined opposition from the City.

The next M.M.A. scheme, introduced, in 1875, was subjected to a still more vehement attack. Even the modifications of Lord Elcho could not save it from being denounced by Lowman Taylor as 'crude' and 'ill-contrived'.[23] Another prominent Councilman, J.T. Bedford, thought it 'a sham from beginning to end'.[24]

The parliamentary debates on Kay-Shuttleworth's resolutions of 1878 suggested to some M.P.s that the City's attitude was changing. The Liberal philanthropist, Alderman Sir Sydney Waterlow, expressed his confidence that provided Shuttleworth dealt leniently with the Corporation's privileges he would not find it hostile or obstructive to his attempt to provide one large municipal body for the metropolis. Waterlow declared his own personal allegiance to the principle of a single municipality. His words were echoed by a City M.P., the banker and future cabinet minister, G.J. Goschen, who predicted that while the Corporation 'would keep a watchful eye on their own interests, they were ready to look with favour on a well-considered scheme of reform in a totally different spirit from that of a few years back'.[25] Goschen too gave his blessing to the resolutions.

The reformers, of course, were delighted. Elcho seized upon Waterlow's intimation that the City would not oppose the proposed changes and pronounced the news 'a great gain'.[26] Others, however, were not so certain. The Home Secretary, Cross, had information of a different kind which showed that the City remained committed to the principle of localised, not centralised, administration, as proclaimed in the Common Council resolution of 1870. Goschen, a Liberal, might choose to interpret the silence of his three Conservative co-members for the City as a sign of acquiescence, but few others can have shared his optimism. Cross was much closer to the truth. In view of the Conservatives' reluctance to meddle with the 'London' issue it was a convenient argument, but it was an accurate one nonetheless:[27]

It had been agreed on all hands, and by both sides of the House, that if this matter were to be undertaken by any Government, the first thing to do was to get the City of London on their side; but at the present moment the Government had not got the City on their side.

Standing aloof

In later years the politicians' desire to 'get the City on their side' grew less and less compelling. Conquest, not compromise, became the objective. This, therefore, is the point at which to ask whether there was any plan at all which could have won acceptance. It is, in fact, a difficult question to answer. Very few positive statements emerged from Guildhall. One or two Councilmen dared to pronounce in favour of 'extension'. In 1870 Deputy Robinson urged his colleagues to 'extend the benefits which they themselves had enjoyed for many centuries'. He was supported by J.T. Bedford who thought the time had come for 'resuscitating' the Corporation which was 'gradually dwindling away'.[28] These were isolated voices, more cries of exasperation than realistic proposals. The only considered response to the reformers' plans came from the pen of Benjamin Scott, the Chamberlain. His *Statistical Vindication of the City of London* (1867)* suggested the establishment of a 'Federated Corporation' as London's superintending body, to comprise 'the Corporation of the City, reinforced by representatives of the metropolis, so as to possess all the necessary powers, privilege and dignity, and to become, for all purposes of aggregate action, the *crème de la crème* of municipal representation'. Scott emphasised that he was speaking for himself alone and not in his official capacity, but he felt sure that the City would rise to the challenge of this new role:[29]

To be absorbed into a board elected by the vestries, to remain standing aloof if London-extra be incorporated, to submit, after centuries of independence, to the control of a board at Whitehall, would be to them impossible, and, if possible, intolerable. They would, we believe, march with the times, adapt themselves to their new position, accept their fresh responsibilities, and maintain proudly, and perpetuate, so far as in them lies, the fair fame, the freedom and the dignity of their ancient City.

---

*It was subsequently suggested that it was James Acland, erstwhile champion of the unfree shopkeepers (above p. 42), who 'wholly compiled' the work. H.J. Hanham, *Elections and Party Management* (1959), p. 238. But though Acland may have been responsible for collecting data and drafting the more prosaic parts, Scott himself was surely the author of the positive and personal passages which concern us here.

Despite their rhetorical clothing and their (intentional) vagueness, Scott's proposals merit attention because they came from such an important and experienced City official. Scott wanted, and expected, the Corporation to take the initiative and to assume some responsibility for governing the metropolis. Yet it is difficult to discern the basis for his confidence. To be sure the City would not have tolerated absorption into a reconstituted M.B.W. nor submitted to Government control. But did it really object to 'standing aloof' from the incorporation of the extra-mural districts? There is no sign that it did. Councilmen were constantly enjoining their colleagues to 'do nothing' and not to meddle in things which did not concern them. To 'take the initiative' was to invite interference. How much better to wait on events.

In March 1868 Common Council considered a motion which called for the introduction of municipalities in the metropolitan boroughs, the preservation of the Corporation intact and its complete separation from the M.B.W. The debate ended inconclusively because members felt that the City should avoid declaring in favour of any specific plan for municipal government and should not interfere with the rest of the metropolis. Both the motion itself and the reason for its failure provide a perfect illustration of the City's attitude to London reform.

Internal changes were contemplated with almost equal suspicion; and for the same reasons. When the appointment of a committee to consider whether any, and if any, what alteration might be made in the City's constitution was vetoed by 51 votes to 39 in 1865 a Deputy declared:[30]

. . . nothing was more probable than that if they were once to move in the matter, the Government, which always looked with great jealousy upon the privileges of the Corporation, would step in and take it out of their hands, and proceed much further than they ever intended or desired.

Nonetheless, though no comprehensive reform was ventured, the City did succeed in making itself more acceptable and less anomalous. While it is impossible to prove the point, this was undeniably a conscious decision. The threat of interference and the relentless pressure of public opinion concentrated the civic mind wonderfully. At last something was done about the anachronistic franchise and fast-dwindling electorate. In 1867 the freedom qualification for ward elections was abolished and £10 ratepayers (as well as those on the parliamentary register) admitted instead. There were also a number of 'improvements' to the square mile. The most notable was the construction of the Holborn Viaduct in 1869 at a cost of almost £2.5 million. Whereas the 1840s and '50s had seen a most undignified resistance to the removal of the cattle market from Smithfield, the '60s and '70s marked the building of the Deptford Cattle Market and the rebuilding of Billingsgate and Leadenhall Markets, together with the establishment of a dead-meat market on the Smithfield site. The Corporation could also point to the reconstruction of Blackfriars Bridge (1869) and the eleven-year-long battle to reclaim and preserve Epping Forest (1871–82).

In connection with the latter George Shaw-Lefevre, founder and chairman of the Commons Preservation Society, which had urged the Corporation to take up the cause, later remarked that the City:[31]

... with a keen eye on their advantage, perceived that great popularity might be achieved by fighting for the interest of the public in a case of such importance and magnitude, and were the more inclined to embark on it at a time when the separate exclusive rights of the Corporation were threatened by the general demand for a single Municipal Government of London.

(The project had the added advantage of providing a thoroughly acceptable pretext for extending the life-time of the controversial metage dues.)

A soulless Corporation

As far as the calibre of City officials is concerned, it is tempting to suggest that here too there was some improvement. The debates in Common Council reveal that introspection was still rife in Guildhall, but complacency was a little less conspicuous. The City, it might be thought, was beginning to attract men of weight and ability again. Such would be the inference from the career of the banker Sir Robert Fowler. In his early years he regarded the Lord Mayor's Show with detached amusement and spoke caustically of the mode of electing Sheriffs. In 1862 he was asked to stand for Alderman, but refused. His diary reads:[32]

Told him I had not time to take it; that I regretted that Lombard Street men refused these offices, but I doubted whether I should be the first to break through it. If I was much urged under other circumstances, it might be a duty.

In the following year Fowler wrote an article on 'City' men avoiding the Corporation. The request was repeated in 1866 and again declined, though not without much struggling with a nagging conscience. 'If respectable people refuse [these Corporation offices], they must fall into lower hands.'[33] In 1878 Fowler relented and as Alderman for Cornhill Ward embarked on what was to prove a momentous civic career. Whether his 'conversion' reflects any general pattern is difficult to say. The abstention of financiers from Guildhall life, of course, was one of the major preoccupations of the early reformers. Bankers like George Glyn were persuaded to break with family tradition and shun the office of Alderman; indeed a House rule explicitly proscribed 'interference in elections, parliamentary or civic, in the City of London.'[34] Others like Baron Lionel Rothschild and

G.J. Goschen sat as M.P.s for the City but had no connection with the Corporation. (Fowler himself had been made leader of the City Conservatives before he became an Alderman.) In later years the divide between the financial and corporate 'City' became less marked, and it may well be that Fowler's career hints at a turning-point in the process.*

It certainly became more and more difficult for the reformers to dismiss the Corporation's members as a rump of self-interested shopkeepers. 'Corruption' became harder to detect. In 1879 there were revelations of misdeeds in the Remembrancer's office, but no amount of huffing and puffing about this 'Painful Story' could turn it into a major scandal or represent it as typical of City administration.

All this should have afforded the Corporation great comfort. But it did not. Two or three decades earlier a programme of public works, an enlarged franchise and an improved system of government might have sufficed to disarm criticism. Now they were minor issues. Not only was there a general acknowledgement of the need to reform London's government, but the failure of the separate municipalities scheme had given enormous impetus to the alternative plans for a unified metropolis. The future, or at least the immediate future, lay with the centralisers and radicals. They cared little about the City's internal arrangements. They saw no point in following Grey's hapless foray into the tangled thickets of the Livery franchise, the allocation of Councilmen and so on. They were scathing about such legislation and contemptuous of any compromise with the City. As their leader J.F.B. Firth remarked in his celebrated *Municipal London* (1876):[35]

. . . *if the history of attempted Corporation Reform teaches anything at all, it teaches this, that for the fullest concessions that any minister dare make, the City care not one iota: that they denounce the very mildest measure in the most revolutionary language, and that there are no means fair or foul within the compass of a soulless Corporation to which they will not stoop to defeat it.*

If any worthwhile reform of London's government was to be accomplished, the City would have to be defeated:[36]

*For the present, however, traders not bankers predominated. Alderman Sir Benjamin Phillips (1811–89) is an excellent example of these latter-day Whittingtons. 'He was a man about whom there was non nonsense. He never claimed to be anything but what he was – a plain citizen, and a self-made man. Although extra-ordinarily wealthy, he was never tired of referring to the day when he came up to London without even the proverbial sixpence in his pocket, and commenced life upon the very lowest rung of the ladder. Upon one occasion he took me to the Commercial Road in his carriage, and pointed out a little bead-shop there, remarking as he did so: 'And there, my boy, is the place where my wife and I first began business by selling beads". From such small beginnings grew the great house of Faudel, Phillips & Co., whose premises now occupy a great portion of Newgate Street.' Montague Williams, *Leaves of a Life* (1890), I, p. 268.

Can it be that there is no honest statesman who dare enter the lists with the Corporation of London, and give form and substance to the opinion of the House of Commons and to the aspirations of the capital City?

CHAPTER VI

Worn out and effete

Firth and his friends did not confine their malevolent attentions to the Corporation; they mounted a frontal assault on the Livery Companies as well. The two institutions, in their minds, were inseparable and equally unacceptable. Indeed in some respects the Companies provoked even more anger than the Corporation. They were thought to be squandering their enormous endowments on fees and feasts. They were also a somewhat more vulnerable target than the resilient Corporation; contemporaries were more likely to respond to talk of embezzlement than to demands for democratic representation. And the difficulty of finding a remedy for the defects of Company government was in no way comparable to the metropolitan dilemma. A redistribution of the Companies' revenues, or the abolition of the Companies themselves, could be decided upon with relative speed. Once started, therefore, the campaign quickly gathered momentum and since it came to a head before the attack on the City this is the place to consider it.

The Companies had fared badly during the nineteenth century. The Municipal Corporations Commission of 1833–7 had listed a total of eighty-nine 'Companies', of whom all but four were undoubtedly Livery Companies. In 1884 no less than thirteen were pronounced extinct, *viz.* the Combmakers, Fishermen, Gardeners, Hatbandmakers, Longbowstring-makers, Paviors, Pinmakers, Silk Weavers, Silk Throwers, Soapmakers, Starchmakers, Tobacco-pipe Makers and Woodmongers. In a few cases the last rites were premature and the Company survived, but the majority did indeed disappear; and it is incontestable that the middle years of the century mark the nadir of Company fortunes. The threat to the Livery franchise, the dismantlement of the freedom regulations, the final severance of contact between most Companies and their trades, the declining interest in the civic life of Guildhall, all these interrelated factors tended to sap Company strength and undermine morale. The largest Companies, it is true, continued to attract new members by virtue of their prestige and wealth. The smaller ones, however, were in serious difficulty. Beyond the opportunity to vote in Common Hall for those prepared to purchase the Livery, they had very little to offer. Their numbers dwindled alarmingly. The overall Livery roll declined from 12,000 in 1832 to 5,500 in 1855; and behind these general figures there lay some equally dramatic individual ones. In 1832 the Liverymen of the Waxchandlers' Company, for example, numbered 93 and the freemen 59; fifty years later the totals had fallen to

41 and 25. Court attendances tell a similar story. The Glass-sellers were obliged to reduce their quorum in 1858, while the Master and Clerk were the sole persons present at the Tinplateworkers' business meetings from 1872–5. Other evidence confirms the pattern, even if it is not as quantifiable or dramatic. Company histories speak of atrophy among the Horners, Musicians, Pattenmakers and Turners; and the description of the Coachmakers in 1867 as 'worn out and effete'[1] may serve for all.

Whether we may apply to the other Companies the rest of the assertion, that the Coachmakers 'had drifted into a wretched chaos of mismanagement', is another matter. The general impression is that though the Companies were complacent or moribund they were not actually corrupt. But, of course, as Trollope's *The Warden* (1855) reveals, there was more to trusteeship than strict adherence to the benefactors' literal instructions. If the needs of a new age were to be met, then the spirit of an endowment was more important than its letter. So at least argued Victorian reformers, and the Companies could not expect to escape censure if they failed to adjust. Surplus revenue, whether derived from trusts or from the Companies' own corporate estates, would have to be devoted to worthwhile causes if criticism was to be avoided.

The great awakening

For much of the century the Companies made no such attempt. Public opinion was treated with blithe disdain. Then in the 1870s came what one Company historian termed the 'great awakening'.[2] The Livery Companies began to take an interest in the work of their crafts and decided to give some assistance to 'technical education'. Quite when the movement got under way is a point of some controversy. Some Company loyalists, anxious to disprove imputations of self-interest, have pointed to instances of generosity which pre-date the radicals' campaign; and certainly the Coachmakers, Painter-Stainers and Turners deserve credit for leading the way in relatively settled times. But it is hard to deny that co-ordinated work was not undertaken until lowering clouds began to darken the sky. A Mansion House resolution of January 1872 on the subject came *after* the first threatening noises in Parliament and the first practical steps were taken a year or two *after* a public appeal by Gladstone for some such initiative and after the start of J.F.B. Firth's rumbustious agitation. The foundation of the City and Guilds Institute in 1877–8 proved to be the start of a remarkably successful venture, but in view of the novelty of such co-operation between the Corporation and sixteen participating Companies and the dissension which anyway broke out periodically in the early years, it is hard to see how the momentum could have been sustained had it not been for the threat of interference or abolition. One of those associated with the Institute from the outset, Professor Thomas Huxley, likened the benefactors to a kind of collective donkey: 'the animal is moving and by a judicious exhibition of carrots in front and kicks behind we shall get him to a fine trot presently'.[3] Constant attacks in the press, repeated questions in the House, and the prospect of a Royal Commission, must all have administered a series of most salutary blows to Company rumps. Much later, when the Institute was faced with a financial crisis in 1904–5, the Clothworkers decided to shoulder the burden, despite a poor response from its fellow-benefactors, because 'the abandonment of a national and valuable work which has conferred such lustre on the Livery Companies would be disastrous on public grounds and would undoubtedly cause a revival of serious attacks on the constitution of the Companies'.[4]

The 'great awakening' manifested itself not only in those Companies still strong and wealthy in the 1870s, but also in Companies which had fallen into decay. A considerable number were either expanded or revived. This was true, *inter alios*, of the Basketmakers, Founders, Gardeners, Glaziers, Horners, Loriners, Needlemakers, Playing-Card Makers and Shipwrights. Once again the reasons are much debated. The Companies themselves argued that increased revenues enabled them to be more expansive. Certainly these were good times for owners of property in the square mile; and in the period 1870–9 the Companies' yearly income increased by almost fifteen per cent. or £100,000. But though this may explain the largesse lavished on good causes at this time (the City and Guilds Institute received no less than £800,000 between 1878 and 1909), it cannot be the reason why some of the smallest Companies, with little or no real estate, also took on new life. Some people explained the revival in terms of personal initiative, and again it is true that certain individuals played a vital role in resuscitating their guilds. The Musicians in large measure owed their revival to William Chappell, the musical antiquary; the Fanmakers to Sir Homewood Crawford, the future City Solicitor; the Tinplateworkers to E.A. Ebblewhite, their Clerk and historian; the Coachmakers to George Hooper; and the Turners to John Jones, vigorous champion of the Livery's rights in Common Hall. But of course, such men could scarcely create guild loyalty *ex nihilo*; their success depended heavily on an existing enthusiasm.

Where then did that interest come from? It was surely a consequence of the radical agitation itself. The remorseless public attention to which the City was subjected made 'citizens' take a second look at their ancient institutions. Some obviously decided that Guildhall and the Companies were worth preserving from Firth and his friends. As clubs and agencies of philanthropy the Companies had much to commend them, and businessmen who had hitherto remained aloof began to replenish the dwindling ranks. As Liverymen, of course, they could be entitled to a vote in parliamentary as well as civic elections and the City's opponents, Liberals and radicals alike, claimed that the expansion in numbers was a deliberate contrivance designed to bolster the Conservative cause. They were able to point to the transformation of the City from a Liberal stronghold into a Tory one. In

1874 only one Liberal, Goschen, was elected; in 1880 there was none at all. (This was despite the effect of the so-called 'minority clause' of the Second Reform Act (1867), which prevented City voters from casting more than three votes each. Without it Goschen would doubtless not have been elected.) How tempting it was to associate this with the substantial increases in the Livery bodies of some of the Companies. The Loriners, Needlemakers and Spectacle Makers each sent three or four hundred voters along to the polls and aroused considerable suspicion. Cries of 'faggot votes' became still more strident when the Aldermen permitted Companies to increase their Liveries beyond the limits prescribed in their constitutions. It is impossible to be certain that there was no truth in the allegations – City Solicitor Crawford's revival of the Fanmakers has an undeniably suspicious look to it; but it is generally easy to accept the Companies' defence that they were admitting new members simply for the sake of their finances. Companies without property could only survive by levying fines and fees and it would have taken an act of extraordinary self-denial to turn away the lengthening queues of applicants. As for the new Liverymen themselves, it is more likely that they were activated by a new-found interest in the Companies than by a desire to add to the Conservatives' electoral strength. No doubt they were impelled by a Conservative determination to resist the radical marauders, but it is hard to see them as pawns in some party-political game.

Gluttony and fraud

So much for the Companies and their members. What now of their assailants? As the Commission of 1833–7 had shown, there were always those who nursed grievances against their Companies and who were prepared to fight their cause in public or in print. In 1872 J.R. Taylor urged the guilds to reform themselves before the State did it for them. He was convinced that he had been denied his rightful place on the court of his own Company, the languishing Innholders, simply because of his radical views. He stressed the innocence of his intentions, but thought the Companies had to be 'useful' if they were to survive. Taylor was a familiar figure and his warnings had little impact. Other less conventional critics were not so easily dismissed. In 1876 the formidable J.F.B. Firth took up the fight. The third chapter of his *Municipal London* made it clear that the agitation for a centralised metropolitan authority would be directed as much against the Companies as the City Corporation. For this there were various reasons. For Firth, of course, it was axiomatic that the Livery vote in Common Hall made the Companies an integral part of the Corporation. An attack on the City would have to include an attack on the guilds. It was also argued that the Livery 'lobby' sustained the Corporation in its fight for survival. Again, the Companies were vulnerable, an easy first step in the demolition of the civic edifice. Finally their wealth could be used as a spectacular endowment for the proposed new Council. No taxes, just a splendid windfall.

There is no proof positive on the point, but Firth seems to have followed up his remarks in his book with the foundation of a City Guilds Reform Association. At the very least Firth was the inspiration behind it. The speech delivered by the chairman, H.D. Seymour, to the St. Pancras Working-Men's Club in April 1876 was largely taken from *Municipal London* and one of the other fly-sheets published by the Association consisted entirely of extracts from the same work. The message was resoundingly clear. The Companies should be, if not abolished, then thoroughly reformed and their revenues 'reappropriated', for public purposes. Tradesmen should rise up and call for 'Reform and Restitution'.[5] Their guilds had neglected them for too long. A Royal Commission of Enquiry should be appointed to start the process.

The Association gained valuable support from James Beal, now Firth's adjutant in the cause of centralization. Beal's contacts were put to good use. He persuaded his own St. James's vestry to initiate a vestry and district board memorial to the Home Secretary urging the appointment of a Royal Commission; and he also contributed some racy and vehement letters over the signatures 'Nemesis' in the *Weekly Dispatch* and 'Father Jean' in the *Echo*. The 'Nemesis' ones, as reprinted by the Reform Association in their fly-sheet series, leave Beal's earlier moderation far behind. The City Corporation is that 'great civic Juggernaut', that 'fathomless court of corruption'; and the Companies are dens of 'gluttony and fraud'.[6]

Other writers on the subject included William Gilbert, author of *The City* (1877), which castigated the Companies particularly for ejecting the poor from their property and forcing them to live in squalor outside the square mile. J.R. Phillips, a barrister and police magistrate, contributed to various journals on the question: he was 'Censor', for example, in the *Weekly Dispatch*. He thought that the Companies' endowments should be pooled and distributed as Parliament saw fit; as for the Halls, they should be sold, every one of them.

Judicial munificence

This agitation 'without doors' was consciously designed to lend weight to similar agitation within Parliament. The subject of the Livery Companies had been raised by M.P.s before this time, but it was not until 1876 that the questioning became insistent. In May of that year, in a move that may well have been orchestrated by Firth and his band, W.H. James (Gateshead) moved an address to the Crown asking for a full return of the Companies' income and property. He used the occasion to raise a host of threatening charges and dark questions. He might protest that he had no wish to see the Companies 'obliterated and swept away', only that 'they should be more fully alive to the altered circumstances and necessities of the present day',[7] but his attack must have made Liverymen ponder the thin line that separated 'alteration' from 'abolition'.

The responses to James's motion were predictable enough, and there is no need to dwell on Kay-Shuttleworth's support nor on the Lord Mayor's opposition. Equally predictable, but more important, were the speeches of Gladstone and R.A. Cross. Gladstone may not have been convinced of the constitutional propriety of such an address, but he was certain of the need for enquiry. Although there might be instances of 'judicial munificence', Gladstone thought that 'much of the revenue of these Companies is positively and utterly wasted, and very imperfectly and doubtfully bestowed'. The Lord Mayor, Alderman Cotton, might find himself supported by a majority of M.P.s in a predominantly Tory House that day, 'but can he guarantee the permanence of that balance of parties? Can he guarantee that that state of public opinion will endure?'[8] And though Gladstone agreed with James that the Companies should not be abolished, who could say what should happen if they persisted in their obscurantist resistance to change? These were ominous, prophetic words. But, of course, for the present a Conservative ministry was in charge and when Home Secretary Cross declared his opposition to the motion James withdrew it.

In the following year James made two further attempts. In February he managed to persuade the House to order a return of the oathes and declarations taken by the members and officers of the Companies (with a view to investigating the ways in which the Livery franchise was obtained), but two months later a much larger number of M.P.s heavily rejected a motion pronouncing it 'the duty of Her Majesty's Government to introduce some legislative measure empowering the Crown to make full investigation into the present condition and revenues' of the Livery Companies.[9] The Solicitor General denounced such a 'general Communistic enquiry'[10] as a threat to private property. His views were widely shared.

It was clear that no Tory-controlled Commons would entertain an assault on the Companies as private corporations but in their public role, as custodians of the municipal franchise, they were distinctly vulnerable. Little wonder therefore that James's next assault, in March 1879, was occasioned by the recent increase in the Fanmakers' Livery sanctioned by the Aldermen. He moved that 'the sale of the parliamentary franchise by the City Guilds with the consent of the Court of Aldermen is an abuse and should be abolished'.[11] City M.P.s and their friends denied the allegations of political chicanery, argued that many of the Liverymen would qualify for a vote in other capacities anyway and explained the Livery increases as quite innocent attempts to raise more revenue. Their words carried the day by 153 votes to 114. Three weeks later James raised the sensitive matter again, though this time only in the form of a question to the Home Secretary, who played a straight and defensive bat in reply.

James's campaign had the important effect of keeping the Company question in the public eye, but it could not hope to find consummation in the statute book while the Conservatives were at the helm. In 1880, however, the Liberals were returned to power with a comfortable majority of

M.P.s at their command and the ageing but still formidable Gladstone at their head. This in itself was enough to make the Companies, and the Corporation, tremble. What was worse, their chief assailant, J.F.B. Firth, had established close links with the ministry.

Something to keep me quiet

It was not long before these fears were confirmed. In May 1880, in what was doubtless a carefully rehearsed gambit, Firth asked whether the Government intended to appoint a Commission of Enquiry into the Livery Companies. Gladstone would not commit himself to the form of the investigation but agreed that Parliament should get full information on the subject. A fortnight later the Home Secretary, Sir William Harcourt, announced that the Government had indeed decided upon a Royal Commission. With remarkable ease the reformers had achieved their objective.

The nomination of the Commission appears to have been the work of Harcourt; and in some ways it was not an easy task. The prospect of immersion in the delights of Company charters and constitutions was not enticing. One Commissioner recalled that Harcourt had conscripted him with the rather chilling words that he 'would give me something to keep me quiet for a year or two'.[12] Nonetheless the subject was of such importance and by now so controversial that when finally assembled the Commission bore an impressive stamp. It was headed by the former Conservative minister, the Earl of Derby (son of Disraeli's former leader), who was soon to take office in the Liberal government. Then came the Duke of Bedford; the former Liberal minister Robert Lowe, now Viscount Sherbrooke; the Lord Chief Justice, Baron Coleridge; the former Conservative Home Secretary, Sir Richard Cross; Sir Nathan Rothschild, head of the British branch of the banking family and Liberal M.P. for Aylesbury; Sir Sydney Waterlow, City Alderman but Liberal member for Gravesend and noted philanthropist; the staunchly Conservative Alderman W.J.R. Cotton (who as Lord Mayor in 1876 had been elected chairman of the 'Guilds Defence Association', a post he still held); the Conservative authority on agriculture and poor relief, Albert Pell; the radical Thomas Burt; and last, but in no respect least, those two scourges of the Companies, W.H. James and J.F.B. Firth.

On a count of heads it was undoubtedly a 'Liberal' Commission which could be expected to confront its task without sentiment or indulgence. But it was equally clear that there were at least two members who would want to go much further than most of their colleagues and one or two who would be opposed to any change at all. There was every indication that the Commission would be unable to speak with anything approaching a united voice. Firth on the one side, and Cotton on the other, would see to that.

The Commissioners began their labours by asking the Companies to complete a lengthy questionnaire covering every aspect of their activities. Most Companies complied, though usually, on legal advice, they protested

against the enquiries as an illegal infringement on chartered privileges and
declined to reveal their title to 'private' corporate property. These complaints notwithstanding, the response was a great deal better than it had
been for the previous Commission in 1833–7. Four fat volumes of evidence testify to the difference.

All this took time and it was not until 1882, two years after their
appointment, that the Commissioners began oral hearings. The first witnesses to be called were the Charity Commissioners, Thomas Hare and
Henry Longley, who expressed themselves satisfied with the way the Companies were discharging their formal charitable commitments but thought
they could do much more with their corporate income. Next followed the
critics of the Companies. Beal had his eyes on what he imagined to be an
income of around £1m a year, and he wanted it pooled and distributed
through his centralised 'municipality' for the sake of worthy causes. The
Companies' Halls should be sold and the proceeds devoted likewise to
public purposes. J.R. Phillips had similar ideas, while William Gilbert used
the opportunity once more to berate the Companies for their treatment of
their poor tenants. There were also two tradesmen who had complaints to
level against the Companies with which they were connected. E.J. Wather-
ston thought the influence of the Goldsmiths over his craft positively harm-
ful, while W.H. Williamson spoke harshly of the Fishmongers' dealings
with the London Fish Trade Association.

The Commission also received deputations from those anxious to benefit
from a redistribution of Company revenue. University College London,
King's College, the London Society for the Extension of University Teach-
ing and the London School Board, all came to press their claims. So too did
Magee College, Londonderry, on the grounds that the Companies had an
obligation to their Irish tenantry. The tenants themselves appeared as well,
urging that they be given the chance to purchase their property on favourable terms should the Companies be forced to sell.

Incorporated philanthropists
The case for the defence was presented partly by representatives from the
City and Guilds Institute. The Lord Chancellor, Sir Frederick Bramwell
(Chairman), and three Company Clerks, all emphasised the importance of
the Institute's work. But in some ways even more helpful to the Companies' cause were the remarks made by the Lord Chancellor, Selborne, in
an almost casual exchange with the Commission's chairman. In the course
of explaining how the Institute came into existence Selborne said that
James's motions in Parliament had played no part in the decision, at least
as far as he personally was concerned. 'I have always thought that the City
Companies, assuming them to be (as I believe them to be in law) absolute
and perfect masters of their own property, as distinct from that which they
held on trust, could do nothing better with their property than promote

objects which were for the public interest . . .'. Derby at once pressed him on the point:[13]

Are we to take it from you that the City Companies are entitled to their property in the same manner and as fully as a private owner would be? — In point of law they are in my opinion absolutely entitled to it, and under no trust whatsoever. It will, of course, be understood that I do not speak of estates which have been given to them on any special trusts. Morally, I do not think that I, as a member of a City Company [Selborne was a Mercer], should choose to be a party to using it in exactly the same way as I should use what was my own as an individual.

You acknowledge a great moral responsibility to the public in the case of private property, but not any greater legal right? — That is my impression. I do not know that I can express it much better. They are ancient institutions; the funds which I call their own property were derived, as far as my knowledge extends, from their own subscriptions, and gifts by their own members and others, intended to be for their absolute use; and although I do not think the present generation ought to put those gifts into their pockets, yet, on the other hand, I cannot admit for a moment that they are upon the footing of public trusts.

From the highest legal authority in the land these were portentous remarks and the Companies were later to seize on them with relish and with a complete disregard for the way in which they were delivered and the qualifications they contained.

For the rest the Commission's hearings were devoted to memorials, letters and deputations from the Companies themselves. Their case was a simple one. They were not public charities but rather (as a later historian was to phrase it) 'incorporated philanthropists'.[14] They were not, nor ever had been, *trade* guilds, but friendly societies established to provide fellowship and succour for their members. Their trading role was a later, extraneous and temporary one. Nor were they *municipal* institutions; they were *not* constituent parts of the City Corporation. Some of their members might be entitled to vote for, or nominate, Corporation officers, but that was the only connection with Guildhall. As to their charitable obligations, they were discharging their trusts with scrupulous care. Their *corporate* revenues were theirs to use as they pleased, though in fact they were often applied lavishly to objects of public concern.

Such was the compound of special pleading, legal subtlety and antiquarian research which confronted the Commissioners when they came to writing their report. Since they did not publish their conclusions until April 1884, there was ample opportunity for 'leaks' and plenty of scope for speculation. Firth gave a somewhat misleading preview to a meeting of the Chelsea Radical Club at the end of 1882, while the *Standard* a year later carried a rather more accurate forecast. Questions in Parliament increased the suspense.

A right at any time to disestablish and disendow

When it finally appeared the report was signed by only nine of the Commissioners, namely Derby, Bedford, Sherbrooke, Coleridge, Waterlow, Pell, James, Firth and Burt. The remaining three, Cross, Rothschild and Cotton, had felt constrained to compose their own minority report. What first of the majority report? It was prefaced by a long survey of the factual evidence. Much of this was familiar enough, but the section dealing with finance aroused great interest. In the first place, the figures showed just how wealthy the Companies were. Their total income for 1879 or 1880 was estimated at £750,000–800,000, more than the combined income of the Oxford and Cambridge Universities and Colleges as revealed in the recent Royal Commission. The capital value of the Companies' property was at least £15m. It was also clear that the revenues were increasing fast. In the preceding decade, 1870–9, income had risen by £100,000. And the signs were that it would go on rising, to the extent that £15m would become £20m in the next twenty-five years. This was despite the rather rash acceptance of expert advice that 'the value of City house property – the principal property of the Companies – has reached its culminating point'.[15] The report then analysed how the money was spent. The £750,000–800,000 comprised about £200,000 in trust income (i.e. explicitly committed to certain charitable causes) and £500,000–600,000 in corporate revenue (i.e. the Companies' own 'private' resources). How was the second and more controversial sum spent? The Commissioners calculated that £425,000 was available for use each year from corporate stock. From this source £175,000 was spent on maintenance; £100,000 on entertainments; and £150,000 on worthy objects. The 'maintenance' category, critics noted, included not just the upkeep of property but also attendance or court fees for Company members (£40,000), and salaries for regular officials (£60,000). On the other hand, due attention was paid to the frequently lavish way the Companies supplemented their trusts out of their corporate revenue. The most spectacular instance concerned the Merchant Taylors' recent expenditure of no less than £140,000 on their re-sited London school; but there were many other examples.

After this summary of the evidence came the Commissioners' recommendations. They went straight to the heart of the controversy and confronted the Lord Chancellor's, and the Companies', contention that corporate income cannot legally be investigated or redirected. The Commissioners, or majority who signed the main report, could not agree. 'It appears to us obvious that the State has a right at any time to disestablish and disendow the Companies of London, provided the just claims of existing members to compensation be allowed.'[16] However, this was not in fact what the

Commissioners recommended. Rather, the State should intervene firstly to prevent the alienation of Company property (the recent examples of Doctors' Commons and Serjeants' Inn had raised fears that Company members might conceivably sell their estates and pocket the proceeds); secondly to secure the permanent commitment of a considerable part of the corporate income to useful purposes; and thirdly to reorganize those trusts where a better application of the revenues attached to them was thought necessary. The justifications for such intervention, or interference, were predictable enough: the Companies were public, municipal bodies; their trusts had not, and (*pace* the lawyers) should have, benefited from the increase in property values; and so on. More interesting were the ways in which the general principles were to be given practical effect. A new standing Commission was to be instructed to make a radical reappraisal of Company expenditure along the following lines. Trusts more than fifty years old should be applied to useful causes irrespective of the intentions of the benefactors; a settled portion of corporate revenues devoted to approved 'public' purposes; and Company constitutions, if practicable, reformed. The Commission should serve for a maximum of five years, during which time the Companies had either to devise suitable 'redistribution' schemes of their own or have schemes imposed upon them. As for the claims of the City and Guilds Institute, the London Colleges and others, these were to be left to the judgement of the new supervisory body. On two other points the report made no pronouncement. The question of Common Hall was left, no doubt with much relief, for separate consideration by the Government as germane to the plans for reorganizing London's municipal government; while the Ulster estates were thought to raise the problem of Irish tenure which lay outside the Commission's scope.

Reappropriation

These disavowals were disappointing, but they did not detract over-much from a powerful and persuasive report. There is much to admire in the blend of flexibility and common-sense which the Commissioners displayed. Much would have depended, of course, on the conduct of the supervisory Commission but the general guidelines established for it are hard to fault. Hard to fault, at any rate, in the eyes of the 'reasonable man'. Those other more demanding judges, the lawyer and historian, might argue otherwise. So at least thought three of the Commissioners, Cross, Rothschild and Cotton. The law, they declared, protected corporations from the predatory instincts of the State. Their private property was as immune from interference as an individual's. Trust income, it was true, had to be disbursed in accordance with the legator's wishes, but it was not at all clear that subsequent increments had to be spent in the same way. History was invoked to show that the Companies were basically private fraternities, friendly societies, whose charity began and ended at home. Their trading role belonged merely to a temporary, if protracted, period in their lives, beginning some while after their birth and ending in the late sixteenth and seventeenth centuries. History also revealed that the Companies had only been rescued from the near-fatal effects of royal oppression (especially under the early Stuarts) and the Fire of 1666 through the prodigious and unaided efforts of their members. This notion of a 'second foundation' reinforced the assertion that the Companies' property was not public but private. For good measure equity was used to complete the argument. The Commissioners' proposals were not only illegal and unhistorical, they were unfair as well. The Companies did not deserve to be treated as errant knaves. They were doing a great deal to help worthy causes; and apart from the fulminations of Firth and his *coterie* there was no sign of public dissatisfaction.

Alderman Cotton signed the dissenting report but also added his own 'Protest' which predictably consisted of a warm vindication of the Companies' conduct and a fierce denunciation of legislative interference. Firth too had to make his own separate report and defended, point by point, the propositions in *Municipal London* on which he had based his call for disestablishment and disendowment. He had tried to persuade the Commission to endorse his proposals, but had lost his motion by ten votes to two; and his support for the majority report was tempered by the feeling that it did not go far enough. His 'Observations' on his signature made his position plain. He failed to see 'what useful purpose can be served by the continued preservation of such Companies as are dissociated from trade' and he thought that 'the best course to pursue will be to dissolve them and to vest their property in an Official Trustee unless or until a Representative Municipal Authority be established in London'.[17] That Municipality of London was certainly a better agency for the 'reappropriation' of Company funds than the proposed Commission.

There the report ended, and the debate began. Even the publication of the Commission's findings aroused controversy, for the secretary, H.D. Warr, wrote a circular letter to newspaper editors drawing their attention to the volume, and emphasising the need to educate 'Liberal electors' in the provinces before the Government introduced legislation on the subject in 1885. He also claimed, quite wrongly, to be acting on the authority of Lord Derby and his colleagues. Harcourt was obliged in Parliament to condemn this 'most indiscreet and improper proceeding'.[18] But, of course, more important was the question whether the controversy would produce any tangible results. There had been heat and fury before, but no legislative action. What would happen this time?

A grievous violation of private right
Sir William Harcourt, as Home Secretary, faced a barrage of such questions in 1884. Despite the Government's deep involvement in the prob-

lems of the Franchise, Ireland, Egypt and Afghanistan, there is no reason to doubt the sincerity of the assurance that though legislation 'at an early date' might not be possible, the ministers 'were not only willing, but anxious, to deal with the subject'.[19] But it was obvious that such a complicated matter did not stand high on the agenda. The only legislation even attempted before the budget in June took the modest form of a Corporate Property Security bill, designed to prevent corporations such as the Companies from 'alienating' their property. Introduced by Dilke and the Attorney General on 20 February, it was dropped on the second reading.

Little could have been expected from Salisbury's stop-gap Conservative Government (July 1885–January 1886). It was left to a member of the Opposition, the former President of the Local Government Board, the radical Sir Charles Dilke, to introduce a 'London Livery Companies Bill' in July, and though there was no real chance of it becoming law, it deserves some attention as a possible blue-print for subsequent legislation. The bill took its general format from a similar measure for the reform of the Universities and Colleges of Oxford and Cambridge in 1877 and most of its specific provisions from the recommendations of the Derby Commission. The Companies were given three years in which to frame schemes for devoting more of their corporate resources to purposes of 'public utility', reallocating their trust funds, and altering their constitutions as appropriate. A standing commission was to be appointed to approve such schemes and intervene when necessary. A few further provisions may be noted: Companies were to be prevented from alienating their property; their accounts to be properly audited; and no Liveryman henceforth admitted to be allowed to vote in Common Hall.

There was a predictable response. In the Commons the Lord Mayor, R.N. Fowler, came close to asking that leave to introduce the bill be refused – a most unusual, unseemly ploy. Outside the House the 'Associated Guilds' condemned the measure and two Companies, the Saddlers and Fishmongers, managed to get up petitions of protest. From the 'Liberty and Property Defence League' came Lord Bramwell's denunciation: 'If this was done by an autocratic legislator, it would be a simple act of tyranny. It is not less so that it is done by Parliament. It is a grievous violation of private right, and a most dangerous precedent'.[20] Much of this, of course, was simply 'for the record'. It must have been obvious that the bill was doomed; as indeed it was. Dilke dropped his measure on the second reading.

The general election of November 1885 left the Conservatives at the mercy of the Irish Nationalists and it was not long before Gladstone was back in office. There was scarcely time, however, even for a tentative enquiry about the Government's intentions before Home Rule forced the Liberals to go back to the electorate, who promptly returned the Conservative-Unionists with a sizeable majority. There Salisbury and his associates stayed until 1892 and during that period, though they made an important contribution to the problem of London's government, there was little likelihood that they would take up the question of the Livery Companies. When the member for Bethnal Green S.W. dared to ask about the ministry's plans, he received an almost supercilious reply from the Chancellor of the Exchequer, Lord Randolph Churchill: 'I should not feel justified in saying that the attention of the Government has hitherto been very closely given to the Report of the Commission on the City Livery Companies'.[21]

The Government's indifference made effectual action impossible, but the reformers persisted in their campaign. Inside Parliament there were bills for abolishing the Livery franchise and for preventing charities from alienating their property;* while outside there were the usual polemical publications. In his *Reform of London and of City Guilds* (1888) Firth reiterated his well-worn theme:[22]

It is difficult indeed to see, now that the Companies as a whole fail to discharge any useful function in connection with the purpose of their incorporation, why they should be preserved. The best course to pursue would appear to be to dissolve them, and to vest their property in a representative London municipal authority.

As for the Companies themselves, they too were active, though in a rather different way. The Royal Commission and its aftermath made them realise just how close to the precipice they had come. They redoubled their efforts to make themselves 'useful'. In 1886, for example, the Carpenters decided to devote their surplus revenue to the encouragement of their craft and the well-being of their East End tenants. The Commission also gave further impetus to the revivification of dead or dying Companies. The Gardeners, for instance, rose Phoenix-like from the ashes in 1890. Whether these developments would prove sufficient to protect the Companies from interference or abolition remained to be seen. Much would depend on the attempts to reform London's municipal arrangements and it is to that parallel campaign that we must now return.

---

*There were also enquiries into the Irish Society, which had been set up by the Corporation and the Livery Companies in 1613 to administer the 'Londonderry' lands granted by James I. Two Select Committee reported on the Society in 1889 and 1890–1, but though the second recommended dissolution nothing resulted. The 'Irish Society' issue was connected with the Livery Company campaign but was interlaced also with the emotive question of Home Rule.

CHAPTER VII

Rather transformation than death

The return of the Liberals to power in 1880 boded as ill for the City Corporation as it did for the Livery Companies. Gladstone himself acknowledged the need for some kind of reform of London's government and, provided other pressing concerns, such as Ireland, permitted, he was prepared to push legislation through Parliament. And he had colleagues, particularly Sir William Harcourt at the Home Office and Sir Charles Dilke, who were ready to tackle the mundane details. Action, however, was unlikely to be forthcoming without a judicious combination of encouragement and pressure. With so many other issues demanding attention, 'London' had to be kept in the ministry's eye. This was the self-appointed task of J.F.B. Firth.

We have already met Firth as the author of *Municipal London* (1876) and the antagonist of the Companies. Now is the time to introduce him properly. He was a Yorkshireman by origin, a Quaker by religion and a lawyer by training. In 1880 he was at the height of his powers and influence, in his mid-thirties and M.P. for Chelsea. His knowledge of the intricacies of metropolitan and civic administration was enormous. He even took the trouble to purchase the large library of a former member of the City Corporation to garner the necessary facts. Whether he brought any personal charisma to his crusade is difficult to say. Photographs show a serious, possibly dour man. Yet he was capable of inspiring great respect, as the words of his close associate, John Lloyd, make clear. More important perhaps was his capacity for hard work, his skill as a polemicist, and his political shrewdness. A rare combination. He had the sense to realise that only by keeping the message loud, insistent, and above all simple, would people take note. Over and over again Firth demanded a single centralized municipality for London. He would have nothing to do with appeasing the M.B.W. and the City. Compromise was quicksand which had engulfed his predecessors. First establish the principle, he declared; the details, and the difficulties, can follow later.

His first move in 1880 was to introduce a bill in Parliament, not so much with the hope of securing its passage, as to have his proposals considered and circulated. There was to be a central Municipal Council, comprising a Lord Mayor, forty Aldermen and two hundred Councillors. The City was to be one of forty districts, each returning one Alderman and five Councillors at triennial elections. Precious few concessions were made to the City's anomalous privileges. Existing Liverymen retained their vote, but new creations did not unless also qualified as ratepayers or parliamentary electors. And existing Aldermen who had not passed the Chair were to be continued in office during the first Council. Otherwise the City, like the M.B.W., was to be 'merged' in the new authority. The Livery Companies too, and the City police, would come under democratic, metropolitan control. Firth paid some attention to the Corporation's indignation:[1]

A recent Lord Mayor has termed these proposals destructive; but under them, whilst it is true that the present Corporation, in its narrow and stinted character, would disappear, it would be rather transformation than death, and there would arise from its ashes a new and powerful body possessing the confidence, and representing the wishes, of the whole metropolis.

But his words carry little conviction. He can hardly have expected the City to acquiesce in its enforced demise in the hope of a glorious reincarnation.

Dramatic and courageous
In due course the bill was lost, but it had served its purpose. The question of a new Central Municipal Council for London was very much alive; and Firth was soon admitted to the highest councils to assist in framing Government legislation. Proposals were first laid by the Home Secretary before the Cabinet on Lord Mayor's Day 1881. To Dilke the choice of date seemed 'dramatic and courageous . . . We all dined with the Lord Mayor, and as the men came in I felt that, knowing what I did as to Harcourt's resolution, we were there under false pretences'.[2] What influence Firth had in precipitating this initial decision is hard to determine, but his was certainly a decisive voice when it came to the details of the plan. Dilke says that when he met Harcourt at the beginning of 1882 he discovered 'he had adopted all the ideas of Beal and Firth and of myself. We formed a committee, consisting of the four [of us], which met daily at Harcourt's house for some time.' Dilke adds: 'On January 7th a committee of the Cabinet on the London Government scheme was appointed, but it met only once, for the informal committee of Harcourt, Beal, Firth and myself did the whole work . . .'[3]

Firth almost certainly dominated the quartet's deliberations. Beal alone could challenge his intimate knowledge of the problem, and by this time Beal was something of a spent force, working now for a centralized municipality but unready to lose his independence by serving under Firth. It was more, one suspects, in deference to the past than the present that Beal was allowed to join the inner sanctum. Firth it was who provided the impetus. It is true that when the bill was made public the ministers pointed to the provision for district councils as evidence that Firthite dogma had been eschewed. Dilke claimed, for instance, that the plan was the same as that embodied in the Shuttleworth resolutions of 1878. But this was a smokescreen, whether deliberately contrived or not. There were local councils, it cannot be denied, but they had very little power and have all the appearance of a sop to public opinion. Most of the effective power was vested in a strong unified Central Council of the kind envisaged in Firth's bill of 1880. The City was given a little more perhaps in the way of special treatment: it was to have, for example, the disproportionately large representation of thirty out of 240 seats; but otherwise the outlook was quite as bleak. Firth, in very large measure, had got his way.

A sea strewn with many wrecks

The Government announced its intention to legislate for London in the Queen's Speech of 1882, yet it did not introduce the bill until 1884. Why the delay? Thanks to the researches of Dr. Young, Dr. Nicholson and others, we know the answer. In the first place, there was a serious dispute over the police clauses. Harcourt, mindful of the threat of Irish terrorism (so shockingly manifested by the Phoenix Park murders), insisted on the Home Office having control of the London police; Gladstone, Dilke and Joseph Chamberlain, on grounds of principle, held out for local control. It was a good while before agreement was secured for the obvious compromise, *viz.* the metropolitan force coming under Government control and the City force under Council control. Secondly, the ministers, as so many of their forerunners had done, found it very difficult to spare the necessary parliamentary time for a complex and comparatively gratuitous reform. Ireland and the Franchise pressed much harder on the ministerial consciousness.

When finally the London bill was laid before the House in April 1884, there was more than a hint of trepidation. Harcourt likened his task to that of 'a navigator who enters a sea strewn with many wrecks and whose shores are whitened with the bones of many previous adventurers'.[4] He went out of his way to mollify the City. He had great respect, he protested, for the Lord Mayor and his office; he was anxious, he declared, to 'build on ancient foundations'.[5] The bill was not a bill of confiscation; it 'merely magnifies and enlarges the power, dignity and influence of the Corporation of London'.[6]

For the most part the words fell on deaf ears. The City's supporters were not convinced; and most of the other M.P.s were simply not interested. It was a minority question. Dilke wrote to his agent:[7]

One unfortunate thing about the London bill is that no-one in the House cares about it except Dilke, Firth and the Prime Minister, and no one outside the House except the Liberal electors of Chelsea. This is the private hidden opinion of Harcourt and of the Metropolitan Liberal members except Firth. I am personally so strong for the bill that I have not at any time admitted this to Harcourt, and I have only hinted it to Firth. . .

A RESPITE.

Sir William Vernon (the Wicked Baronet). "HA! (Aside.) FOILED AGAIN! BUT A TIME WILL COME—"!!!

This is difficult to check (and Dilke was always conscious of his audience), but certainly Harcourt recognized that his measure would arouse little excitement. He called it his 'big suet pudding', a 'stodgy *pièce de résistance*' in the legislative programme.[8] And when the second reading came up in July the Chamber was woefully thin. On one occasion the Opposition estimated the attendance at between fifteen and fifty and on another twice called, unsuccessfully as it transpired, for the debate to be declared inquorate.

Apart from the Chelsea contingent the only real passion came from the City's Tory supporters. There were fierce outbursts of indignation from C.T. Ritchie (Tower Hamlets), of whom we shall hear more later, and from two Aldermen, Sir John Whittaker Ellis and R.N. Fowler. Ellis contributed a marvellously patriotic harangue:[9]

The Corporation of London was now the most perfect municipal government which existed in the world; and the bill which sought to abolish the Corporation was so full of absurdities and inconsistencies, in the name of unity was creating so much disunity, so stultified itself in its details, that he should be wanting in his duty to the Corporation of which he had so long been a member if he did not raise his voice in protest against it.

Fowler, whose reluctant conversion to civic life we have traced earlier, was equally vociferous and as Lord Mayor from 1883–4 and again in 1885 he spoke with special authority.

The second reading of the bill in July proved to be its last. It would be easy to assume that the inauspicious reception in the House was responsible for the bill's failure. But this was almost certainly not the case. What really killed the bill was the full-scale crisis provoked by the Lords' rejection of the Franchise bill. The ministers decided to make the issue a test of confidence, and this meant clearing the decks of other major pieces of legislation. Such an outcome had long been expected and there is some reason for believing that by July at least the Government was going through the motions on 'London' as testimony of good intentions and with an eye on a forthcoming general election. Hence, in part, the indifference of the House.

The reformers were understandably angry and vent their wrath principally on the Prime Minister. But their vituperation was a little unfair. Local government may not have been one of Gladstone's political priorities, but there was no question of wilful obstruction. It was quite absurd to argue from the G.O.M.'s acceptance of a Guildhall address in October 1881 marking his fifty years' public service to some devious antagonism towards municipal reform. His attitude to the City was diplomatic but unequivocal:[10]

We say that we ought not to leave, in its present state of isolation, the historic

Corporation of London. We do not admit that that historic Corporation,
with all its traditions — and very great traditions many of them are — is the
property of the small handful of persons contained within the limits of the
City. We affirm that the Corporation belongs to the metropolis, and that the
metropolis should have the power to do honour to the Corporation. This is
not spoliating, but enriching it. The riches, dignity, power, authority, and
desirableness of belonging to that Corporation will be infinitely greater when
it has undergone its just extension, and become the representative of the
whole metropolis, than ever it can be as long as it remains within its present
narrow limits.

In due course Gladstone, or at least his party, would have another opportunity of 'extending' the City's limits. For the present the Corporation
could take comfort that yet another assault on its independence had come
to grief.

The trumpets of the League

Before passing on to the next stage in the saga it is necessary to look once
again at that extra-parliamentary agitation which invariably formed the
backcloth to Victorian legislation. It is all the more important to do so on
this occasion since the tactics employed aroused considerable controversy
and in themselves contributed to the argument for abolishing the Corporation. The Harcourt bill induced almost millenarian enthusiasm in the
reformers' camp and near apoplectic anxiety in Guildhall.

First the reformers. In October 1880 a middle-aged aspirant lawyer from
Brecknorshire, John Lloyd, placed an advertisement in the press suggesting a gathering of all those interested in London reform. The response was
initially cautious but soon wholehearted. By mid-1881 Lloyd had collected
most of the great names of the movement, including Firth himself (as
President) and W.H. James, in what was called the London Municipal
Reform League. James Beal joined too, though his Metropolitan
Municipalities Association maintained a separate, if rather enervated, existence. Adherents were also found among the prominent politicians and
public figures of the day: some, like Kay-Shuttleworth familiar enough,
others like Sir Arthur Hobhouse and the banker B.W. Currie, less so.

The aim of the League was utterly straightforward. At Firth's insistence
it stuck strictly to the simple demand for One Municipality. Public meetings, letters to the press and pamphlets, all were employed with great
determination. One of its members declared:[11]

Nothing has ever been done in this country except by sound agitation, and
such was necessary before they could move the Corporation of the City of
London, but which, like Jericho of old, would speedily fall to the trumpets of
the League.

Readers who have come this far in the story will not be surprised by the City's reaction to these unlovely black-coated Sirens. It treated them all with a mixture of proud disdain and massive caution. It refused to make any positive step whatsoever. In October 1881 Common Council was urged by Deputy Rudkin to acknowledge its readiness to assist in extending 'an improved and more uniform system of local government' over the metropolis and instruct a committee to prepare a draft scheme as well as to consult with the Government and other representative metropolitan bodies. This after all, he pointed out, was in accordance with the Court's resolution of 1870. He argued in vain. An amendment pronouncing it 'unwise, if not uncalled for, for the Corporation of the City of London to take the initiative in drafting a scheme affecting representative bodies outside the City' was carried by a substantial majority. Councilman Judd spoke for many when he declared:[12]

This is not the time or place, nor were they the individuals to move in this matter. They were at that moment threatened by the Government, and he thought it would be better to let sleeping dogs lie. At all events this was not the time when those having glass houses should throw stones. When the day came that they had to defend their rights and privileges, they should be able to meet their enemies in the gate; but for them to sally out and attack others was about the most suicidal thing they could do.

When the Government's bill did finally materialise in April 1884 Common Council's orators shed their reticence and revamped their trusty *clichés*. It was a 'bill of disturbances', of 'pains and penalties', of 'confiscation'. It would destroy local self-government, promote centralization and create a Monster Municipality. It was the work of a junto of malevolent agitators, the artificial contrivance of the Municipal Reform League. Worst of all, 'the bill, while professing its extension and enlargement, practically extinguishes the ancient Corporation of the City of London, with its charters, liberties and traditions.'[13]

Sir William Harcourt had expressed himself desirous of building on ancient foundations. But permit him to say that if the measure were carried the old Corporation of London would be entirely extinguished; not a fragmentary portion of it would exist; the old City of London, with its Lord Mayor, great and respected, would be no more.

Few dared to counter such furious rhetoric. One dissentient, the Liberal Sir John Bennett, could scarcely make himself heard. Others, such as Councilman Dresser Rogers and Alderman Sir William McArthur, suspected of favouring a single municipality, were denounced and called upon to resign.

A MIDSUMMER PANTOMIME.

"OH, THE LITTLE DARLING! I'LL PUT HIM IN THE OVEN, AND KEEP HIM NICE AND WARM *TILL NEXT YEAR!*"

Like mummies in a glass box
It is perhaps superfluous to add that amid the flurry of destructive indignation there was no room for positive contributions to the metropolitan
debate. The only City schemes publicly propounded at this time came from
unorthodox sources. In 1882 Benjamin Scott dusted down his proposal,
first advanced in 1867, for a Central Corporation to superintend the work
of the City and the metropolitan boroughs. It was to be no more than
primus inter pares. The City undoubtedly valued its Chamberlain's work,
but there was no official endorsement of the plan. It appeared as a personal
contribution to the *Contemporary Review*. A more original, but less realistic, suggestion was published by Henry Clarke in letters to the *City Press*
in 1881. Clarke wanted to extend the boundaries of the Corporation to
Charing Cross in the west, Euston Road in the north and Nightingale Lane
in the east. Four new satellite boroughs would be created, together with a
Central Government Council dealing with metropolitan matters. This
brought Clarke to the notice of the Bishopsgate electors who returned him
as one of their Councilmen in 1882, but it had no other discernible impact.
It certainly did not arouse the interest of his new colleagues at Guildhall.
Clarke even failed to secure the appointment of a Metropolitan Government Committee to deal with the question of reform. It was not until
Harcourt's bill had been dropped that the Special Committee asked for,
and was given, permission to consider the general issue of London's government and to treat with interested parties. And all that resulted from the
Committee's deliberations was a brief report in November 1885, hurriedly
prepared in time for the General Election, which reaffirmed the resolution
of 1870 and suggested the creation of nine other borough corporations and
a nebulous 'central organisation'. Despite occasional instructions and
promises, the plans became no more specific or practical.

For some Councilmen such inaction was absurd:[14]

*They wanted a committee who would let the public know why the Corpor-
ation existed, and not a committee which contented itself by saying the
Corporation had been there so long and ought therefore not to be touched.
They were not to be preserved because they were like mummies in a glass box.*

But most were indeed content. They were only too aware of the fragility of
that glass box. Throwing stones, as Judd had told them, was madness.

To work up our opposition
Such at any rate was the public face which the City presented to a watching
nation. Behind the scenes and outside the Council chamber rather more
active steps were being taken to preserve the Corporation's independence.
In February 1882 a Special Committee was appointed to deal with the
impending London bill. It was given a free hand; and most Councilmen had

little knowledge of its activities. Discretion was the watchword. Not that it took much imagination to guess at its tactics. These were obvious enough: to publicise the case against the bill; organize opposition from interested bodies (the M.B.W., vestries and ratepayers); and orchestrate support for the alternative strategy of separate municipalities. For securing these ends the Committee authorised the expenditure of no less than £19,500, but how much it knew about the precise way the money was being spent is impossible to determine. It certainly placed a great deal of trust in the City's full-time officials. Not so much the Chamberlain who, as Scott was quick to point out, merely honoured the warrants presented to him, as the Solicitor (Sir Thomas Nelson), the Remembrancer or parliamentary agent (G.P. Goldney) and the Town Clerk (Sir John Monckton). On such men devolved the day-to-day task of taking 'the different steps that were necessary to work up our opposition'.[15]

Principally this meant employing 'agents'. Some were merely experienced local politicians, such as Common Councilman E.J. Stoneham; others were professional party men, such as H.B. Taylor in south London and C.H. Palmer north of the river; while one or two were apparently unattached mercenaries, such as the distinctly dubious journalist J.H. Johnson. Men of this kind were a familiar breed in Victorian politics and their work was not in itself illegitimate. But close supervision was essential, particularly when a public body like the City Corporation was providing the money. It was all very well for Common Council to put its faith in its Special Committee and for the Committee to put its trust in the officials; but someone had to take responsibility. The question is, did Nelson, Goldney and Monckton? The answer has not been found. Nelson took his secrets with him when he died in 1885, while Goldney and Monckton denied all knowledge of improper conduct. But at the very least it seems likely that they did not enquire as thoroughly as they ought to have done into their agents' activities. They certainly did not make it plain enough how far 'opposition' could go; and when dealing with men such as Johnson that was a grave mistake.

It was reasonable enough perhaps to spend money encouraging opponents of the Harcourt bill, but not so reasonable to contrive an impression of opposition. At least one of the Associations supported by City money was in existence before the agitation began, but others, such as Johnson's Metropolitan Ratepayers' Protection Association and W.J. Devenish's Anti-One Municipality League, were creations of the moment. To what extent they harnessed genuine opposition to centralization is hard to say. We do not have to accept all the charges of their opponents to acknowledge that there were grounds for suspicion. On one occasion Johnson asked Lord Clifton publicly to subscribe to his M.R.P.A. and promised to reimburse him for the £100 suggested – out of City funds, of course.

Similar question-marks hang over the 'charter movements' sponsored by

"THE VOICE OF THE TURTLE."

THE TURTLES, IN THE MOST UNSELFISH MANNER, ARE PREPARED TO SACRIFICE THEMSELVES IN THE INTERESTS OF THE CORPORATION.

[" I shall look with very grave suspicion upon any proposition for altering the government of the Metropolis."—*Speech of Lord Mayor Elect to the Liverymen.*]

the Corporation. The Remembrancer's explanation was gloriously poker-faced: the City 'have always recognized the great advantages they have themselves derived from being incorporated, and they have always endeavoured to extend those advantages to other people'.[16] It was, one supposes, purely coincidental that incorporation of the London boroughs would preclude the establishment of the dreaded Single Municipality? Perhaps cynicism should not go too far. There was some pressure for charters before 1882 and the necessary petitions to Privy Council could not be obtained without organization. But there can be no denying that the charter fever which suddenly infected Lambeth, Southwark, Finsbury, Marylebone, Tower Hamlets, Greenwich and Woolwich in 1882 owed much to Guildhall 'encouragement'. And when the Harcourt bill was dropped, so too was the charter agitation.

If 'Associations' and petitions were susceptible to the machinations of the unscrupulous, so also were meetings. The City claimed that over two hundred meetings were held to express opposition to the proposed legislation. Again there was a perfectly plausible justification for the 'organization' involved. Town Clerk Monckton declared:[17]

'I found in my part of the town the men whom I was in the habit of meeting said "What an absurdity this One-Municipality Movement is"; and I said, "If you think so, why not attend meetings and say so"; and they said, "A fine thing to attend them and get your head broken"; and then I saw that meetings must be in some way organized; that you must take some trouble to get them up and get people to attend them.'

But 'getting up' meetings proved to be something of a euphemism, at least as far as some of the less scrupulous or more zealous agents were concerned. Supporters who were deemed 'too enthusiastic'[18] were paid not to remain at a Guildhall meeting where they might have conveyed the wrong impression. On the other hand, some 'supporters' were hired to increase the size of the audience when numbers were deemed important. Alternatively audiences might be kept deliberately small and select so as to ensure they were 'pretty harmonious' (in Johnson's brazen words).[19] Meetings held outwardly in the name of the Reform League might be packed to make the opposition more numerous than the supposed convenors.

The press, of course, was an essential part of the campaign and large sums were spent on 'advertisements', i.e. reports on the meetings described above. Small contrived gatherings could be made to seem large and representative with judicious penmanship. Reporters too were encouraged, indeed paid, to attend the meetings and, according to Johnson at least (though his testimony must be treated with caution), they tended, for some strange reason, to take 'a pleasant view'[20] of the City's side of the question.

"THE LOVING CUP."

(MINISTERIAL BANQUET AT THE MANSION HOUSE.)

The Lord Mayor. "HERE'S TO OUR NEXT MERRY MEETING, SIR WILLIAM! 'THREATENED MEN LIVE LONG'!" *(Drinks.)*

" We are tol that London wants no reform or changes in its admirable Institutions. . . . . London never had a Government worth speaking of to look after its interests . . . . it had no Government. Where was the Corporation of London ? . . . . You come to me for a remedy. . . . . I see only one remedy, in constituting London into a body able to take care of itself. When it is once so constituted," &c., &c., &c.—*Sir W. V. Harcourt's reply to the Anti-Water Companies' Deputation, vide " Times " Report, August 1.*

London was in two great camps

The most controversial tactic of all was to interfere with the meetings of the L.M.R.L. Nothing could be done perhaps to prevent hot-headed supporters, such as Captain Sewell (unfortunately also a clerk in the Chamberlain's office) and his militia men, from taking the fight to the enemy, as occurred at a League meeting in 1881; but it need not have been Corporation policy virtually to follow their example. Of course, the Remembrancer was able to find a suitable form of words to lend legitimacy to the strategy. The City, he said, could not allow it to be thought that Firth's meetings were a true reflection of London opinion. This was an understandable anxiety, but no excuse for confrontation. For once the principle of interference was conceded, a string of dangers followed. If 'speakers' were to move amendments at league meetings then they would have to be protected. And 'protectors' might not confine themselves to their appointed tasks and indulge in provocative heckling or fisticuffs. Again, if men were required to lend some visible numerical strength to the City's cause and counterbalance the League's supporters, then there was a temptation to introduce hired bands. And if men were to be hired, transported and 'refreshed', why not make sure they were tough enough to make themselves heard and felt? Finally, if the League resorted to the device of making 'open' meetings invitation-only affairs, why not make one's own tickets and distribute them among friends?

To all these temptations the City's agents succumbed. How far City officials were cognizant of the more reprehensible practices will never be known. But they certainly stand indicted of failure to forbid interference at the outset. They had plenty of other weapons at their disposal without having to resort to provocation of this kind. It was unworthy and undignified.

What now of the City's opponents? Their annalist, John Lloyd, painted a vivid contrast between:[21]

. . . the London Municipal Reform League, working openly by public meetings, letters to the Press, and pamphlets,and supported only by the funds of its subscribers, and the Special Committee of the City Corporation working in secret, with practically unlimited Corporation funds at its disposal, and perfectly unscrupulous as to how they were spent, so long as the League's meetings could be obstructed and their efforts to obtain reform rendered vain.

This was absurd. The League too had 'stewards': in one case twelve, in another forty, all 'honest but powerful'[22] hammermen from a Chelsea engineering works; it too hired 'organizing agents'; and it too knew the power of the purse (witness the £4 paid for information on the forged tickets). But it remains true that the League's record was better than the

City's. The former may not have had the widespread, spontaneous support it claimed, but it certainly did not feel the need to descend to some of the 'dirty tricks' practised by Johnson and Co.

The scenes of near-anarchy which resulted from clashes between the two groups are difficult to recreate. At a League meeting in St. James's Hall in June 1883 the reformers filled the front of the building with friends admitted by ticket through a special door. The City sent 70–80 of its own supporters and serious trouble ensued. Agent Palmer stayed long enough to see a man thrown over some bannisters and then departed hastily. At the Kensington Town Hall nearly a year later the League placed three hundred adherents next to the platform and another phalanx at the rear of the audience. The precautions were no more than was required, for the City's agent sent almost as many of his own men. One episode in the ensuing *fracas* was initiated and later described by Lloyd: 'a powerful, big man, the fugleman of the City-hired gang, was tossed from the platform and forced through the door. He troubled the meeting no more . . .'[23]

Verdicts on these unseemly events depended on the point of view. The Remembrancer likened it to a parliamentary contest: 'We were fighting a great general election you might say, for more than two years, over the whole of the metropolis.'[24] Lloyd, on the other hand, preferred military metaphors. 'London was in two great camps, the City and its hirelings, and the People and their leaders'; it was a 'prolonged battle royal'.[25]

The apple had fallen from the tree into our lap
We left Gladstone's ministry in July 1884 embroiled in parliamentary reform. This proved to be only the start of many months of political instability, with Home Rule for Ireland at the centre of the turmoil. A short-lived Conservative ministry (July 1885 – January 1886) was followed by Gladstone's equally brief Third Government. It was only in July 1886 that the electorate gave a conclusive verdict. With the support of the Liberal Unionists the Conservatives could command 118 more seats than the Liberal Home Rulers and Irish Nationalists. The Prime Minister was the shrewd and intellectual Lord Salisbury.

The arrival of any Conservative Government, of course, was likely to evoke a sigh of relief from Guildhall. And the situation certainly looked promising. Salisbury, it was true, was no stickler for tradition and had clever plans for bringing his party face-to-face with democratic reality. He had already expressed himself publicly in favour of a reform of local government, that most sensitive of issues for the Conservative party; and indeed a bill had already been drafted. But he was most unlikely to countenance anything that smacked of centralization. Even more encouraging was the appointment to the Presidency of the Local Government Board of C.T. Ritchie, the leading Conservative opponent of the Harcourt bill in 1884.

The City, therefore, had reason to hope that, if change were unavoidable, the longed-for separate municipalities would be the chosen scheme. For tactical reasons it refused to enter into details, much (as we have seen) to the exasperation of some of its supporters, but its preference was obvious enough. The other interested parties had similar, though independent plans: a deputation of vestrymen impressed the merits of the two-tier system on the Home Secretary in December 1886, while some metropolitan M.P.s tried to secure legislation embodying the same principle in 1887 and 1888.

Ritchie's own preference lay somewhere between this unabashed localism and the centralist alternative. The provisions for London in his bill establishing County Councils in England and Wales envisaged a central metropolitan 'county' authority subsuming the M.B.W. but working alongside both an independent City Corporation and a set of district councils of quasi-vestry status. This was scarcely the full-scale decentralization the City had been hoping for, but at least it was something. District councils, however weak, did represent a serious impediment to future radical assaults. But for reasons connected with the Local Government measure as a whole the Cabinet decided to drop the second tier clauses, and so the bill laid before Parliament in 1888 created a powerful and unencumbered London County Council – that is to say, the very Monster Municipality the City had dreaded so much and had laboured so hard to prevent.

This time there was no reprieve. Partly because the time for replacing the indirectly elected and ramshackle M.B.W. had palpably arrived. (A 'corruption' scandal only hastened the inevitable.) Partly also because the City Corporation was virtually unaffected by the measure. There was, therefore, no hope of a backbench revolt of anti-reform Tories, at least not on the scale required to endanger major Government legislation.

The City was thus obliged to suffer in pained silence the creation of the L.C.C. How could it complain? There were some irritating alterations in its government, on which it could, and did, make a stand; but fundamental changes there were none. Even the City police retained their independence. All it could do was hope that when the Government's provisions for the metropolis were complete – Ritchie promised further legislation in the near future – that the County Council would be counter-balanced by some effective local authorities.

The reformers, on the other hand, were delighted. They had obtained what they had always wanted: a democratic, powerful Central Authority. They were confident that it would be only a matter of time before the L.C.C. swallowed up that isolated anachronism, the City Corporation. Firth gave the following appraisal of the bill:[26]

*The general position is, that the Metropolitan Board of Works dies at once —
like a man who is beheaded — but the City of London is only to die gradu-*

ANOTHER "BITTER CRY."

Alderman. "OH, BUMBLE! JUST TO THINK OF IT!—NO MORE HALDERMEN!!"
Bumble. "AR SIR! IT'S WUSS THAN THAT!—NO WESTRIES! NO BEADLES! NO NOTHINK!!"
Both (*despairingly*). "OH, WERDANT 'ARCOURT! WERDANT 'ARCOURT!"—— [*They bust into tears.*

ally. It is to be surrounded by a pure and free organization, and the life at its centre cannot be prolonged for any considerable time. The Chairman of the London Municipal Council, as it may be called, will look upon the operations of the citizens in the square mile embracing the City very much as Lemuel Gulliver looked upon the operations of Mildendo, the capital of Lilliput, and before long the City will become part of a great municipal organization.

Firth and his friends affected not to be completely content with the bill: they were keen to commit Ritchie to further reform on specific points, and they complained about the exceptions made for the City's anomalies. But privately they could scarcely believe their luck. As John Lloyd recalled:[27]

Our long anxiety and labour were at an end, our victory had come, none the less valued, by a stroke of good fortune and without our raising a finger. The apple had fallen from the tree into our lap!

When the turtle is turned on its back

The excitement engendered by the County Councils legislation tended to overshadow another assault on Guildhall. On this occasion it was an attempt to impugn the City's integrity by means of a full-dress investigation of the City's opposition to the Harcourt bill of 1884. There had been complaints at the time, in both Parliament and the Press, about the City's conduct: Firth had publicly denounced the expenditure of City funds as 'unmanly, un-English, and disgraceful'.[28] But no firm evidence had emerged. It was only later that the chance to substantiate the allegations arose. Before handing over his account-book to City Solicitor Nelson, J.H. Johnson had taken the trouble of making a shorthand copy – 'mostly as a curiosity',[29] he claimed. In 1886 he passed the evidence on to the secretary of the Chelsea Liberal Association, whence, strange to tell, it came into the hands of J.F.B. Firth. Firth immediately recognized the importance of the book, but since the London issue was then dormant, he decided to wait for a more opportune moment. This came a year later when the City again got its parliamentary agents to work – this time to secure the renewal of the controversial Coal and Wine dues. After suitable 'revelations' in the press, Firth (temporarily without a seat) persuaded George Howell, M.P. for Bethnal Green N.E. and erstwhile 'organizing agent' for the L.M.R.L., to raise the matter in Parliament and call for an investigation. There was little opposition and on 4 March 1887 a Select Committee was duly appointed to consider the alleged 'improper use and malversation of public funds of the Corporation of London . . .'[30] Five M.P.s headed by the Marquess of Hartington were to be assisted by two interrogators: Charles Bradlaugh M.P. for the 'prosecution' and J.C. Lawrance Q.C. for the defence.

A familiar spectacle ensued, with Firth and his friends labouring hard to make their mud stick and the City officials, including the seventy-three year-old Scott, doing their agile best to avoid the missiles. A diverting side-show was afforded by the personal tussle between the remorseless Bradlaugh and the impulsive Lord Mayor, R.N. Fowler. Fowler had been a noisy and energetic leader of the resistance to Bradlaugh's attempt, as an atheist, to avoid the Christian oath imposed on new M.P.s; and he had also been impetuous enough to dismiss the malversation charges as 'anonymous tittle-tattle'[31] and (or so it was alleged) call Howell a 'damned liar' in the Commons lobby.[32] This set the scene for a heated, though inconclusive, clash. Fowler was plainly not party to any misdeeds.

Bradlaugh's insistent questioning, however, reaped a rich harvest elsewhere and by the end of the hearings much of the prosecution's case had been upheld. The Committee had little difficulty in coming to some firm conclusions. The City's expenditure on 'advertisements' in the newspapers had been extravagant and excessive, if not actually corrupt; the supervision of the agents' activities had been inadequate and the money disbursed to them used for indefensible purposes; subsidising so-called political bodies, such as the Metropolitan Ratepayers' Protection Association, had been improper for a public authority; and placing corporate funds in the hands of irresponsible and unknown persons for the manufacture of public opinion had been calculated to mislead Parliament.

All this constituted proof of the 'improper use' of City funds as mentioned in the Committee's instructions. It was only on the question of 'malversation' that the Committee demurred. The City claimed a legal right to spend its own private corporate funds in whatever way it chose, and the Committee decided that the claim could only be refuted in a court of law. (According to the recollections of one L.M.R. Leaguer, it was Hartington's casting vote which saved the City from a complete indictment; but there is no hint of this in the Committee's minutes.)

From this last conclusion the City derived considerable comfort and there was much heart-searching among the radicals concerning the inclusion of that over-precise term 'malversation' in the Reference. But in most respects they had achieved their aim. Direct parliamentary action may not have been forthcoming (though Firth was only quite narrowly defeated in an effort to have the Commons call for statutory restrictions on City expenditure), but the indirect consequences were far from negligible. The Hartington findings may not have played a part in the expiration of the Coal and Wines due, which were almost certainly doomed anyway; but they undoubtedly shocked a number of the City's friends and made the task of defending the Corporation all the more difficult. Firth once remarked that 'when the turtle is turned on its back it is not able to fight very hard'.[33]

CHAPTER VIII

THE METROPOLITAN BOROUGHS (1888–99)

Home Rule for London

Before 1888 the City had comforted itself with the reflection that positive innovatory action was necessary before its position could be threatened. After the establishment of the London County Council the situation was reversed. The City had to trust that the Conservatives would complete the work of 1888 and introduce those local councils which alone offered any hope of long-term security. But as the radicals themselves had discovered so many times in the past, it was easier to prevent than to pass legislation. Home Secretary Ritchie did not abandon his district council plans, but he could not, or would not, press them on his colleagues with compelling urgency. Other matters took priority. A bill was actually prepared in 1891, but nothing had been effected before the General Election of the following year returned the Liberals to power.

The change of Government was a calamity for Guildhall. Not simply because its old adversaries were back in office, but also because the call for reform or abolition had reached new heights. From its inception the London County Council was dominated by 'anti-City' sentiment. The 'Progressives', as the Liberals and radicals called themselves, heavily outnumbered their 'Moderate' or Conservative opponents. London Municipal Reform Leaguers, with the redoubtable Firth at their head, were well represented. There was unconcealed animosity towards the Corporation. Indeed, this was one of the reasons why Harcourt persuaded Lord Rosebery, former Liberal foreign secretary and one of the City's representatives, to become chairman of the Council. 'Firth', he said, 'would be a red flag to the City'.[1] (It was also felt that his election as chairman would render Rosebery's position as a member for the City less difficult and embarrassing.)

Firth, who took the influential and salaried post of deputy-chairman, died six months later on holiday in Switzerland – a premature end to a remarkable career. But his followers remained to further his schemes. 'Home Rule for London'[2] was the battlecry, and there was much excited agitation for the millenium 'by return of post'.[3] 'Unification' was at the heart of the demands; and that meant the end of the City, and almost certainly the Companies too, in their traditional form. In 1889 the Councillors voted by 57 votes to 17 in favour of a motion that the Livery Companies be reformed in accordance with the abortive bill of 1885; and three years later they adopted recommendations for 'the possession of full municipal powers and the removal of the exceptions and immunities now secured to the City'.[4]

Successive chairmen of the Council, Lord Rosebery (1889–90 and 1892) and Sir John Lubbock (1890–2), tried to restrain this militancy. In a celebrated review of the Council's first year's work, Rosebery offered the following advice:[5]

As you are aware, in some respects London is one already, but the Corporation and privileges of the City are maintained intact. Our duty, it seems to me, is to respect that arrangement in all courtesy and good faith. The present condition of things, as I have said, must in its nature be provisional. In the fullness of time the Metropolis will be one — one in all respects. It will not be easy to solve that great problem, to reconcile and blend all the various elements, to mingle the pomp and splendour of the City with the simple democracy of our body, to sew the purple of the City with the linen of the County Council together, but in any case it is not our work. It will be the work of statesmen and of Parliament, and no action of the Council, as far as I know, will either further or facilitate it. I hope it will be accomplished, when it is accomplished, with the least possible friction and the least possible irritation, but in the meantime I believe that our duty in the matter is perfectly clear and that our relations with the City should be marked by dignity and friendliness and fair dealing; not encroaching on the privileges of the City nor allowing the City to encroach on ours; not allowing the interests of the community of London at large to suffer any neglect on our part either in action or in representation, but not unnecessarily interfering with that ancient body where we have no direct interests of the community to serve.

These were skilful words, full of studied moderation. But it is important to note their substance as well as their tone. Rosebery was as committed to a unified London as the Firthites. The debate concerned the means not the end. In 1892 he decided to relinquish his rather embarrassing City seat and stand for East Finsbury. He told his new and more radical constituents in unequivocal terms that 'the object of Parliament and of reformers must be that the City should be united with London as soon as possible, and with as little friction as possible'.[6]

Unification

From the Foreign Secretary, and future Prime Minister, in the incoming Liberal Government, these were indeed portentous words. 'Unification' was in the air: 'the City turtle is on its back, the knees of Gog and Magog are shaking, the Griffin is rocking on his pedestal'.[7] In the House of Commons on 21 February 1893 John Benn, prominent L.C.C. Progressive and M.P. for Tower Hamlets St. George, asked whether the Government was going to take any steps to bring about the amalgamation of the City and County of London. H.H. Fowler, the President of the Local Government Board, replied that the Government had come to the conclusion that 'the

THE BOGIE MAN.

"HUSH! HUSH! HUSH!   "THEN HIDE YOUR HEADS, MY DARLINGS;
HERE COMES THE BOGIE MAN!   HE'LL CATCH YOU IF HE CAN!"

administration of London must be considered imperfect and anomalous until arrangements have been made for including the City in the general system of the Metropolis'. He had decided, therefore, to appoint a small Royal Commission 'to consider the proper conditions under which the proposed amalgamation can be effected and to make specific and practical propositions for that purpose'.[8]

The reasons for this decision are not easily determined. Perhaps Rosebery had impressed the importance of the question on his fellow ministers. Perhaps the cabinet was responding to back-bench pressure. There was, after all, a group of virulently anti-City metropolitan members making themselves felt at this time. Whatever the explanation, the Government decided to tackle the question in the most direct way possible. As Dr. Young has pointed out, the Parish Councils bill of 1894 afforded a perfect opportunity for the unostentatious reform of London's local authorities. Instead the party was to be granted the chance to bring the City down by means of a public enquiry followed by separate legislation.

The Commission comprised only five members. The chairman was L.H. Courtney, a respected Liberal Unionist of an intellectual disposition; the two 'municipal' experts were E.O. Smith, Town Clerk of Birmingham, and R.D. Holt, Mayor of Liverpool; and the two representatives of the interested parties were Sir Thomas Farrer, Progressive member of the L.C.C. and Henry Homewood Crawford, the City Solicitor.

Their terms of reference were exactly as Fowler had stated them to be in the Commons. The Commissioners were simply to consider *how* the amalgamation of the City and County of London could be effected. But the City thought the Commission should also consider *whether* such an amalgamation should take place. This, it claimed, had been implied by a letter from Fowler at the outset of the enquiry and only on that basis had the City decided to participate. The City wanted to be allowed to present evidence against amalgamation itself and to advance the claims of the other local authorities in London. The Commissioners, however, stood firm. They interpreted the reference to mean that 'such an amalgamation is desirable if it is practicable';[9] and they resisted the City's attempts to widen the scope of the hearings.

With painful deliberation the City withdrew from the enquiry. Neither side wanted to appear unreasonable and there was a good deal of self-justification and hesitation; but the breach was inevitable. The hearings began in June; by mid-November Common Council, on the advice of its Special Committee, had resolved that:[10]

The Corporation, whilst ready and anxious to continue to tender evidence, can only proceed upon the assumption and an assurance that the Royal Commission will be ready to hear evidence when tendered upon the question of the desirability as well as of the convenient practicability, of an amalgamation of the City and County of London.

PUTTING IT PLEASANTLY!

County Council Cook. "DILLY, DILLY, DILLY! COME AND BE—*AMALGAMATED!*!"

Fowler persuaded the City to continue submitting evidence for a time, but it was only a temporary truce. In February the City witnesses withdrew and Crawford asked for leave to resign. It had proved a futile exercise. The Commissioners felt that the City had been wilfully wasting their time by providing too much information on the irrelevant general points and too little on the relevant practical ones. The City, for its part, regarded the Commission as the creation and mouthpiece of the L.C.C. and felt that it had been 'absolutely precluded from suggesting anything but its own extermination.'[11]

Amalgamation

The four remaining Commissioners continued to hear evidence until June and published their findings in August. Their recommendations were drastic indeed. The 'Old City' and County of London, they said, should be merged in a new Corporation of the City of London. All the old City's traditions and ceremonies, including the office of Lord Mayor, should be transferred to the new body. The Old City would relinquish all its 'public' responsibilities and institutions, such as the markets, bridges, the Guildhall Library, the Museum, the School of Music, and the Mansion House. The freedom would be abolished, except that the new Corporation could continue to grant honorary freedoms. The Old City would be left with a few 'private' trusts, but otherwise was reduced to the level of the existing vestries and district boards. It was to concern itself simply with 'local administration' duties and the constitution of the 'Council of the Old City,[12] as it would be called, was to be brought into line with other such bodies.

The reactions to the proposals may be surmised without difficulty. The City, of course, was disgusted. Its Special Committee tried to make something of the Commissioners' plans for local councils with considerable, if undefined, powers, and there was talk of extending the boundaries of the City so as to enable it to stand alongside any such municipalities. But on the core of the report, the amalgamation scheme, there was unqualified hostility. Alderman Sir George Faudel-Phillips denounced the 'Mammoth County Council'[13] that would be created. 'Amalgamation', as a celebrated cartoon (p. 127) showed, meant not expansion but destruction.

The LCC Progressives, equally obviously, were delighted. The recommendations bore a striking resemblance to the proposals their Special Committee had tendered to the enquiry. They were disappointed that the Commissioners had not recommended that the united London police force be placed under the control of the new Corporation and they had misgivings about the plans for strong local authorities. But the removal of their *bête noire*, the City Corporation, was ample compensation. The cherished goal was in sight. The Special Committee – Sidney Webb, J. McKinnon Wood and W.H. Dickinson – set to work on the necessary bill.

All now hinged on the reaction of the Government. In March 1894 Gladstone had been succeeded as Prime Minister by Rosebery. How propitious it seemed! The Progressives pestered their associate for action and, despite concern about the likely opposition from the Lords, Rosebery agreed to introduce a measure. The bill was duly promised in the Queen's Speech of January 1895 and a Cabinet committee got down to preparing a bill – which differed little from the L.C.C.'s draft. Spring Gardens, the L.C.C.'s new home,* was alive with excited expectation. It was firmly believed that the end of the City had come.

Then time ran out. Once again a Government committed to reforming the Corporation found itself unable to spare the necessary parliamentary time. On 7 March the Chancellor of the Exchequer, Sir William Harcourt, told the House that the bill would not be introduced before Easter; and that was the last public mention of it. In June came the unexpected resignation of the Government and in July a General Election which gave the Conservatives a majority of 152. The City had escaped yet another attempt on its life.

Bolstering up the stupid old City
It was Salisbury and his colleagues who completed the salvation of the City by creating the longed-for separate municipalities. Why did they finally commit themselves to devolution in London? External pressure certainly played a part. The City Corporation itself continued to urge the merits of the plan. The vestries too, or at least the wealthier and more ambitious of them, petitioned to be granted greater powers. And there was also a little less pressure in the opposite direction from the L.C.C. Certainly during the years 1895–8, when the Progressives only maintained control through their Aldermanic majority, a more accommodating attitude was evident in Spring Gardens. Some functions, it was acknowledged, might be more properly performed by smaller local bodies.

But it was really the polarization of metropolitan politics along party lines which explains the Government's determination to pass legislation. The decisive step was taken in 1894 with the foundation of the London Municipal Society. There had been one or two previous 'private' attempts to galvanize Conservative opposition to the Progressive L.C.C., but the 'party' had remained aloof, partly for reasons of principle and partly through sheer lack of interest. The L.M.S. received the backing its predecessors had missed. Salisbury himself was persuaded to become involved in the enterprise, in part to ensure that Conservatives and not Joseph Chamberlain's ex-Liberal Unionists held sway in the new Society, but mainly because an offensive in London was considered essential to protect

---

*In its first year or so the L.C.C. met, ironically enough, in the City's Guildhall. Later it moved into the former headquarters of the M.B.W.

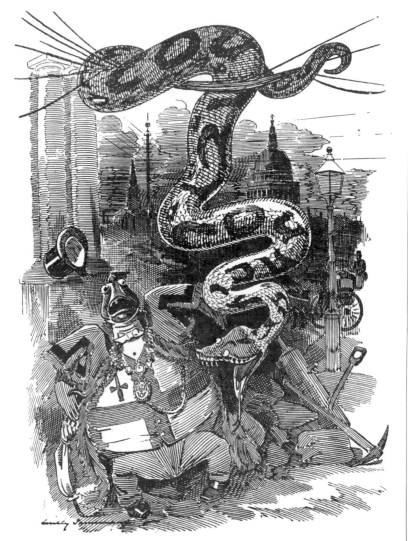

THE CIVIC TURTLE AND THE COUNTY COUNCIL BOA CONSTRICTOR.

the party's parliamentary representation. With no less than 59 seats now at stake following the Redistribution Act of 1885, the Conservatives could not afford to permit the Progressives to translate their municipal majority into a parliamentary one. The General Election, as well as the L.C.C. elections, due in 1895 made the issue a pressing one and Salisbury intervened in London's politics for the first time in November 1894. Carefully briefed by the party agent, Salisbury made a fierce attack on the Progressive County Council as 'the place where Collectivist and Socialistic experiments are tried. It is the place where a new revolutionary spirit finds its instruments and collects its arms'. At the same time he declared his opposition to any assault on the City which might result from the recent Royal Commission: 'this proposal to put the County Council in the place of the Corporation . . . will dispossess a body which has inherited great reverence and respect from many generations of Englishmen and is now held in high esteem . . .' The City must not be touched:[14]

> . . . any attempt to degrade and to spoil the City will not be patiently submitted to. The City has deserved well of England. It has a splendid record and there are many among us who will refuse to allow it to be swept away by an accidental swing of the pendulum when, for the moment, the powers that attack it may seem to be in the ascendant.

The Progressives, naturally enough, were disgusted at the sight of the Conservatives siding with Guildhall in the metropolitan debate. Sir Thomas Farrer, the L.C.C.'s representative on the Amalgamation Commission, wrote of Salisbury 'bolstering up the stupid old City'.[15] But the City, of course, was delighted and immediately recognized the L.M.S. as a valuable ally. There were soon negotiations about financial assistance, and though the precise outcome of a 'confidential interview' with Alderman Faudel-Phillips and Solicitor Crawford is unclear, £2,000 was expected.[16] The Companies too had an interest in the L.M.S., which had avowed its opposition to 'attacks made upon the trust and corporate property of the Livery Companies.' The Clothworkers subscribed £100 for the purpose of organizing 'a constitutional and legitimate league of defence against the wanton, systematic and unjustifiable misrepresentation of the detractors and enemies of the Corporation and Guilds of London'.[17]

The Conservative initiative had important consequences. It almost turned the tables on the Progressives in the L.C.C. elections of March 1895 and it placed London high on the agenda when a Conservative Government was returned after the General Election in July. L.M.S. members were well represented in Salisbury's cabinet and there was general agreement on the need for some form of devolution. But there was much less harmony and confidence over details. When finally a scheme was devised, the advocates of caution prevailed. The political and administrative difficulties were thought to allow only a limited transfer of powers – more limited indeed than even the L.C.C. had once been prepared to contemplate. The twenty-eight new local authorites were to be called 'boroughs', though they scarcely deserved the term. (It was, in fact, only included in the bill at a very late stage.) But, however hamstrung the bodies may have been, their mere creation was enormously beneficial to the City. A two-tier system of London government, no matter how top-heavy, gave sanctuary to the City Corporation.

A municipal mausoleum asylum

The Progressives were greatly relieved by the measure. One of them dismissed it as a 'legislative mouse', a 'modest Vestry Reform bill'.[18] But they nevertheless decided to whip up as much opposition in Parliament as possible, not so much on practical as on ideological grounds. The bill had a symbolic importance since it tampered, albeit gently, with the L.C.C. and also because it left the City intact. It was pressure from the London Liberals which ensured that the legislation was given a warm reception in the House.

When he introduced the bill on 23 February 1899, Arthur Balfour, the First Lord of the Treasury, explained why the City had been excluded: 'The City of London is already a highly organized local authority. It already possesses the dignity which we desire to increase in the case of the vestries, and to give to the new authorities we propose to create, and therefore, it naturally falls outside the scope of this measure'.[19] Sir Henry Campbell-Bannerman, the leader of the Opposition, was not so convinced:[20]

. . . sooner or later the City of London, like all the other parts of the metropolis, must fall into line with the neighbouring districts. There can be little doubt that it cannot be regarded as a permanent arrangement that there should be this great dignity and importance centred in one part of the metropolis – a dignity and importance almost overshadowing the dignity and importance of the London County Council itself.

There were few Liberal speakers who did not echo Campbell-Bannerman's sentiments. One of the most vigorous denunciations of the City came from John Burns, Progressive member of the L.C.C. and M.P. for Battersea:[21]

Whether honourable Members opposite like it or not, the City has got to be dealt with some day. (Hear, hear) Yes, the City has got to be dealt with some day, and I believe that day is not so far distant as many so-called representatives of the City are apt to think. We hear about the Corporation being the embodiment of the highest civic traditions, of historical continuity and all that sort of thing, but there are some of us who think that where it is not a

"I'M GETTING A BIG GIRL NOW!"

Miss Unified London putting away all her pretty Toys and Playthings.

municipal mausoleum asylum it has a tendency to become a glorified
Bucket-shop. There are some of us who believe it ought to take a keener and
closer interest in the life of poor and struggling citizens than it does. And
when the City is to be dealt with, amalgamation must take place.

More prominent members of the party spoke in similar vein. Herbert
Gladstone, for example, asked:[22]

How long will (the City) be content to remain a mere speck in the administra-
tive county of London, luxuriating in its enormous wealth, unburdened,
unbalanced, uninspired by any responsible discharge of duties in the least
degree adequate to its position? How long will it be content to occupy that
position, which every day becomes more of a reproach and an anomaly,
neglecting each successive opportunity of once more becoming the great and
vitalizing centre of the greatest metropolis of the world?

The Opposition was convinced that the bill should embrace the City in
its provisions. H.H. Asquith, the future Prime Minister, declared that 'a
bill which does not deal, and which does not profess to deal, with the
position, prerogatives, and powers of the City Corporation is a bill which
stands confessed upon the face of it as a bill whose authors are afraid to
deal with the essence of the problem which lies before them'.[23] An attempt
to include the City was made in committee, but the amendment was defeated by 208 votes to 103. The bill duly became law in July.

The London Government Act (1899) represented a decisive stage in the
City's struggle for survival. In the first place, it placed serious practical
obstacles in the path of future abolitionists. This had been clearly recognized by the Act's opponents. R.B. Haldane had said:[24]

To my mind the chief objection to this bill, as regards that part of it which
concerns the City, is not what it does not do – not that it leaves the City, in a
sense, intact – but that it makes the work of the reformer almost an impossi-
bility, in the future. Therefore, from that point of view, Her Majesty's minis-
ters may be congratulated, from the point of view of the City, on the creation
of these new municipalities, for they will surround the City with a sort of
Praetorian guard which cannot easily be broken through by those who wish
hereafter to tread the pathway of reform. And when Her Majesty's ministers
next go to the Mansion House – although I am not in the confidence of the
City – I think I can promise them a right royal welcome from the City, not as
far as the affairs of the Empire are concerned – nor as reformers of the great
municipality of London – but as men who have rescued the City from all
danger of attack upon its ancient privileges as an old and unreformed Cor-
poration.

In the second place, the Act identified the Conservatives with the cause of the City. As the Liberal Unionist Duke of Devonshire (formerly the Marquess of Hartington) remarked in debate, 'the Conservative party . . . are almost unanimously pledged against any attack upon the privileges and constitution of the City of London . . .'[25]

The City, therefore, had good reason to be pleased. There was a general recognition at Guildhall that a battle, if not the war, had been won. L.C.C. member Henry Clarke thought it no longer necessary to remain on Common Council:[26]

Before entering the Corporation in 1882, and ever since, I have laboured with others to defeat those who sought to impose upon London a policy of centralization which menaced the very existence of the Corporation. The happy termination of this struggle brought about by the present Government removed the principal motive which for some years past has induced me to seek re-election . . .

The Special Committee in its report to Common Council congratulated the Court that 'the Act in question by its various provisions constitutes the corner-stone of the Great Rebuilding of Local Municipal Government for London'; 'the principles for which the Court has for many years consistently or persistently contended are embodied in the Act'.[27] It was a sweet triumph.

THE MARQUIS AND THE MUNICIPAL MONSTER.

Salisbury Frankenstein. "SORRY I EVER PUT YOU TOGETHER, YOU GREAT HULKING BOOBY! BUT JUST YOU WAIT A BIT. I'LL SOON TAKE YOU TO PIECES AGAIN!"

CHAPTER IX

GUILDHALL AND COUNTY HALL (1900 onward)

All their gorgeous paraphernalia
The establishment of the Metropolitan Boroughs in 1899 undoubtedly made the City's position much more secure. For the immediate future at least there would be no more talk about 'unification' or 'amalgamation'. But this did not mean that the Corporation's separate powers were inviolable. Even a Conservative government felt obliged to legislate for the metropolis as a whole. Sensible provision for education, water and the Port of London could not be made without trespassing on the City's anomalous status. In 1904 Common Council re-formed its Special Committee in order to protect the 'rights, interests and privileges of the Corporation.' The City, it was said, was not prepared 'to take it lying down'.[1] There was a danger that gradual erosion might succeed where comprehensive assaults had failed.

But, of course, the chief source of danger remained the L.C.C. and relations could never be entirely amicable while the Progressives ruled Spring Gardens. Old animosities died hard and recurrent problems of services and rates were always likely to revive them. Further friction was caused by the sensitive issue of ceremonial and protocol. When the Council had to present its Address to the new King Edward VII in February 1901, the chairman, W.H. Dickinson, wrote in his diary:[2]

At St. James's we met the City Corporation who assembled in a separate room and went into the throne room before us. I think the King must have been struck by the contrast. They had all their gorgeous paraphernalia — gold mace, red and blue gowns, etc. etc. We had nothing . . . * *I'm glad we managed it as it once and for all places the Council on a level with the City and must sooner or later strike the public how absurd it is to perpetuate this dual system of London government.*

---

*The L.C.C.'s austerity was deliberate and self-conscious. As Margaret Cole has explained, the Council was 'much too proud to try and vie with the Lord Mayor and all his pomp and circumstance; the dislike of ceremonial is deeply rooted in the history of the L.C.C.' *Servant of the County* (1956), p. 25. Herbert Morrison relished the contrast between the City and the Council: 'Guildhall impresses one with a sense of history, antiquity and tradition, whereas the County Hall gives one a sense of authority and the pressing responsibilities of twentieth-century civic government'. All at County Hall was designed to enable members 'to save time and get through the greatest practicable amount of municipal hard labour'. *How Greater London is Governed* (1935), pp. 38–9.

Nonetheless, there was less ideological fervour than there had been. Ritualistic noises were still uttered but not very often and sometimes even then with more than a hint of pragmatism and resignation. Even J.W. Benn, *doyen* of the Progressives, couched his 'anti-City' polemics in conciliatory or at least ambiguous terms:[3]

The popular notion is that the L.C.C. thirsts for the blood of Gog and Magog, and has but scant admiration for their past or present belongings. 'Down with the City' is supposed to be the Progressive war-cry. 'Down with the L.C.C.' is rather mine, if it be held to convey the extension of the rights and dignities of the old City to all its children who now gather round its walls . . . I would gladly see the L.C.C. abolished tomorrow if some such comprehensive scheme could be carried. A house divided against itself cannot stand. If the City does not absorb the L.C.C., the L.C.C. must sooner or later absorb much of the City, and it would be vastly better that the old civic rod should swallow the socialistic serpent. It will be impossible for much longer to maintain this divorce of dignities from drainage.

There were a number of reasons for this shift of emphasis. In the first place, the 'defeat' of 1899 was recognized to be a major impediment to further reform. The 'dual system of London government' may have been 'absurd', but it was likely to remain for the conceivable future. Secondly, the issues of unification or amalgamation were regarded not merely as impracticable but also rather *passé*. The 'old guard'[4] Progressives, such as Dickinson and Benn, might wish to renew old campaigns, but their younger colleagues concentrated on new questions, such as housing and the extension of the Council's boundaries to embrace the new suburbs. Thirdly, the Moderates or Conservatives were threatening the Progressives' electoral position. Theoretical schemes for London's future government could be considered otiose, indeed even a political liability. So at least argued the Liberal M.P., T.J. MacNamara, at a 'Debate on the Reform of London Government' at the National Liberal Club in December 1906.[5] He had no love for the City – 'I have had enough of flummery to last me a lifetime' – but there was no point in upsetting the Corporation. The immediate concern was to win next March's elections.

Exploited London

The advice was sound for in 1907 the Moderates, now called Municipal Reformers, turned a deficit of forty-seven seats into a majority of forty-two. It was the beginning of twenty-seven years of Conservative rule in the L.C.C. The difference this made to the City was exemplified by the resolution of the Spitalfields dispute. Between 1899 and 1902 the Progressive County Council and the City had been at odds over the ownership of the market; but when an offer of control was made to the Council in 1911 the

Moderates were content to pass the market on to the Corporation and explicitly acknowledge the City's ancient monopolistic claims. Outside the Council chamber the Conservative L.M.S. continued to strive for the City's preservation. There were personal and tactical differences it is true: in December 1903 four City dignitaries resigned from the Society and in the following year the L.M.S. branch in the City was dissolved. But they were all fighting the same battle for localism and independence. In 1911 the L.M.S. promised to 'resist the threatened destruction of the City and Borough Councils in London'.[6]

The Progressives, of course, were maddened by the electoral rebuff, not least because a Liberal Government had just come to power. Beatrice Webb wrote: 'We always thought that the first Liberal ministry would see us defeated'.[7] (Sir Harry Haward remarked about a similar instance: 'What would have happened in London government if the party complexion of Parliament and the County Council had invariably been the same, may be left to the imagination)'.[8] The disappointment revived some of the traditional animus towards the City. John Lloyd was moved to publish his *History of a Great Reform 1880–1888* partly because of the City's contribution to the defeat of the radicals, including Lloyd himself, at the 1907 election. A Guildhall 'Ratepayers' Association' attacking Progressive 'wastrels'[9] recalled the bad old days of Johnson and Co. and Lloyd was determined to show the public who the real 'Municipal Reformers' were. His associates had similar feelings. The recently knighted Sir John Benn, for example, summarised Progressive aims in 1909 as 'a United London, an equal rate, the land bearing its due burden, the property of the ancient trade guilds devoted to works of public utility in the City for which they laboured'.[10] Three years later he concluded a celebrated speech on 'Exploited London' with an appeal to the City to take the lead in 'the reunion and reconstruction of London'.[11] Otherwise, 'if the City once more fails us', the Progressives were ready to implement Harcourt's bill of 1884.

There was, of course, the hope that the radicals could by-pass Spring Gardens and appeal directly to the Liberal ministers. But the approaches met with a distinctly lukewarm reception. Even the presence of an erstwhile colleague at the head of the Local Government Board afforded the Progressives no joy. In December 1911 John Burns told the M.P. and L.C.C. Liberal Percy Harris that he could not 'at present make any promise of legislation on the subject of London government next session'.[12] This merely confirmed what should have been obvious. The ministers would not contemplate venturing into such difficult territory without the support of London's representative body. The Progressives had to accept that unpalatable democratic fact.

Meanwhile civic life in the square mile was flourishing. The 'great awakening' of the late nineteenth century had proved to be no mere transitory phenomenon. A permanent change of attitude had been effected in

City circles. There were new clubs, such as the Cordwainer Ward Club (founded in 1902), the Guild of Freemen (1908) and the City Livery Club (1914). There was even a new Company, the Solicitors, formed in 1909 (though not made a *Livery* Company till 1944). This was the first new creation for two hundred years; and it was to prove the start of a trend. Perhaps the most reliable barometer of City vitality is afforded by the size of the Livery, which confounded the cynics by remaining at or around 8,000 despite the defeat of the radical assailants and despite the loss of electoral rights in 1918.[13]

A solid phalanx of opposition

During the First World War the two parties in the L.C.C. sank their differences to deal with the national emergency; and this co-operation continued afterwards during the period of 'reconstruction'. This had an important consequence for the City, for in return for an electoral pact the Municipal Reformers agreed to support the Progressives in their call for an enquiry into Greater London government. More extended and more centralized powers were needed for the County Council, it was claimed. The suburban authorities, especially the threatened counties, reacted vehemently. The L.C.C. was a 'wolf on the prowl', they declared. The City too proclaimed its opposition. In December 1919 the *City Press* attacked the L.C.C. for its 'megalomania'; interpreted the plans as 'the setting up of one huge autocratic authority that will control London's millions on the principle of water-tight compartments, without taking into consideration for one moment the peculiar characteristics, the individual needs, and the distinctive limitations of the local areas to be lumped together and formed into the new metropolis'; and warned the L.C.C. of 'a solid phalanx of opposition if it decides to go ahead with the scheme'.[14] Some while later a deputation took the Corporation's anxieties to the Minister of Health, Addison, who was dealing with the matter.

The localists lost the struggle. Late in 1921, after enduring two years of badgering from the L.C.C., the Government finally agreed to appoint a Royal Commission:[15]

> . . . *to enquire and report what, if any, alterations are needed in the local government of the administrative county of London and the surrounding districts, with a view to securing greater efficiency and economy in the administration of local government services and to reducing any inequalities which may exist in the distribution of local burdens as between different parts of the whole area.*

The Commission comprised a number of experts and worthies of various political complexions and was headed by the former Speaker of the House of Commons, Viscount Ullswater.

The chief witness for the L.C.C. was R.C. Norman, who, though a Conservative Municipal Reformer, supported unification. For fear of arousing further suburban hostility he decided not to proffer detailed proposals. That, he argued, was the business of the Commission. He doggedly refused to be drawn, despite insistent pressure from his questioners. This was nowhere more apparent than in his attitude towards the City. Tactical cunning and political timidity were manifest in every sentence:[16]

... the City is in such a peculiar position that I should like to consider its own view, and if the City says, 'We will have nothing to do with it, we will stay as we are', I think that would be an important element for consideration. But I hope the City will decide to take in the future a much larger part than it has been used to take in the immediate past in the local government of London.

No amount of persistence on the part of Commissioner Sir Albert Gray could penetrate the fog:[17]

In what direction do you suggest that the City should take a larger part in local government? — I do not want to formulate any part which the City should play; I think it is for the City to make its own proposals. I should be very glad if the City counted for a good deal more in the government of London.
But surely you might be asked in what direction? — No; I want to hear their views first.
But you are out to claim that they should take a larger part? — Yes, I am.
And I rather expected you to say in what direction you made such a claim.
(Chairman) You are each waiting for the other? — The City Corporation is by so far the senior body that I should like them to advance first into the field.

Norman's stance made the Corporation's task in reply an easy one. It was able to dismiss the L.C.C.'s proposals as precluding worthwhile comment. The suggestions were vague and contradictory. The City's representatives did certainly have to deal with some interrogation from one of the Commissioners, Robert Donald, who wanted to see if the Corporation was prepared to take the lead in a new 'Greater London Authority'; but otherwise they were able to fall back on platitudinous appeals for the preservation of local independence and the maintenance of the *status quo*. The nearest to a positive statement the City came was in its written submission:[18]

... the Corporation recognizes that in London by reason of the size of the area and population and the diversity of conditions in different parts of the

area, some system of dual administration is essential. But the Corporation strongly urges that any alterations that may be contemplated should go as far as possible in the direction of independent powers and undivided responsibility.

Such sentiments, amply reinforced by the other local authorities, weighed heavily with the Commissioners. They were conscious of the political difficulties of implementing the L.C.C.'s plans. They even troubled to refer to Lloyd George's earlier warning to a County Council deputation: 'A report that would get 128 local authorities up in arms against you is not a report that any government would face with equanimity'[19] The Majority report brushed aside the L.C.C.'s suggestions as both insubstantial and impracticable and advised that no effectual alterations be made. Only one of the two Minority reports, signed by Donald and Labour M.P. Stephen Walsh, advocated further 'centralization'.

Pretentious buffoonery
Even before the Royal Commission finished its deliberations, the coalition which had been responsible for its inception was breaking down. London politics reverted to their traditional 'adversary' pattern. But almost immediately the Liberal-Progressives plummeted into an irreversible decline: forty seats in 1919 became twenty-six in 1922 and only six in 1925. Their place as the chief Opposition party was taken by Labour. The national trend was mirrored in London. A new genuinely lower class and socialist party had entered the fray. It soon became evident that one day the new County Hall opposite the Houses of Parliament would be governed by Labour.

Here indeed was a fresh and potent threat to the City. Labour leaders made no secret of their contempt for the square mile. Their vision of an 'enlarged, simplified, unified'[20] London had no place for the Corporation. In 1917 Herbert Morrison, secretary of the London Labour party and later to become Labour's first L.C.C. leader, asked:[21]

. . . is it not time London faced up to the pretentious buffoonery of the City of London Corporation and wiped it off the municipal map? The pioneer of civic liberty, the City, is now a square mile of entrenched reaction, the home of the devilry of modern finance and that journalistic abortion, the stunt press. The City is an administrative anachronism, and in our scheme of London government we must consider twentieth-century needs as well as tenth-century history.

Five years later, when explaining his party's plans to the Ullswater Commission, Morrison was less histrionic but still quite firm about the Corporation. Stephen Walsh asked him:[22]

I do not see in your statement that there is any specific mention of the position of the City of London. Have you had regard at all to the very anomalous position held by the City in this matter? — That opens up quite exciting considerations, but I am quite sure that the Labour party in London would divest the City Corporation of a good many of its financial and economic assets and a good deal of its administration which is unsatisfactory, and which is related to the City Livery Companies and so on. The London Labour party would desire reform.

You say there is much to be said for the amalgamation into one area of the counties of London, Middlesex, Essex, Hertford, Kent and Surrey. Here there is no direct mention of the City of London as an authority? — That is quite so. I think our feeling generally is that whilst in order to preserve the peace we might agree that certain of the ancient history and dignity of the City Corporation should be preserved, we do not see why it should be the markets authority, for example, within a seven mile radius, or why it should have certain financial privileges which it has, and otherwise it ought to be content with the general powers of a minor local authority.

His basic hostility to the City again surfaced in 1925 during a debate about the L.C.C.'s use of 'London' as its motto. The objections were avowedly historical and legalistic, but Morrison detected another more sinister influence:[23]

. . . the City might never have been mentioned but, nevertheless, the City was beneath the opposition. He was one of those who asserted that the Council was the true Corporation, and not a small body in one square mile of the City. The real question was whether the Council was the great authority representing London, and whether they were prepared to defend their position against the small body which usurped the name of London. He hoped they would vote for their City and against the small and privileged section in the middle of that City.

In 1928 Morrison spelt out his planned reform: 'The ideal would be one great Corporation of London – a new City Corporation with the Lord Mayor and Sheriffs and Aldermen, heads of a new civic authority – popularly elected – with minor authorities to discharge local functions.'[24]

Labour's opportunity to implement its schemes came in 1934 with a conclusive victory in the L.C.C. elections. Morrison was now the unchallenged leader of both his party and London. But he did nothing to alter the structure of metropolitan government and made no assault on the City. He seems to have been preoccupied with a desire to show that Labour could *govern*. The accent was on responsibility, efficiency and caution. There was to be no ideological gimmickry, no gratuitous radicalism. The risk of opposition from the other London authorities, not least the City, was enough to dissuade Morrison from promulgating his 'Greater London' plans. The issue was quietly shelved.

In 1935 Morrison wrote a book explaining *How Greater London is Governed*. Instead of lambasting the City for its 'pretentious buffoonery' as he had done in 1917, he now dispassionately traced what 'might-have-been' had the Corporation extended its powers beyond its walls. He refused to accept that the 'Great Refusal' was due merely to 'narrow mindedness and selfishness' and he tried hard to find other explanations. The conclusion was startlingly devoid of recrimination:[25]

So we can only sigh our regrets that the great City of London Corporation did not develop and expand as it might naturally have been expected to; that it has become largely shut off from the pulsating life of the far-flung London of the twentieth century; and that Greater London does not share in the enjoyment of the rich historical traditions, the civic glory and the dignity of Guildhall and the Mansion House.

The only significant call for change in these years came not from a politician but an academic. W.A. Robson's *The Government and Misgovernment of London* (1939) was to prove extremely influential and deserves brief notice. Robson wanted to see a new authority taking responsibility for the whole of Greater London. The two-tier system was to be retained but there was to be much simplification and rationalization. Among those local bodies to be given administrative surgery was the City:[26]

The ancient City presents a spectacle today which is both tragic and comic. There is something heart-rending in the thought of all the lost opportunities which resulted from the refusal of the City Corporation to share its inheritance with the wider community of the metropolis, and the memory of the pusillanimous failure of successive Parliaments and ministries to insist on its participation in the full task of London government. There is something ludicrous in the sight of the square mile of the City, with its vast wealth and long traditions, entirely divorced from the rest of London, a heart cut off from the living body of the metropolis, like the heart removed from a dissected animal beating in a scientist's laboratory.*

Various reforms were suggested: enlarging the electorate, reforming the constitution and subjecting the City's corporate wealth to the Greater London rate. Robson could see no point in trying to install the Corporation at the head of the new authority. 'The time for that has passed'; there was 'no future for the City Corporation in the Greater London we are contemplating, only its past'.[27]

*'Obsolete appendix' was the simile used by the Liberal journalist A.G. Gardiner in *John Benn and the Progressive Movement* (1925), p. 89.

The City Corporation cannot, however, any longer be permitted to have a monopoly of the insignia and the nomenclature of civic life. The denizens of Greater London must be designated citizens and not mere inhabitants. The Greater London region must have its Lord Mayor; and the Lord Mayor of Greater London must have the precedence to which he is entitled by the substance of present things rather than by the shadow of the past.

The City, of course, could afford to treat such pronouncements with a certain amount of disdain. It had no real cause for anxiety while Morrison kept a tight rein on his Labour followers on one side of the Thames and a National Government continued on the other. A watchful silence was all that was required. One City zealot gave vent to his apprehensions in the course of a commentary on the Livery Companies Commission of the 1880s:[28]

It is to be hoped that such an attack will not be repeated, but funds and property provided by the beneficence and foresight of by-gone citizens, however well and faithfully applied and administered, always offer a peculiarly tempting bait to predatory politicians. Some of us, therefore, may again have to join together with our brethren of the other Companies in repelling and defeating the enemy.

But for the most part the mood was one of confidence and expansion. An Air Pilots' and Air Navigators' Company was established in 1929; a Master Mariners' Company, after incorporation by royal charter in 1930, received a grant of Livery from the Court of Aldermen two years later; and in 1933 the Stationers' Company amalgamated with the recently formed Company of Newspaper Makers. Overall Livery numbers began to rise substantially and by the end of the 1930s had nearly reached 10,000.

No, not at present

The Second World War revived the slumbering debate about London's government. The need for physical reconstruction and economic revitalization prompted a good deal of theoretical discussion, but no practical results were forthcoming. In part this was due to an instinctive feeling that the problem was simply too vast and complex for resolution. The opposition to any reform would be ferocious and it would be all too easy to unleash an uncontrollable municipal leviathan. Far better to leave well alone even if this meant perpetuating muddle and inefficiency. In part too the inertia was based on political considerations. The Labour party, still in control of the L.C.C., had no wish to tamper with its electoral base by taking in 'Greater' London or altering borough boundaries. (From 1947 to 1965 the Leader of the Council was Sir Isaac Hayward, Morrison's former adjutant and just as determined as his mentor to eschew ideological controversy – a

Morrisonian L.C.C. was no threat to the City.) Both at national and local level, London was too precious an asset to be risked in this way. On their side, the Conservatives, though out-of-place, remained averse to change on principle; and it was some while before political frustration turned their thoughts towards administrative reform.

The stalemate, of course, suited the City admirably. Its anomalous privileges virtually disappeared as a political issue. One of the few exceptions proves the rule. In July 1951 Dr. H.M. King asked the Labour Minister of Local Government and Planning whether he would introduce legislation to reform the government of the City of London, so as either to give the vote to all who lived or worked there or to integrate its government into that of the L.C.C. 'No, not at present',[29] was the brief reply.

Not that the City was without its set-backs during this period. Enemy action destroyed eighteen of the thirty-six Company Halls and damaged fifteen others. Rebuilding costs and the loss of rents were heavy blows to Company finances which State compensation did little to cushion. Damage of another kind was inflicted by the Representation of the People Act (1948) which abolished the 'business' vote and therefore amalgamated the tiny City constituency with Westminster. It was the end of an ancient tradition. Yet despite these difficulties and changes Livery Company life continued to thrive. Two new Companies, the Furniture Makers (1952) and the Scientific Instrument Makers (1955), were formed in these years; an old one, the Tobacco Pipe Makers, was revived (1954); and three more, the Solicitors (1944), the Farmers (1952) and the Air Pilots and Air Navigators (1956), were granted Liveries. The Livery as a whole increased from 9,500 at the end of the War to 13,000 little more than a decade later. The City was acquiring vitality, strength and friends.

A living piece of history

Ironically enough it was the London Conservatives who shook the City out of its complacent security. For many years the Conservatives had been uncertain as to the propriety of entering local politics as a party. Hence the 'Moderate', 'Municipal Reform' and 'Municipal Society' subterfuges. But now they abandoned their compunction and confronted Labour on openly party-political terms. At the same time they decided that something had to be done about the apparently impregnable Labour majority on the L.C.C. One obvious gambit was to press for a 'Greater London' which would incorporate the traditionally conservative suburbs. Without such a reorganization there seemed to be no hope of a Conservative London.

These arguments carried weight both in national party circles and, more specifically, in the Ministry of Housing and Local Government, where Harold Macmillan included local government reform among the 'skeletons' in his 'ministerial cupboard'. The L.M.S. was encouraged to prepare proposals for reform and, though the 'Powell Plan' (named after its main author, Enoch Powell) was subjected to extensive criticism and modification, the issue was very much alive. Duncan Sandys, Macmillan's successor at the ministry, took up the initiative, though he concentrated rather on local government in general than London in particular. He was followed by Henry Brooke, who though equally non-committal on London, did agree (under pressure from his civil servants) to appoint a Royal Commission in 1957:[30]

> ... to examine the present system and working of local government in the Greater London area; [and] to recommend whether any, and if so what, changes in the local government structure and the distribution of local authority functions in the area, or in any part of it, would better secure effective and convenient local government ...

The chairman was an eminent solicitor, Sir Edwin Herbert, and he had six colleagues.

The City, of course, was among the interested parties required to present evidence to the Commission. Its written submission describing its constitution, functions and services was prefaced by the customary defence of its unique position in national and local life. 'Institutions with deep roots are a source of stability at home and of admiration abroad;' the City is 'an historical asset to be safeguarded'; and so on.[31] Later its witnesses had to deal with some questions about the Corporation's role as a local authority. But there was no radical discussion of the City's right to exist. The Commissioners were interested in other issues.

When the Report appeared in 1960 it recommended the establishment of a Council for Greater London to govern a wider area than the L.C.C. There were also to be fifty-two powerful borough councils, including the City. The preservation of the City was justified in some paragraphs which were later to arouse considerable controversy. The Commissioners accepted that the City's separate status was anomalous but argued that the anomaly should continue. That, they said, was a definite not a provisional recommendation:

> If we were to be strictly logical we should recommend the amalgamation of the City and Westminster. But logic has its limits and the position of the City lies outside them.

The loss of the City's ancient traditions and ceremonial 'would leave an unfillable gap in our national life'[32] and to divorce the ceremonial element from the purely municipal functions of the City would deprive the former of all meaning. Nor was it valuable or practicable to combine the offices of Lord Mayor and chairman of the proposed G.L.C. There might be need to give special consideration to certain 'public' services, such as the Thames bridges, which the City administered, but otherwise the City should remain unchanged.

It was one thing, however, for the Corporation to receive this support as a mere recommendation and quite another to have it enshrined in statute. All now depended on the reaction of the Government. The national party machine had become convinced of the electoral arguments in favour of extension and it was Central Office's energy and pressure which turned the Report into legislation. The London Government bill, as it finally transpired late in 1962, differed somewhat from the Commission's suggestions, but none of the changes, which included a marked reduction in the number of boroughs, affected the City. The Corporation was no longer actually to be designated a borough but it was to possess all the powers of one.

Throughout the early stages of the bill there was some sniping at the City from Labour M.P.s. K. Robinson (St Pancras, North) found it 'very difficult to take seriously a bill which purports to modernize London's government and yet preserves that ludicrous anachronism the City of London'.[33] J. Parker (Dagenham) argued that the government was 'frightened of the City',[34] while George Brown thought the explanation party-political: 'there is no case for the City remaining and having these powers except that it is a Tory stronghold which the government believe they can hold'.[35] A number of M.P.s were convinced that the 'destruction' of the L.C.C. and the preservation of the City exposed the bill's essentially political character.

As to alternatives, the most favoured one was that recently advanced by Professor W.A. Robson. The City should be incorporated in a large central borough embracing Holborn, Finsbury, Westminster and part of Marylebone, St. Pancras, Shoreditch and Stepney. Michael Cliffe (Shoreditch and Finsbury) turned an academic point into a personal plea:[36]

If the Conservative government are to destroy one of the world's finest institutions, the L.C.C., I see no reason why the City should be considered sacrosanct simply because it is the hub of the Commonwealth, merely because the Bank of England, the Mansion House and the Stock Exchange are there. People speak of the Lord Mayor of London, but he is the Lord Mayor of one of the smallest bits of London. I was the mayor of a borough with a population much larger than the City's. It would be a wonderful thing if Shoreditch and Finsbury were linked to the City of London. We could spend a great deal of the City's money which is made on the Stock Exchange. The money is made quickly enough there and we could help spend it in these boroughs where it is needed.

The Opposition mounted its main attack on the City provisions in committee. The chief speakers were Shadow Housing minister Michael Stewart and the Islington M.P. Albert Evans. Both were maddened by this 'outrageous anomaly in London's local government life'.[37] But they had a redoubtable opponent in Sir Keith Joseph. Minister for Housing and Local Government, whose father had been Lord Mayor and who had himself been a Common Councilman and Alderman. He began by sketching out the common ground:[38]

There were occasions during the last century when, had the City been more outward-looking and more venturesome, the whole history of the local government of the metropolis might have been very different. Last century, government after government begged the City to take responsibility for the growing mass of the metropolis, but, time after time, the City turned its back on what would have been a very heavy duty and very heavy responsibility but which might have solved a lot of our problems today.

So much was agreed, he said. What was now to be decided was whether the City should survive as an independent local authority. The minister had no doubts:[39]

Here is a living piece of history with much benefit flowing from it . . ., fulfilling its limited duties as well as other authorities do, doing harm to no one, bringing benefit to many, whose virtues cannot be transferred and whose extinction, therefore, would do no one a jot of good. . . . Here is a local authority which is unique. It has qualities which benefit the nation and the citizens of the nation. It pays for its own ceremonial, pageantry and hospitality out of private not public funds and its history reaches back to the Middle Ages. Here is a local authority providing, without any expense to the taxpayer or ratepayer, bridges, parks and schools. Here is a local authority paying its own way and, in addition, out of its rates, contributing to London as well.

The argument carried the day on a party-political division of 236 to 186 against the amendment.

An egalitarian Orwellian drabness

The London Government Act became law in July 1963, but before its provisions could be implemented in July 1965 the Conservatives lost their thirteen-year hold on power and Harold Wilson's Labour party formed the new government. It was doubtless the hope that the new ministers would give effect to their earlier criticisms before it was too late which explains a motion presented by Hugh Jenkins (Putney) in March 1965. He asked for leave to introduce a bill:[40]

. . . to dissolve the Corporation of the City of London and make provisions consequent thereto; to make provision for the administration of the City; and for related purposes.

He was prepared to leave the question of City ceremonial to debate, but he had no doubt of the need to abolish the City 'as a municipality'. It was, he said, 'an intolerable rotten borough'. John Harvey (Walthamstow, East), a regular defender of the City in Commons debates, countered thus in his peroration:[41]

What, then, would this mean little bill seek to do? Is it hoped to maraud and plunder funds providently built up and long devoted to a whole host of good works — funds which are not the State's to take? Or does the hon. gentleman consider the existing burdens of London's ratepayers and taxpayers to be insufficient, so that he wants them to pay for the maintenance of Epping Forest, Burnham Beeches, the bridges across the Thames and all the cultural amenities I have mentioned? Or does he conceive that there is some puritanical virtue in ending the pageantry that flows from the long pages of London's history so that we can all be plunged into an egalitarian Orwellian drabness?

Jenkins was refused leave by 214 votes to 103. It was interesting how many prominent Labour leaders did not trouble to attend. Michael Stewart, the City's fierce critic in 1963, was a particularly conspicuous absentee. The inference must be that reforming the City was considered too gratuitous and too controversial a measure for even a Labour government to undertake. The London Government Act went ahead without hindrance or change.

For a number of years the issue lay dormant and the City's future looked as secure as it had ever been. But then in the early 1970s Labour activists in London began to adopt a much more aggressive attitude to the City as part of their plans for a radical readjustment of the capital's ill-balanced economic and social structure. The party's manifesto for the 1973 G.L.C. elections, *A Socialist Strategy for London*, declared that:[42]

The continued anachronism of the City of London within the G.L.C.area is something Labour in London will not accept. It will press for legislation aimed at abolishing the City as a local government unit.

A little over a year later Tony Banks, the Labour chairman of the Council's General Purposes Committee, promised that when a majority Labour government was returned the G.L.C. would 'urge upon it the need to reform London Government in line with our manifesto pledge'.[43] A Labour government was indeed elected with a sizeable majority in October 1974 and the anti-City lobby set about preparing its case.

In June 1975 a 'City of London' Working party set up by the Greater London Regional Council of the Labour party (the successor of the London Labour party) submitted its report. It castigated the City for its low rates and undemocratic government and recommended abolishing it in its present form. It decided against absorption or sub-division and recommended instead that the City be administered by a special committee of the G.L.C. Its local authority functions were to be transferred variously to G.L.C. departments, the Inner London Education Authority and other London boroughs. The City Police were to be absorbed by the Metropolitan force, no further Aldermen created, and the duties and title of the Lord Mayor given to the G.L.C. chairman. The report was duly approved and forwarded to both the Minister of Planning and Local Government and the party's National Executive Committee. How it was received there is hard to say, but it certainly found favour with the ruling Labour group on the G.L.C. In March 1976 Tony Banks expressed his hope that it would soon prove possible 'to make the abolition of the City a matter of Council policy'.[44] In December Banks persuaded his General Purposes Committee to recommend the abolition of the City as a local government unit (though he failed in plans to levy a differential rate). He regarded it as 'the fulfilment of one of our pledges, the abolition of the most undemocratic local government institution in the whole of the country'.[45] Two months later the Committee's report was 'received' by full Council on a division of 40 votes to 31.

Even this official imprimatur, however, failed to stir Parliament. A Ten-Minute Rule bill introduced by Bryan Davies (Enfield, North) in March 1977 to give effect to the G.L.R.C. and G.L.C. plans was defeated by 198 votes to 157. Davies's invective against 'an island of wealth in a sea of poverty' was dismissed by Geoffrey Finsberg (Hampstead), veteran anti-L.C.C. and G.L.C. campaigner and Opposition spokesman on London, as the repetition of a 'phoney, fraudulent and loaded London Labour party report'. 'The City should not be abolished to suit the jealous little men of the Far Left'.[46]

Death wish

What now of the future? The City's opponents remain strong and strident. The G.L.C. elections of 1981 brought into power a Labour group committed to radical socialism and their leader, the controversial Ken Livingstone, makes no secret of his disdain for the Establishment. All this appears to bode ill for the Corporation. The G.L.C. majority will not fail to seize an opportunity to 'democratize' or abolish the City and redistribute its rateable and corporate wealth. But will such an opportunity arise? At present the Labour group are preoccupied with attempts to revive London's ailing economy and resolve its mounting social problems. It will be hard for them to find the time or indeed the justification for an assault on the square mile. And if they were to attempt the task, there is no sign that Parliament will give them any assistance. Only a left-wing Labour Government would sponsor the necessary legislation and the smallest dose of pragmatism or timidity will be sufficient to impede progress. The external threat, therefore, is more apparent than real.

As far as the City's internal strength is concerned, here too the signs are propitious. No less than nine Livery Companies have been created since 1977: the Chartered Surveyors, Chartered Accountants, Chartered Secretaries and Administrators, Builders Merchants, Launderers, Marketors, Actuaries, Insurers and Arbitrators. This has brought the total number of Livery Companies to 93 and the size of the Livery to over 20,000. The links between the City and the business community are therefore closer than they have been for many generations. There is also a new and refreshing expansiveness of outlook. Ever since a media consultant allegedly discovered something close to a 'death wish'[47] in Corporation circles in 1974, 'public relations' have been carefully fostered. At a deeper level, Corporation members and officers are more than willing to discuss the City's position and do so with candour and conviction. The City is not only fit and healthy, it is also seen to be so.

There are, however, a few clouds in the sky. The City's constitution continues to baffle and irritate outside observers. Why should the Aldermen be allowed to veto the election of new Aldermen? Why not make the Aldermen seek re-election every few years? To this the City replies that there is need to keep the closest eye on the suitability of would-be Aldermen as future Lord Mayors and to provide for a continuous period of training and experience. There is much to be said for this argument, but the City cannot afford any repetition of the controversies aroused by the rejection of Edwina Coven in 1973–4 and Donald Silk in 1979–80. 'Democracy' is an emotive clarion-call which could quickly rally neutral opinion against the Corporation. The ward franchise also causes disquiet. The resident population is too small and too unevenly spread to provide an acceptable base; and the 'business vote' of certain owners and tenants permits some 'multiple voting' which also offends the purists. Again the City is alive to the problem and has the matter under discussion. Its dilemma is a real one. A 'rate-paying' electorate, in its proper sense, is hardly feasible in an area of highly-rated corporate concerns and a 'working population' electorate would be impossibly large. But in this instance too the City will have to do something to soothe democratic sensibilities. Perhaps it should seek to introduce a vote for limited liability companies in order that its franchise should reflect the area it serves. Finally, there are continuing complaints about the City's rates. The G.L.C. and the Inner London Education Authority want more money from the square mile to sustain and train London's needy population. The City, on its side, points to the vast increase in rates over the past decade and the fear that bankers and brokers will leave the square mile, indeed the country, if pressed too hard. The money-earning business City is as much a national 'resource' as its rates are a London one. This is fair enough; and it is equally true that a hefty proportion of the City's revenues is spent on the metropolis as a whole. But as London's social and economic difficulties increase the pressure for a still higher contribution will mount and the City will have to make its case with yet more clarity and vigour if it is to avoid criticism.

It is, of course, possible that faced with these problems the City could take the line of least resistance and jettison its local government responsibilities and retain only its civic and ceremonial role. This is what a number of pundits, including some friends, have urged the City to do. But it does not seem very likely. There is a determination to retain both functions, however ill-assorted they may sometimes appear. Corporation officers are proud of the practical part they play in running the square mile. If their methods are unusual, they say, then so are their responsibilities. The City cannot be governed on conventional lines and if political idealists are disturbed that is not such a high price to pay for a contented and prosperous financial community. The business City would receive little consideration if it were governed by one or more of the inner boroughs politically antipathetic to the capitalist system and weighed down as they are with pressing problems of social and urban blight. Such confidence is compelling. The City Corporation has found a *raison d'être* which has often been lacking in the last century or two. And, for the present at least, it seems capable of imparting this sense of purpose to Parliament and the nation at large. It will need to maintain and extend its efforts at self-publicity and explain its constitutional difficulties more openly, but otherwise the future looks bright. The remarkable survival of the City of London and its Livery Companies seems set to continue for many years to come.

LIVERY COMPANIES HALLS

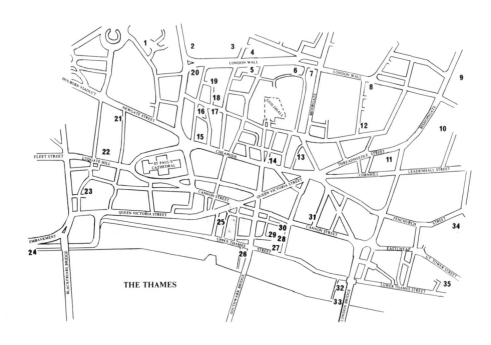

1 Butchers' Hall	**19** Pewterers' Hall
2 Ironmongers' Hall	**20** Plaisterers' Hall
3 Barbers-Surgeons' Hall	**21** Cutlers' Hall
4 Salters' Hall	**22** Stationers' Hall
5 Brewers' Hall	**23** Apothecaries' Hall
6 Girdlers' Hall	**24** Master Mariners' Hall
7 Armourers' and Brasiers' Hall	**25** Painters' Hall
8 Carpenters' Hall	**26** Vintners' Hall
9 Coopers' Hall	**27** Innholders' Hall
10 Leathersellers' Hall	**28** Dyers' Hall
11 Merchant Taylors' Hall	**29** Skinners' Hall
12 Drapers' Hall	**30** Tallow Chandlers' Hall
13 Grocers' Hall	**31** Founders' Hall
14 Mercers' Hall	**32** Fishmongers' Hall
15 Saddlers' Hall	**33** Glaziers' Hall
16 Goldsmiths' Hall	**33** Scientific Instrument Makers' Hall
17 Wax Chandlers' Hall	**34** Clothworkers' Hall
18 Haberdashers' Hall	**35** Bakers' Hall

REFERENCES TO CHAPTER I

1. V. Pearl, *London and the Outbreak of the Puritan Revolution, 1625–42* (1961), p. 18.
2. Printed as Chapter 1 in the Appendices to J. Stow, *A Survey of the Cities of London and Westminster*, ed. J. Strype (1720).
3. Pearl, *London*, p. 1.
4. G. Unwin, *The Gilds and Companies of London* (3rd edn., 1938), p. 277.
5. As reported by J.J. Baddeley, *The Guildhall of the City of London* (7th edn., 1939), p. 29.
6. N.G. Brett-James, *The Growth of Stuart London* (1935), p. 226.
7. *Ibid.*
8. *Ibid.*, p. 244.
9. *Ibid.*, p. 245.
10. Pearl, *London*, pp. 1, 71.
11. R. Ashton, *The Crown and the Money Market, 1603–40* (1960), p. 77.
12. Pearl, *London*, p. 74.
13. *Seventeenth-Century Economic Documents*, ed. J. Thirsk and J.P. Cooper (1972), p. 635.
14. *The Diary of Samuel Pepys*, ed. R. Latham and W. Matthews (1970), VII, p. 271.
15. T.F. Reddaway, *The Rebuilding of London after the Great Fire* (1948), p. 181.
16. W.G. Bell, *The Great Fire of London in 1666* (2nd edn., 1920), p. 271.
17. *A Dialogue between Francesco and Aurelia, two unfortunate Orphans of the City of London* (1690), p. 7.
18. *A Collection of the Debates and Proceedings in Parliament in 1694 and 1695 upon the Inquiry into the late Briberies and Corrupt Practices* (1695), p. 93.
19. *Report from the Select Committee on the Orphans' Fund* (Parliamentary Papers (Cmd. 308), 1829, III, 365), p. 20.
20. *The Times*, 6 Jan. 1928.
21. 'Mr. Comptroller's Account of the City's Estate etc.', in Corporation of London Record Office, Misc. MSS. 237.7.
22. *Journals of the House of Commons*, VII, p. 178.
23. W. Herbert, *The History of the Twelve Great Livery Companies* (1834–6), I, pp. 182–3.

24. W.M. Williams, *Annals of the Worshipful Company of Founders of the City of London* (1867?), p. 36.
25. N. Burt, *A New Year's Gift for England, and all her Cities, Ports and Corporations* (1653), p. 15.
26. J. Levin, *The Charter Controversy in the City of London, 1660–1688, and its Consequences* (1969), p. 2.
27. *Ibid.* p. 55
28. H.M. Hyde, *Judge Jeffreys* (2nd edn., 1948), pp. 184–5.
29. *The Diary of John Evelyn*, ed. E.S. de Beer (1955), IV, pp. 342–3.
30. Levin, *Charter Controversy*, p. 2 and n.
31. Herbert, *Twelve Great Livery Companies*, I, p. 217.
32. T. Girtin, *The Triple Crowns. A Narrative History of the Drapers' Company* (1964), pp. 266–7.

REFERENCES TO CHAPTER II

1. S. and B. Webb, *English Local Government: the Manor and the Borough* (1908), p. 703.
2. *Ibid.*, p. 714.
3. J.K. Buckley, *Joseph Parkes of Birmingham* (1926), p. 129.
4. G.B.A.M. Finlayson, 'The Politics of Municipal Reform, 1835' *English Historical Review*, LXXXI (1966), p. 674.
5. *Idem*, 'The Municipal Corporations Commission and Report, 1833–5', *Bulletin of the Institute of Historical Research*, XXXVI (1963), p. 49.
6. *Ibid.*, p. 42.
7. *Hansard*, 3rd Series, XXVIII, col. 243.
8. *Ibid.*, col. 571.
9. W. Thomas, *The Philosophic Radicals* (1979), p. 290.
10. British Library, Additional MS. 40553, f. 214v: Palgrave to Peel, 3 Nov. 1844.
11. Guildhall Library, MS. 110, f. 206.
12. *Report of the Royal Commission on Municipal Corporations (England and Wales): London and Southwark; London Companies* (Parliamentary Papers (Cmd. 239), 1837, XXV), p. 283 (35).
13. *Ibid.*, p. 303 (55).
14. Herbert, *Twelve Great Livery Companies*, II, p. 41.
15. *Royal Commission Report* (1837), p. 178.
16. Undated letter preserved in John Stewart's collection of 'Newspapers, Cuttings, Pamphlets etc. relating to the Corporation Reform bill, 1856' in the Guildhall Library.
17. *Royal Commission Report* (1837), p. 2.
18. *Ibid.*, p. 11.

19. G. Wallas, *The Life of Francis Place* (4th edn., 1925), pp. 347–8.
20. *Ibid.*, pp. 346–7.
21. D. Cecil, *Lord M., or the Later Life of Lord Melbourne* (1954), p. 221.
22. *Royal Commission Report* (1837), p. 4.
23. *Ibid.*
24. *The Corporation Commission. Report delivered to the Committee in aid of Corporate Reform* (1833).
25. Palgrave to Laurie (no date), in Stewart Collection.
26. 'The Decline and Fall of the Corporation of London' (Part IV), *Fraser's Magazine*, XLIX (1854), p. 457.
27. Allen, *Corporation of London*, p. 68.
28. *Hansard*, 3rd Series, LXVII, col. 238.
29. 'The Corporation of London and Municipal Reform', *Westminster Review*, XXXIX (1843), p. 498.
30. *Ibid.*, pp. 565 – 6.
31. *The Substance of an Address delivered by Charles Pearson, Esq. at a Public Meeting . . .* (1844), p. 202.
32. *Ibid.*, p. iv.
33. Carpenter, *Corporation of London*, p. 4.
24. *Ibid.*, pp. 58 – 9.
35. Fletcher, 'Statistical Account of the Police of the Metropolis', *Journal of the Statistical Society of London*, XIII (1850), p. 235.
36. Carpenter, *Corporation of London*, p. 6.

REFERENCES TO CHAPTER III

1. *Letters of the Rt. Hon. Sir George Cornewall Lewis Bart. to various friends*, ed. G.F. Lewis (1870), II, p. 272.
2. R. Lambert, *Sir John Simon and English Social Administration* (1963), p. 132.
3. F.H.W. Sheppard, *London 1808–1870: the Infernal Wen* (1971), p. 281.
4. *Report of the Royal Commission on the Corporation of the City of London* (Parliamentary Papers (Cmd. 1772), 1854, XXVI), p. vii.
5. *Disraeli, Derby and the Conservative Party. Journals and Memoirs of Edward Henry, Lord Stanley 1849–69*, ed. J. Vincent (1978), pp. 140–1.
6. *Ibid.*, p. 149.
7. *TheTimes*, 30 October 1856.
8. *Royal Commission Report* (1854), p. x.
9. *Ibid.*, Question 146.
10. *Ibid.*, QQ, 147 and 151.
11. *Ibid.*, Q. 647.

12. *The Times*, 4 November 1853.
13. *Royal Commission Report* (1854), Q. 2787.
14. *Ibid.*, Q. 2682.
15. *Ibid.*, Q. 5184.
16. T.B. Macaulay, *The History of England from the Accession of James II* (Everyman edn., 1905), I, p. 272.
17. *Royal Commission Report* (1854), Q. 656.
18. *Letters of Cornewall Lewis*, II, p. 274.
19. 'Decline and Fall', *Fraser's Magazine*, XLIX (1854), p. 5.
20. *Royal Commission Report* (1854), p. xvii.
21. *Ibid.*, p. xxxviii.
22. *Ibid.*, p. xxxv.
23. *Letters of Cornewall Lewis*, II, p. 264 (misdated).
24. *Hansard*, CXXXVII, col. 190.
25. *Ibid.*, CXXXVIII, col. 2242.

REFERENCES FOR CHAPTER IV

1. *Hansard*, CXLI, cols. 314–15.
2. *Ibid.*, col. 332.
3. Palgrave to Laurie (no date), in Stewart Collection.
4. *The Times*, 15 April 1856.
5. *Ibid.*, 12 April.
6. *Ibid.*, 14 April.
7. *Civil Service Gazette*, 19 April.
8. *The Times*, 16 April.
9. *Ibid.*, 23 April.
10. *Morning Herald*, 28 April.
11. *Morning Advertiser*, 17 April.
12. *Ibid.*, 14 April.
13. Item in Stewart Collection.
14. *Morning Advertiser*, 17 April.
15. *The Times*, 2 April.
16. *Ibid.*, 16 April.
17. *Ibid.*, 24 April.
18. *Morning Advertiser*, 25 April.
19. *Ibid.*, 12 April.
20. *Morning Star*, 16 April.
21. *Morning Herald*, 14 April.
22. *Ibid.*, 16 April.
23. *Morning Advertiser*, 8 May.
24. *Hansard*, CXLII, cols. 1993–4.
25. *The Times*, 30 October.

26. *Morning Advertiser*, 16 April.
27. *Ibid.*, 27 June.
28. *The Times*, 30 October.
29. *Ibid.*, 29 October.
30. *Hansard*, CXLVIII, col. 738.
31. *Ibid.*, col. 742.
32. *Ibid.*, col. 743.
33. *Ibid.*, CLI, col. 271.
34. *Ibid.*, cols. 289–90.
35. *Ibid.*, col. 292.
36. *Ibid.*, col. 300.
37. *Ibid.*, col. 302.
38. *Royal Commission Report* (1854), Q. 2782.
39. *Hansard*, CLI, cols. 308–9.
40. *Proceedings in the Bills for the Regulation of the Corporation of London* (1858), p. 229.
41. So Deputy Harrison reported in Common Council. *Morning Advertiser*, 29 June 1858.
42. *Hansard*, CLV, col. 159
43. *Ibid.*, col. 496.
44. *Ibid.*
45. J.F.B. Firth, *Municipal London* (1876), p. 568.
46. *Hansard*, CLVIII, col. 75.
47. *Ibid.*, col. 86.
48. *Ibid.*, CLXI, col. 273.
49. *Report of the Select Committee on Metropolis Local Taxation* (Parliamentary Papers (Cmd. 476), 1861, VIII), p. iii.
50. *Ibid.*, pp. xi-ii (391–2).
51. *Hansard*, CLXX, col. 491.

REFERENCES FOR CHAPTER V

1. W.F. Moneypenny and G.E. Buckle, *The Life of Benjamin Disraeli* (1910–16), IV, p. 479.
2. E.J. Feuchtwanger, *Disraeli, Democracy and the Tory Party* (1968), p. 20.
3. Moneypenny and Buckle, *Disraeli*, VI, p. 90.
4. *Ibid.*, VI, p. 13.
5. Firth, *Municipal London*, p. 587.
6. *Address of Mr. James Beal delivered at the St. James's Vestry Hall . . .* (1867), pp. 22, 35.
7. *Letter to 'The Times' by James Beal . . .* (1874), pp. 3, 5.
8. *Collected Works of John Stuart Mill* (1963–), XIX, p. 538.

9. *Hansard*, CLXXXVIII, col. 890.
10. *Ibid.*, CXCVI, cols. 1941 and 1943.
11. *Ibid.*, CCI, col. 856.
12. *Ibid.*, CCXXXIX, col. 672.
13. *Ibid.*, CLXXXI, col. 1218.
14. *Report of the Select Committee on Metropolitan Local Government* (Paliamentary Papers (Cmd. 268), 1867, XII), p. vi (440).
15. *Hansard*, CXCVI, col. 1941.
16. *Report of the Select Committee on Metropolitan Local Government* (Parliamentary Papers (Cmd. 452), 1866, XIII), Q. 6856.
17. *Hansard*, CCI, col. 863.
18. *Morning Herald*, 17 May 1867.
19. Leading article in *The Standard* printed in *Stand Fast! Will the Citizens Consent to the Surrender of their Charters to a Foreign Body? What says Chief Baron Kelly?* (1867), p. 16.
20. *Morning Advertiser*, 22 February 1867.
21. B. Scott, *A Statistical Vindication of the City of London* (1867) p. 178.
22. See *Report of the Select Committee* (1866), Appendix no. 9, p. 296 (clause 42).
23. *Morning Post*, 12 February 1875.
24. *Daily Telegraph*, 19 March.
25. *Hansard*, CCXXXIX, col. 731.
26. *Ibid.*, col. 710.
27. *Ibid.*, col. 716.
28. *Morning Advertiser*, 13 May 1870.
29. Scott, *Statistical Vindication*, pp. 190–2.
30. *Morning Post*, 4 November 1865.
31. D. Owen, *The Government of Victorian London* (1982), p. 247.
32. J.S. Flynn, *Sir Robert N. Fowler. A Memoir* (1893), p. 180.
33. *Ibid.*, p. 190.
34. R. Fulford, *Glyn's 1753–1953. Six Generations in Lombard Street* (1953), p. 180.
35. Firth, *Municipal London*, p. 588.
36. *Ibid.*, p. 590.

REFERENCES FOR CHAPTER VI

1. *The Coachmakers. A History of the Worshipful Company of Coach-makers and Coach Harness Makers, 1677–1977*, ed. H. Nockolds (1977), p. 106.
2. Roland Champness quoted in F.W. Law, *The Worshipful Company of Spectacle Makers. A History* (1979), p. 50.

3. J. Lang, *City and Guilds of London Institute Centenary 1878–1978. An Historical Commentary* (1978), p. 15.
4. T. Girtin, *The Golden Ram* (1958), p. 266.
5. *City Guilds Reform Fly Sheets* (1876), no. 3, p. 13.
6. *Ibid.*, pp. 12, 5, 18.
7. *Hansard*, CCXXIX, col. 1137.
8. *Ibid.*, col. 1146.
9. *Ibid.*, CCXXXIII, col. 878.
10. *Ibid.*, col. 909.
11. *Ibid.*, CCXLIV, col. 823.
12. *The Reminiscences of Albert Pell*, ed. T. Mackay (1908), p. 314.
13. *Report of the Royal Commission on the City of London Livery Companies* (Parliamentary Papers (Cmd. 4073), 1884, XXXIX), QQ. 1682 and 1684–5.
14. J.N. Daynes, *A Short History of the Ancient Mistery of the Dyers of the City of London* (1965), p. 74.
15. *Royal Commission Report* (1884), p. 30.
16. *Ibid.*, p. 42.
17. *Ibid.*, p. 87.
18. *Hansard*, CCXCIII, col. 1099.
19. *Ibid.*, CCXC, col. 203.
20. Open letter dated 18 July 1885 in Guildhall Library MS. 17, 132.
21. *Hansard*, CCCIX, col. 1123.
22. Firth, *Reform of London*, p. 116.

REFERENCES FOR CHAPTER VII

1. *A Practical Scheme of London Municipal Reform, being an Epitome of 'The Municipality of London Bill'* (1881), pp. 9–10.
2. S. Gwynn and G.M. Tuckwell, *The Life of Sir Charles W. Dilke* (1918), I, p. 420.
3. *Ibid.*
4. *Hansard*, CCLXXXVII, col. 41.
5. *Ibid.*, col. 51.
6. *Ibid.*, col. 69.
7. Gwynn and Tuckwell, *Dilke*, II, pp. 10–11.
8. A.G. Gardiner, *The Life of Sir William Harcourt* (1923), I, p. 470.
9. *Hansard*, CCXC, col. 532.
10. *Ibid.*, cols. 545–6.
11. *London Municipal Reform Conference . . . to promote Representative Government for the Whole of the Metropolis* (1881), p. 10.
12. *Morning Advertiser*, 7 October 1881.

13. *Ibid.*, 19 April 1884.
14. *Ibid.*, 21 January 1887.
15. *Report from the Select Committee on the London Corporation* (Charges of Malversation) (Parliamentary Papers (Cmd. 161), 1887, X), Q. 1163.
16. *Ibid.*, Q. 1519.
17. *Ibid.*, Q. 2400.
18. *Ibid.*, Q. 1265.
19. *Ibid.*, Q. 2736.
20. *Ibid.*, Q. 2872.
21. J. Lloyd, *London Municipal Government. History of a Great Reform, 1880–1888* (2nd edn., 1911), pp. 39–40.
22. *Report from the Select Committee* (1887), Q. 1634.
23. Lloyd, *History of a Great Reform*, p. 57.
24. *Report from the Select Committee* (1887), Q. 1496.
25. Lloyd, *History of a Great Reform*, pp. 39, 56.
26. *Hansard*, CCCXXIV, col. 1748.
27. Lloyd, *History of a Great Reform*, p. 68.
28. *Report from the Select Committee* (1887), Q. 1564.
29. *Ibid.*, Q. 2883.
30. *Hansard*, CCCXI, col. 1224.
31. *Ibid.*, col. 904.
32. *Ibid.*, CCCXVII, col. 1352.
33. *Ibid.*, CCCXXIV, cols. 1755–6.

REFERENCES FOR CHAPTER VIII

1. K. Young, *Local Politics and the Rise of Party. The London Municipal Society and the Conservative Intervention in Local Elections, 1894–1963* (1975), p. 40.
2. W. Phillips, *'Home Rule for London'. An Appeal and a Warning* (1888?).
3. A.G. Gardiner, *John Benn and the Progressive Movement* (1925), p. 98.
4. *Report of the Royal Commission on the Amalgamation of the City and County of London* (Parliamentary Papers (Cmd. 7493), 1894, XVII–III, p. 22 (Protest prefixed to the City's Statement).
5. H. Haward, *The London County Council from Within* (1932), p. 27.
6. Gardiner, *Benn*, 152.
7. *Ibid.*, p. 132.
8. *Hansard*, 4th Series, IX, col. 35.
9. *Royal Commission Report* (1894), XVII, p. 10.
10. *Ibid.*, Q. 2844.

11. Alderman Faudel-Phillips quoted in *Royal Commission on London Government 1893–4. Report of Special Committee of the Corporation of London* (1895), p. ii.
12. *Royal Commission Report* (1894), XVII, p. 29.
13. *Report of the Special Committee of the Corporation of London* (1895), p. ix.
14. *The Times*, 8 November 1894.
15. Young, *Local Politics and the Rise of Party*, p. 67.
16. *Ibid.*, pp. 68–69.
17. T. Girtin, *The Golden Ram* (1958), p. 257.
18. K. Young and P.L. Garside, *Metropolitan London. Politics and Urban Change, 1937–1981* (1982), p. 100.
19. *Hansard*, LXVII, col. 355.
20. *Ibid.*, col. 367.
21. *Ibid.*, cols. 404–5.
22. *Ibid.*, LXVIII, col. 1580.
23. *Ibid.*, LXIX, cols. 170–1.
24. *Ibid.*, LXVII, cols. 1628–9.
25. *Ibid.*, LXXIII, cols. 9–10.
26. P. Clarke, *Serving his Generation. Being Short Notes on the Public Life of Henry Clarke, J.P.* (1915), p. 33.
27. G.M. Vine, 'Without the Walls', *Transactions of the Guildhall Historical Association*, IV (1969), p. 98.

REFERENCES FOR CHAPTER IX

1. G.H.M. Vine, 'The Special Committee', *Transactions of the Guildhall Historical Association*, I (1948), pp. 29–30.
2. H.C. White, *Lord Dickinson of Painswick. A Memoir* (1956), pp. 35 – 6, 104.
3. *Coming Men on Coming Questions*, ed. W.T. Stead (1906), p. 405.
4. Young and Garside, *Metropolitan London*, p. 125 n.
5. *A Debate on the Reform of London Government* (1906), p. 16.
6. Young and Garside, *Metropolitan London*, p. 122.
7. B. Webb, *Our Partnership*, edd. B. Drake and M.I. Cole (1948), p. 364.
8. *The London County Council from Within* (1932), p. 199.
9. Lloyd, *History of a Great Reform*, p. viii.
10. *The Times*, 6 April 1909.
11. Gardiner, *Benn*, pp. 415 and 513.
12. Young and Garside, *Metropolitan London*, p. 122 n.
13. *Corporation of London* (1950), p. 15.
14. Young and Garside, *Metropolitian London*, p. 130 n.

15. *Report of the Royal Commission on the Local Government of Greater London* (Parliamentary Papers (Cmd. 1830), 1923, XII Part I), p. ix.
16. *Minutes of Evidence taken before the Royal Commission on London Government* (1922), Q. 1174.
17. *Ibid.*, QQ. 1705–9.
18. *Ibid.*, Q. 13,503, para. 11.
19. *Royal Commission Report* (1923), para. 262.
20. B. Donoughue and G.W. Jones, *Herbert Morrison. Portrait of a Politician* (1973), p. 25.
21. *Ibid.*, p. 115.
22. *Minutes of Evidence taken before the Royal Commission* (1922), QQ. 10, 232–3.
23. *The Times*, 28 January 1925.
24. K. Young, 'The Conservative Strategy for London, 1855–1975', *The London Journal*, I (1975), p. 74.
25. H. Morrison, *How Greater London is Governed* (1935), p. 160.
26. W.A. Robson, *The Government and Misgovernment of London* (1939), pp. 380–1.
27. *Ibid.*, p. 387.
28. G. Elkington, *The Worshipful Company of Coopers. With Notes and Recollections, 1873 to 1930* (1930), pp. 83–4.
29. *Hansard*, 5th Series, 491, col. 44 (Written Answers).
30. *Report of the Royal Commission on Local Government in Greater London* (Parliamentary Papers (Cmd. 1164), 1959–60, XVIII), p. 1.
31. *Royal Commission on Local Government in Greater London. Written Evidence* (1962), I, p. 33.
32. *Royal Commission Report* (1960), paras. 935 and 940.
33. *Hansard*, 669, col. 117.
34. *Ibid.*, 670, col. 431.
35. *Ibid.*, 669, col. 329.
36. *Ibid.*, col. 307.
37. *Ibid.*, 671, col. 1370.
38. *Ibid.*
39. *Ibid.*, cols. 1371 and 1373.
40. *Ibid.*, 708, col. 1298.
41. *Ibid.*, col. 1306.
42. *A Socialist Strategy for London. Labour Party Manifesto* (1973), p. 20.
43. *Greater London Council. Minutes of Proceedings 1974*, p. 336.
44. *Ibid.*, 1976, p. 205.
45. *Ibid.*, p. 808.
46. *Hansard*, 927, cols. 1423 and 1426–8.
47. *Evening Standard*, 6 June 1974.

CALENDAR OF EVENTS

National		City and Metropolitan	
1625	Accession of Charles I		
		1636	The 'New Incorporation of the Suburbs'
1642	Civil War		
1649	Execution of Charles I		
1660	Restoration of Charles II		
		1665	Plague
		1666	Great Fire of London
		1682–3	Quo Warranto attack on the City's charter
		1684	Surrender of Company charters
1685	Accession of James II		
1688	Glorious Revolution, Accession of William and Mary	1688	Restoration of old charters by James II
		1689	Reaffirmation of the City's privileges
		1694	Orphans Act dealing with the City's debts
1702	Accession of Queen Anne		
1715	Accession of.the Hanoverian George I		
		1725	City Elections Act
1727	Accession of George II		
		1748	Supplementary Orphans Act
1760	Accession of George III		
		1768–74	John Wilkes's radical agitation
1820	Accession of George IV		
1830	Accession of William IV		
1830–4	*Whig* ministries (Grey, Melbourne)		
1832	Parliamentary Reform		
1834–5	*Conservative* (Peel)		
1835–41	*Whig* (Melbourne)	1835	Municipal Corporations Act
1837	Accession of Queen Victoria	1837	Municipal Corporations Commissioners' report on London
		1839	Failure of bill to amalgamate City and Metropolitan police forces
1841–6	*Conservative* (Peel)		
1846–52	*Liberal* (Russell)		
		1848	City largely exempted from Public Health legislation
1852	*Conservative* (Derby)		
1852–5	*Coalition* (Aberdeen)		
		1853–4	London Corporation Commission

National		*City and Metropolitan*	
1854–6	Crimean War		
1855–8	*Liberal* (Palmerston)	1855	Metropolitan Board of Works established
		1856–61	London Corporation Reform bills
		1856	Abolition of 'freedom' requirement for retailing in the Square Mile
1858–9	*Conservative* (Derby)		
1859–66	*Liberal* (Palmerston, Russell)		
		1861	Select Committee on Local Government and Taxation in the Metropolis
		1863	City and Metropolitan Police Amalgamation bill
		1865	Metropolitan Municipalities Association founded by James Beal
1866–8	*Conservative* (Derby, Disraeli)	1866–7	Select Committee on Local Government and Taxation in the Metropolis
		1867–78	M.M.A. reform bills
1868–74	*Liberal* (Gladstone)		
		1870	Common Council's resolution in favour of separate municipalities
1874–80	*Conservative* (Disraeli)		
		1876	J.F.B. Firth's *Municipal London* published
		1877–8	Foundation of the City and Guilds' Institute
1880–5	*Liberal* (Gladstone)	1880–4	Livery Companies Commission
		1881	London Municipal Reform League formed
		1884	London Government bill
1885–6	*Conservative* (Salisbury)	1885	Redistribution of Seats Act giving more seats to London
1886	*Liberal* (Gladstone)		
1886–92	*Conservative* (Salisbury)		
		1888	Local Government Act
		1889	Formation of the London County Council
		1889–1907	Progressive (i.e. Liberal) control of L.C.C.
1892–5	*Liberal* (Gladstone, Rosebery)		
		1893–4	Royal Commission on the Amalgamation of the City and the L.C.C.
		1894	Foundation of the London Municipal Society
1895–1905	*Conservative* (Salisbury, Balfour)		
		1899	Metropolitan Boroughs Act

National	City and Metropolitan
1901 Accession of Edward VII	
1905–15 *Liberal* (Campbell-Bannerman, Asquith)	
	1907–34 Conservative control of the L.C.C.
1910 Accession of George V	
1914–18 First World War	
1915–22 *Coalition* (Asquith, Lloyd George)	
	1918 Representation of the People Act effectively ending the Livery's parliamentary vote
1921–4 *Conservative* (Bonar Law, Baldwin)	1921–3 Royal Commission on London Government
1924 *Labour* (MacDonald)	
1924–9 *Conservative* (Baldwin)	
1929–31 *Labour* (MacDonald)	
1931–45 *National* (MacDonald, Baldwin, Chamberlain, Churchill)	
	1934–65 Labour control of the L.C.C. (Morrison, Latham, Hayward)
1936 Accession of Edward VIII	
1936 Accession of George VI	
1939–45 Second World War	1939 Publication of W.A. Robson's *The Government and Misgovernment of London*
1945–51 *Labour* (Atlee)	
	1948 Representation of the People Act abolishing the City's 'business vote' and amalgamating the constituency with Westminster
1951–64 *Conservative* (Churchill, Eden, Macmillan, Home)	
1952 Accession of Queen Elizabeth II	
	1957–60 Royal Commission on Local Government in Greater London
	1963 London Government Act
1964–70 *Labour* (Wilson)	
	1965 Greater London Council established
	1965–7 Labour control of the G.L.C.
	1967–73 Conservative control of the G.L.C.
1970–4 *Conservative* (Heath)	
	1973–7 Labour control of the G.L.C.
1974–9 *Labour* (Wilson, Callaghan)	
	1975–7 Labour party attack on the City in the G.L.C. and Parliament
	1977–81 Conservative control of the G.L.C.
1979– *Conservative* (Thatcher)	
	1981– Labour control of the G.L.C.

GLOSSARY AND ABBREVIATIONS

Aldermen. Twenty-five Aldermen now constitute the City's upper Court. They used to be more powerful in everyday administration than they are today. An Alderman is chosen by the residents and certain business owners or tenants in his ward, though the other Aldermen have the right of veto. In theory he can serve for life, but in practice he retires at seventy.

Assistants. The Court of Assistants constitute the governing body of a Livery Company. Assistants are elected or co-opted, usually by seniority, from the Liverymen.

Chamberlain. The City Corporation's chief financial officer.

City's Cash. The City's own corporate revenues, as opposed to its trust funds and rate income.

Common Council. The main assembly of the Corporation, comprising the Lord Mayor, Aldermen, and Common Councilmen.

Common Councilmen. Elected each year by residents and certain business owners of tenants in the wards. They now number 136, though the figure used to be considerably higher.

Common Hall. The gathering of the Liverymen of the Companies for the nomination and election of certain City officers. In the seventeenth and eighteenth centuries it was the forum for outspoken criticism of the Government.

Comptroller. Formerly in charge of the City's property and estates; now also City Solicitor.

Corporation of the City of London. The ancient governing body of the famous 'square mile', originally the walled heart of London and now the centre of London's financial and commercial community.

Freemen. The freedom of the City is acquired in three ways: by patrimony or direct descent from a freeman; by apprenticeship to a freeman (now largely a nominal affair); and by redemption or purchase. In former times only freemen were allowed to exercise a trade in or around the square mile. (The last vestiges of this regulation were removed in 1856.) Freemen were formerly also entitled to elect Aldermen and Common Councilmen, but they lost this exclusive right in 1867. Honorary freedoms are granted to men and women who have performed notable service to the City, the nation or the world.

G.L.C. Greater London Council (1965–).

Guildhall. The City's Headquarters, first built in the fifteenth century. Now integrated into a modern precinct and complex.

L.C.C. London County Council (1889–1965).

Livery Companies. City Companies, formerly craft guilds, entitled to bestow their Livery on members. Their order of precedence is determined by the date of the Court of Aldermen's 'grant of Livery'.

Liverymen. Freemen who on election and payment of a fee become entitled to wear the Livery or clothing of their Company. Collectively they constitute the City's Livery and in Common Hall they nominate or elect various City officers, including the Lord Mayor and Sheriffs. They were formerly able to elect the City's M.P.s.

L.M.R.L. London Municipal Reform League. Founded by John Lloyd in 1881; committed to centralization and root-and-branch reform of the City.

L.M.S. London Municipal Society (1894–1963). The Conservative party's political organization for London and the provinces.

Lord Mayor. The Corporation's chief magistrate and ceremonial head. He is an Alderman chosen, invariably by rote, by his fellows after the nomination of two names by Common Hall. When an Alderman has served as Lord Mayor he is 'past the Chair'. His annual presentation to the judges in November is known as Lord Mayor's Day and the procession to the Law Courts the Lord Mayor's Show.

Master and Wardens. The *cursus honorum* of a Livery Company. The officers have various titles: the Master, for example, is often called the Prime Warden. They are chosen by the Assistants either from their own ranks or the Livery and they serve two or three Wardenships and then the Mastership by turns each year.

M.B.W. Metropolitan Board of Works (1855–89). The inchoate predecessor of the L.C.C.

M.M.A. Metropolitan Municipalities Association. Founded by James Beal in 1865. Initially in favour of a devolved government for London based on the parliamentary constituencies, but increasingly concerned to unify and centralize.

Prime Warden. The Master of certain Livery Companies. See 'Master and Wardens'.

Recorder. The senior law officer of the Corporation.

Remembrancer. Ceremonial officer and parliamentary agent.

Renter Warden. One of the officers of a Livery Company. See 'Master and Wardens'.

Sheriffs. Two legal officers elected each year by Common Hall. One is an Alderman, the other not. Under the Stuarts the office was regarded by the Crown as a source of dangerous independence, while under the Hanoverians it became merely an onerous chore. Now as much a ceremonial as a legal office. An Alderman cannot become Lord Mayor without having served as Sheriff.

Town Clerk. The City's chief administrative officer.

Wards. The City used to contain twenty-six wards, but now Bridge Ward Without, a sinecure, is amalgamated with Bridge Ward proper and the number is twenty-five. Each ward is represented by an Alderman and a certain number of Common Councilmen.

APPENDIX I

LIVERY COMPANIES IN ORDER OF PRECEDENCE

1. Mercers
2. Grocers
3. Drapers
4. Fishmongers
5. Goldsmiths
6. and 7.* Merchant Taylors
7. and 6.* Skinners
8. Haberdashers
9. Salters
10. Ironmongers
11. Vintners
12. Clothworkers
13. Dyers
14. Brewers
15. Leathersellers
16. Pewterers
17. Barbers
18. Cutlers
19. Bakers
20. Wax Chandlers
21. Tallow Chandlers
22. Armourers and Brasiers
23. Girdlers
24. Butchers
25. Saddlers
26. Carpenters
27. Cordwainers
28. Painter Stainers
29. Curriers
30. Masons
31. Plumbers
32. Innholders
33. Founders
34. Poulters
35. Cooks
36. Coopers
37. Tylers and Bricklayers
38. Bowyers
39. Fletchers
40. Blacksmiths
41. Joiners
42. Weavers
43. Woolmen
44. Scriveners
45. Fruiterers
46. Plaisterers
47. Stationers and Newspaper Makers
48. Broderers
49. Upholders
50. Musicians
51. Turners
52. Basketmakers
53. Glaziers
54. Horners
55. Farriers
56. Paviors
57. Loriners
58. Apothecaries
59. Shipwrights
60. Spectacle Makers
61. Clockmakers
62. Glovers
63. Feltmakers
64. Framework Knitters
65. Needlemakers
66. Gardeners
67. Tinplate Workers
68. Wheelwrights
69. Distillers
70. Pattenmakers
71. Glass Sellers
72. Coachmakers and Coach Harness Makers

* The Merchant Taylors and Skinners change places in the order of precedence each year.

73. Gunmakers
74. Gold and Silver Wyre Drawers
75. Makers of Playing Cards
76. Fanmakers
77. Carmen
78. Master Mariners
79. Solicitors
80. Farmers
81. Air Pilots and Air Navigators
82. Tobacco Pipe Makers
83. Furniture Makers
84. Scientific Instrument Makers
85. Chartered Surveyors
86. Chartered Accountants
87. Chartered Secretaries and Administrators
88. Builders Merchants
89. Launderers
90. Marketors
91. Actuaries
92. Insurers
93. Arbitrators

APPENDIX II

LORD MAYORS SINCE 1835 AND THEIR COMPANIES

Election

1835 W.T. Copeland *Goldsmiths*
1836 T. Kelly *Plaisterers*
1837 J. Cowan *Wax Chandlers*
1838 S. Wilson *Weavers*
1839 Sir C. Marshall *Innholders*
1840 T. Johnson *Coopers*
1841 J. Pirie *Plaisterers*
1842 J. Humphery *Tallow Chandlers*
1843 W. Magnay *Stationers*
1844 M. Gibbs *Fishmongers*
1845 J. Johnson *Spectaclemakers*
1846 Sir G. Caroll *Spectaclemakers*
1847 J.K. Hooper *Vintners*
1848 Sir J. Duke *Spectaclemakers et al.*
1849 T. Farncomb *Tallow Chandlers*
1850 J. Musgrove *Clothworkers*
1851 W. Hunter *Upholders*
1852 T. Challis *Butchers*
1853 T. Sidney *Girdlers*
1854 F.G. Moon *Stationers et al.*
1855 D. Salomons *Coopers*
1856 T.Q. Finnis *Bowyers*
1857 Sir R.W. Carden *Cutlers*
1858 D.W. Wire *Innholders et al.*
1859 J. Carter *Clockmakers*
1860 W. Cubitt *Fishmongers*
1861 W. Cubitt *Fishmongers*
1862 W.A. Rose *Spectaclemakers et al.*
1863 W. Lawrence *Carpenters et al.*
1864 W.S. Hale *Tallow Chandlers*
1865 B.S. Phillips *Spectaclemakers*
1866 T. Gabriel *Goldsmiths*
1867 W.F. Allen *Stationers*
1868 J.C. Lawrence *Carpenters et al.*
1869 R. Besley *Loriners*
1870 T. Dakin *Spectaclemakers et al.*
1871 S.J. Gibbons *Salters*
1872 Sir S.H. Waterlow *Stationers et al.*
1873 A. Lusk *Spectaclemakers et al.*
1874 D.H. Stone *Spectaclemakers et al.*
1875 W.J.R. Cotton *Haberdashers et al.*
1876 Sir T. White *Feltmakers*
1877 T. Owden *Innholders et al.*
1878 Sir C. Whetham *Leathersellers*
1879 Sir F.W. Truscott *Stationers et al.*

1880 W. McArthur *Spectaclemakers*
1881 J.W. Ellis *Merchant Taylors*
1882 H.E. Knight *Spectaclemakers et al.*
1883 R.N. Fowler *Spectaclemakers et al.*
1884 G.S. Nottage *Spectaclemakers et al.*
1885 R.N. Fowler *Spectaclemakers et al.*
1885 J. Staples *Leathersellers et al.*
1886 Sir R. Hanson *Merchant Taylors et al.*
1887 P. de Keyser *Spectaclemakers et al.*
1888 J. Whitehead *Fanmakers et al.*
1889 Sir H.A. Isaacs *Loriners et al.*
1890 J. Savory *Goldsmiths et al.*
1891 D. Evans *Haberdashers et al.*
1892 S. Knill *Goldsmiths et al.*
1893 G.R. Tyler *Stationers et al.*
1894 Sir J. Renals *Spectaclemakers et al.*
1895 Sir W.H. Wilkin *Broderers et al.*
1896 G. Faudel-Phillips *Spectaclemakers et al.*
1897 H.D. Davies *Spectaclemakers et al.*
1898 Sir J.V. Moore *Loriners et al.*
1899 A.J. Newton *Fanmakers et al.*
1900 F. Green *Glaziers et al.*
1901 Sir J.C. Dimsdale *Grocers*
1902 Sir M. Samuel *Spectaclemakers et al.*
1903 Sir J.T. Ritchie *Shipwrights et al.*
1904 J. Pound *Leathersellers et al.*
1905 W.V. Morgan *Cutlers et al.*
1906 Sir W.P. Treloar *Loriners et al.*
1907 Sir J.C. Bell *Fanmakers et al.*
1908 Sir G.W. Truscott *Stationers et al.*
1909 Sir J. Knill *Goldsmiths et al.*
1910 Sir T.V. Strong *Stationers et al.*
1911 Sir T.B. Crosby *Turners et al.*
1912 Sir D. Burnett *Loriners et al.*
1913 Sir T.V. Bowater *Girdlers et al.*
1914 Sir C. Johnston *Innholders*
1915 Sir C.C. Wakefield *Haberdashers et al.*
1916 Sir W.H. Dunn *Wheelwrights et al.*
1917 C.A. Hanson *Pattenmakers*
1918 Sir H.B. Marshall *Stationers*
1919 Sir E.E. Cooper *Musicians*
1920 J. Roll *Horners et al.*
1921 Sir J.J. Baddeley *Framework Knitters et al.*
1922 E.C. Moore *Fruiterers*

1923 Sir. L. Newton *Loriners et al.*
1924 Sir A. Bower *Vintners et al*
1925 Sir W.R. Pryke *Painter Stainers*
1926 Sir G.R. Blades *Gardeners*
1927 Sir C.A. Batho *Paviors et al.*
1928 Sir K. Studd *Fruiterers et al.*
1929 Sir W. Waterlow *Stationers*
1930 Sir P. Neal *Bakers et al.*
1931 Sir M. Jenks *Haberdashers*
1932 Sir P.W. Greenaway *Stationers*
1933 Sir C.H. Collett *Glovers*
1934 Sir S.H.M. Killik *Fanmakers*
1935 Sir P. Vincent *Gold and Silver Wyre Drawers et al.*
1936 Sir G.T. Broadbridge *Loriners*
1937 Sir H.E.A. Twyford *Masons et al.*
1938 Sir F.H. Bowater *Girdlers*
1939 Sir W.G. Coxen *Cordwainers et al.*
1940 G. Wilkinson *Stationers*
1941 Sir J.D. Laurie *Saddlers et al.*
1942 Sir S.G. Joseph *Cutlers*
1943 Sir F. Newson-Smith *Turners et al.*
1944 Sir F. Alexander *Shipwrights*
1945 Sir C. Davis *Fanmakers*
1946 Sir B. Smith *Bakers et al.*
1947 F.M. Wells *Haberdashers et al.*
1948 Sir G. Aylwen *Merchant Taylors et al.*
1949 Sir F. Rowland *Horners et al.*
1950 D. Lowson *Glaziers et al.*
1951 Sir L. Boyce *Loriners*
1952 Sir R. de la Bère *Skinners*

1953 N.V. Bowater *Vintners*
1954 S. Howard *Gardeners*
1955 C. Ackroyd *Carpenters et al.*
1956 Sir C. Welch *Haberdashers et al.*
1957 Sir D. Truscott *Vintners*
1958 Sir H. Gillett *Basketmakers*
1959 Sir E. Stockdale *Carpenters et al.*
1960 Sir B. Waley-Cohen *Clothworkers*
1961 Sir F. Hoare *Goldsmiths*
1962 Sir R. Perring *Tin Plate Workers et al.*
1963 Sir J. Harman *Plumbers et al.*
1964 Sir J. Miller *Coachmakers*
1965 Sir J. L. P. Denny *Barber Surgeons et al.*
1966 Sir R. Bellinger *Broderers et al.*
1967 Sir G. Inglefield *Haberdashers et al.*
1968 Sir C. Trinder *Fletchers et al.*
1969 Sir I.F. Bowater *Haberdashers*
1970 Sir P.M. Studd *Merchant Taylors et al.*
1971 Sir E. Howard *Gardeners*
1972 Lord Mais *Cutlers et al.*
1973 Sir H. Wontner *Feltmakers et al.*
1974 M. Fox *Wheelwrights et al.*
1975 L. Ring *Armourers and Brasiers*
1976 Sir R. Gillett *Master Mariners*
1977 P.B.R. Vanneck *Fishmongers et al.*
1978 K. Cork *Horners et al.*
1979 P.D.H. Gadsen *Clothworkers et al.*
1980 R.L. Gardner-Thorpe *Painter-Stainers et al.*
1981 C. Leaver *Carmen*
1982 A.S. Jolliffe *Painter-Stainers*

Titles are as at the time of election. Companies are 'mother' Companies, i.e. the first one joined and the one used for civic purposes.

It is interesting to note the number of Lord Mayors who had two – sometimes four or five – Companies. Whether this was a general practice outside the Aldermanic bench and whether it seriously affects the overall Livery figures is hard to say.

APPENDIX III

PARTY STRENGTH ON THE L.C.C. AND G.L.C.

Year	Moderate, Municipal Reform, Conservative	Progressive, Liberal	Labour	Independent	Seats
1889	45	73			118
1892	35	83			118
1895	59	58		1	118
1898	48	70			118
1901	32	86			118
1904	35	82		1	118
1907	79	37	1	1	118
1910	60	55	3		118
1913	67	49	2		118
1919	68	40	15	1	124
1922	82	26	16		124
1925	83	6	35		124
1928	77	5	42		124
1931	83	6	35		124
1934	55		69		124
1937	49		75		124
1946	30	2	90	2	124
1949	64	1	64		129
1952	37		92		129
1955	52		74		126
1958	25		101		126
1961	42		84		126

G.L.C.

Year	Conservative	Labour	Liberal	Seats
1964	36	64		100
1967	82	18		100
1970	65	35		100
1973	32	58	2	92
1977	64	28		92
1981	41	50	1	92

Taken from K. Young and P. L. Garside, *Metropolitan London* (1982), p. 343.

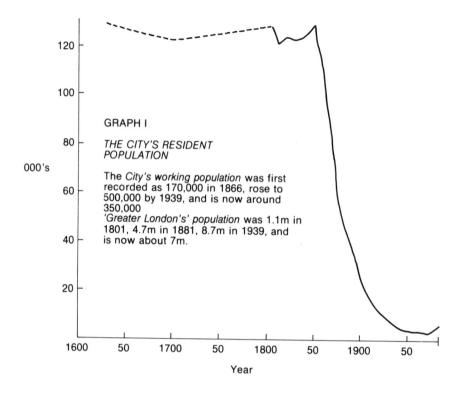

GRAPH I

THE CITY'S RESIDENT POPULATION

The *City's working population* was first recorded as 170,000 in 1866, rose to 500,000 by 1939, and is now around 350,000
'Greater London's' population was 1.1m in 1801, 4.7m in 1881, 8.7m in 1939, and is now about 7m.

000's

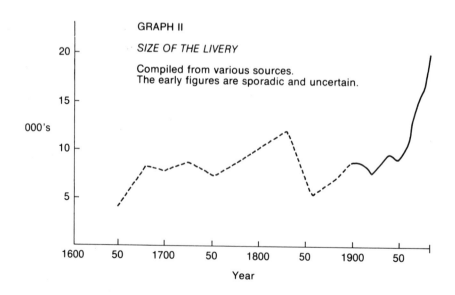

GRAPH II

SIZE OF THE LIVERY

Compiled from various sources.
The early figures are sporadic and uncertain.

000's

BIBLIOGRAPHY

I should like to draw attention to my dependence on two of the sources listed below: John Stewart's collection of newspaper cuttings and other material relating to the Corporation bill of 1856, which was of great help in the writing of Chapter IV; and a set of bound newspapers containing reports of proceedings in Common Council, 1827–88. Both are in the Guildhall Library. Otherwise, apart from a few dips into manuscripts, I have relied on whatever published matter I could find. Much proved to be irrelevant to my theme and only items from which I gained direct assistance have been included here.

Adams, A., *The History of the Worshipful Company of Blacksmiths* (1951).
Address of Mr. James Beal delivered at the St. James's Vestry Hall (1867).
Alford, B.W.E., and Barker, T.C., *A History of the Carpenters' Company* (1968).
Allen, W.F., *The Corporation of London: its Rights and Privileges* (1858).
An Analysis by the Remembrancer of the City of London . . . (1870).
Arundell, T., *Historical Reminiscences of the City of London and its Livery Companies* (1869).
Ash, B., *The Golden City. London between the Fires, 1666–1941* (1964).
Ashdown, C.H., *History of the Worshipful Company of Glaziers* (1919).
Ashton, R., *The Crown and the Money Market, 1603 — 1640* (1960).
— , *The City and the Court, 1603 — 1643* (1979).
Atkins, S.E., and Overall, W.H., *Some Account of the Worshipful Company of Clockmakers of the City of London* (1881).
Ball, M. *The Worshipful Company of Brewers* (1977).
Bamberger, L., *Bow Bell Memories* (1932).
Barker, T.C., *The Girdlers' Company. A Second History* (1957).
— . See also Alford, B.W.E.
— . See also Hatcher, J.
Beaven, A.B., *The Aldermen of the City of London* (1908–13).
Bell, R.W., See Gibbon, G.
Bell, W.G., *The Great Fire of London in 1666* (2nd edn., 1920).
Benn, J., 'Early Memories of the London County Council', *Ways and Means*, IV no. 48 (1920).
Bennett, E., *The Worshipful Company of Carmen of London* (1952).
— , *The Worshipful Company of Wheelwrights of the City of London* (1970).
Blackham, R.J., *The Soul of the City. London's Livery Companies* (1931).
— , *London for Ever. The Sovereign City* (1932).

Blagden, C., *The Stationers' Company. A History, 1403–1959* (1959).
— , 'Charter Trouble', *Book Collector*, VI (1957).
Blake, R., *Disraeli* (1966).
Blakesley, G.H., *The London Livery Companies' Commission. A Comment on the Majority Report* (1885).
Bone, G.A., *The Worshipful Company of Glass Sellers of London* (1966).
Bonner, H.B., *Charles Bradlaugh* (1895).
Brett-James, N.G., *The Growth of Stuart London* (1935).
Briggs, A., *Victorian Cities* (1968 edn.).
— , *Victorian People* (1954).
Brown, K.D., 'London and the Historical Reputation of John Burns', *The London Journal*, II (1976).
— , *John Burns* (1977).
Buckle, G.E. See Moneypenny, W.F.
Buckley, J.K., *Joseph Parkes of Birmingham* (1926).
Burt, N., *A New Year's Gift for England and all her Cities, Ports and Corporations* (1653).
Carpenter, W., *The Corporation of London, as it is, and as it should be* (1847).
Catalogue of the Extensive and Valuable Library of the late Sir Francis Palgrave (1862).
Champness, R., *The Worshipful Company of Turners of London* (1966).
The City Companies and their Property. A Plea for Fair Play (1886).
City Guilds Reform Fly Sheets (1876).
City Men and City Manners (1850).
City of London Directory and Livery Companies Guide (1982).
The City of London: a Record of Destruction and Survival (1951).
The City of London. The Official Guide (n.d.).
The City Solicitor's 'Painful Story' and other papers (1879).
Clarke, E., *The Story of My Life* (1918).
Clarke, H., *London Municipal Reform. An Address delivered at the Bishopsgate Ward Club* (1882).
Clarke, P. *Serving his Generation. Being Short Notes of the Public Life of Henry Clarke* (1915).
Clode, C.M., *Memorials of the Guild of Merchant Taylors* (1875).
The Coachmakers. A History of the Worshipful Company of Coachmakers and Coach Harness Makers, 1667–1977, ed. H. Nockolds (1977).
Cole, M., *Servant of the County* (1956).
The Collected Works of John Stuart Mill (1963–).
A Collection of the Debates and Proceedings in Parliament in 1694 and 1695 upon the Enquiry into the late Briberies and Corrupt Practices (1695).
Collins, B.R., *A Short Account of the Worshipful Company of Fan Makers* (1950).
Collins, W.J., 'The London Government Bill', *Contemporary Review*, LXXV (1899).

Coming Men on Coming Questions, ed. W.T. Stead (1905).

Conacher, J.B., *The Aberdeen Coalition 1852–55* (1968).

Conder, E., *Records of the Hole Crafte and Fellowship of Masons* (1894).

Conington, H., *Reform at any Price? A Question about the London Corporation Bill and the Commissioners' Report* (1856).

The Corporation Commission. Report delivered to the Committee in aid of Corporate Reform (1833).

The Corporation of London. Its Origin, Constitution, Powers and Duties (1950).

Crewdson, H.A.F., *The Worshipful Company of Musicians* (2nd edn., 1971).

Crewe, Marquess of, *Lord Rosebery* (1931).

Cutler, H., *The Cutler Files* (1982).

Davies, A.E., *The Story of the London County Council* (1925).

Daynes, J.N., *A Short History of the Ancient Mistery of the Dyers of the City of London* (1965).

A Debate on the Reform of London Government (1906).

'The Decline and Fall of the Corporation of London', *Fraser's Magazine*, XLIX (1854).

Dexter, J.T., *The Government of London* (1875).

A Dialogue between Francesco and Aurelia, Two Unfortunate Orphans of the City of London (1690).

Dibdin, L.T., *The Livery Companies of London. Being a Review of the Report of the London Livery Companies' Commission* (1886).

Disney, M.H., *The Honourable Company. An Account of the Origin and Progress of the Honourable Company of Master Mariners, 1921–69* (1974).

Disraeli, Derby and the Conservative Party. Journals and Memoirs of Edward Henry, Lord Stanley, 1849–69, ed. J. Vincent (1978).

Do the City Ratepayer Underpay? The Facts (1977).

Donoughue, B., and Jones, G.W., *Herbert Morrison. Portrait of a Politician* (1973).

Doolittle, I.G., 'The Government of the City of London, 1694–1767', (Oxford Univ. D.Phil, thesis, 1980).

—, 'The City's West End Estate: A "Remarkable Omission" ', *The London Journal*, VII (1981).

—, 'Walpole's City Elections Act (1725)', *English Historical Review*, XCVII (1982).

—, 'The City of London's Debt to its Orphans, 1694 – 1767', *Bulletin of the Institute of Historical Research* (forthcoming).

Dummelow, J., *The Waxchandlers of London* (1973).

Dunbabin, J.P., 'The Politics of the Establishment of County Councils', *Historical Journal*, VI (1963).

Durning-Lawrence, E.J., *Family History of the Lawrences of Cornwall* (1915).

Durston, C.M.G., 'The City of London and its Ward Clubs', *The Old Lady of Threadneedle Street*, LII (1976).

An Economic Study of the City of London, edd. J.H. Dunning and E.V. Morgan (1971).

Elkington, G., *The Worshipful Company of Coopers. With Notes and Recollections, 1873 to 1930* (1930).

Englefield, W.A.D., *The History of the Painter-Stainers' Company* (1950 edn.).

Evans, D., *The Life and Work of William Williams* (1940).

Ferris, P., *The City* (1960).

Feuchtwanger, E.J., *Disraeli, Democracy and the Tory Party* (1968).

Finer, S.E., *The Life and Times of Sir Edwin Chadwick* (1952).

Finlay, R., *Population and Metropolis. The Demography of London, 1580–1650* (1981).

Finlayson, G.B.A.M., 'The Municipal Corporations Commission and Report, 1833 – 35', *Bulletin of the Institute of Historical Research*, XXXVI (1963).

— , 'The Politics of Municipal Reform, 1835', *English Historical Review*, LXXXI (1966).

Firth, J.F., *Coopers' Company, London. Historical Memoranda, Charters, Documents, and Extracts from the Records of the Corporation and Books of the Company, 1396–1848* (1848).

Firth, J.F.B., *Municipal London; or, London Government as it is, and London under a Municipal Council* (1876).

— , *A Practical Scheme of London Municipal Reform, being an Epitome of 'The Municipality of London Bill'* . . . (1881).

— , *Reform of London Government and of City Guilds* (1888).

Fisher, F.J., *The Worshipful Company of Horners. A Short History* (1936).

Fitch, C., *The History of the Worshipful Company of Pattenmakers of the City of London* (1926).

Fletcher, J., 'Statistical Account of the Police of the Metropolis', *Journal of the Statistical Society of London*, XIII (1850).

Flynn, J.S., *Sir Robert N. Fowler. A Memoir* (1893).

Foley, D.L., *Governing the London Region. Reorganization and Planning in the 1960s* (1972).

Fortescue, H., *Representative Self-Government for the Metropolis. A Letter to Viscount Palmerston* (1854).

Foster, F.F., *The Politics of Stability. A Portrait of the Rulers in Elizabethan London* (1977).

Foster, W., *A Short History of the Worshipful Company of Coopers of London* (1944).

Franks, R.H., *Corporation Abuses. A Letter to the Right Honourable Viscount Althorp on the Justice and Necessity of Reforming the Livery Companies of the City of London* (1833).

Fraser, M., 'Sir Benjamin Hall and the Administration of London', *Transactions of the Honourable Society of Cymmrodorion* (1963).

Fraser, W., *London Self-Governed* (1866).

Fulford, R., *Glyn's 1753–1953. Six Generations in Lombard Street* (1953).

Gardiner, A.G., *The Life of Sir William Harcourt* (1923).

— , *John Benn and the Progressive Movement* (1925).

Garside, P.L. See Young, K.

George, M.D., *London Life in the Eighteenth Century* (1966 edn.).

Ghewy, A.B., *Real Municipal Government for London* (1898).

Gibbon, G. and Bell, R.W., *History of the London County Council, 1889–1939* (1939).

Gilbert, W., *The City. An Enquiry into the Corporation, its Livery Companies, and the Administration of their Charities and Endowments* (1877).

' "Gilt and Gingerbread"; or, Tom Fool's Day in the City', *Fraser's Magazine*, L (1854).

Girtin, T., *The Golden Ram. A Narrative History of the Clothworkers' Company, 1528–1958* (1958).

— , *The Triple Crowns. A Narrative History of the Drapers' Company, 1384–1964* (1964).

— , *The Mark of the Sword. A Narrative History of the Cutlers' Company, 1189–1975* (1975).

Glover, E., *The Gold and Silver Wyre-Drawers* (1979).

Golding, C., *The City* (1951).

Gomme, G.L., *London in the Reign of Victoria* (1898).

— , *The Governance of London* (1907).

Gooch, G.P., *Life of Lord Courtney* (1920).

Gosling, H., *Up and Down Stream* (1927).

'The Government of London', *Westminster Review*, XLIX (1876).

'The Government of London', *Spectator* (February 1913).

Gray, R., *A History of London* (1978).

'Greater London Regional Council of the Labour Party. Final Report and Recommendations of the City of London Working Party' (June 1975). Typescript.

Greater London Council. Minutes of Proceedings.

Gwynn, S., and Tuckwell, G.M., *The Life of Sir Charles W. Dilke* (1918).

Hadley, G., *Citizens and Founders. A History of the Worshipful Company of Founders, 1385–1975* (1975).

Hanham, H.J., *Elections and Party Management. Politics in the Time of Disraeli and Gladstone* (1959).

Hansard, III–V, 1833 to present.

Hare, T., 'Ideal of a Local Government for the Metropolis', *Macmillan's Magazine*, VII (1862–3).

— , *London Municipal Reform* (1882).

Harris, B., 'Why should the City escape?' *Political Quarterly*, XXXIV (1963).

Harris, P.A., *London and its Government* (1913 and 1931 edns.).

— , *Forty Years in and out of Parliament* (1947).

Harrison, F., 'The Amalgamation of London', *Contemporary Review*, LXVI (1894).

Hart, W. See Jones, G.W.

Hatcher, J., and Barker, T.C., *A History of British Pewter* (1974).

Haward, H., *The London County Council from Within* (1932).

Hawkins, J.W., *History of the Worshipful Company of the Art or Mistery of Feltmakers of London* (1917).

Hazlitt, W.C., *The Livery Companies of the City of London* (1892).

Henderson, A.J., *London and the National Government, 1721–42* (1945).

Henriques, R., *Marcus Samuel, First Viscount Bearsted* (1960).

Herbert, W., *The History of the Worshipful Company of Founders* (1925).

Hibbert, W.N., *History of the Worshipful Company of Founders* (1925).

Hickson, W.E., 'The Corporation of London and Municipal Reform', *Westminster Review*, XXXIX (1843).

— , 'The Apologists of City Administration', *ibid.*, XLI (1844).

— , 'City Administration . . . Case of the Non-Freemen', *ibid.*, XLIII (1845).

The History of 'The Times' (1935 – 52).

History of the Worshipful Company of Paviors of the City of London (3rd edn., 1966).

A History of the Worshipful Company of Tobacco Pipe Makers and Tobacco Blenders (1969).

Hobhouse, A., *Some Reasons for a Single Government of London* (1884).

— , 'The City Companies', *Contemporary Review*, XLVII (1885).

Hobhouse, H., *The Ward of Cheap in the City of London* (n.d.).

Hobhouse, L.T., and Hammond, J.L., *Lord Hobhouse. A Memoir* (1905).

Horton, G., *The Municipal Government of the Metropolis* (1865).

How the City Oppose London Reform (1888).

Hughes, T., 'The Anarchy of London', *Macmillan's Magazine*, XXI (1869 – 70).

Hyde, H.M., *Judge Jeffreys* (2nd edn., 1948).

Imray, J., *The Charity of Richard Whittington. A History of the Trust Administered by the Mercers' Company, 1424–1966* (1966).

Jackson, W.E., *Achievement. A Short History of the London County Council* (1965).

James, M., *Social Problems and Policy during the Puritan Revolution, 1640–1660* (1930).

Jephson, H., *The Sanitary Evolution of London* (1907).

— , *The Making of Modern London. Progress and Reaction* (1910).

Johnson, D.J., *Southwark and the City* (1969).

Jones, G.W., See Donoughue, B.

—, and Hart, W., 'Sir Isaac Hayward, 1884–1976', *The London Journal, II (1976)*.

Jones, P.E., *The Worshipful Company of Poulters of the City of London* (2nd edn., 1965).

—, *The Butchers of London* (1976).

Kahl, W.F., *The Development of the London Livery Companies. An Historical Essay and Select Bibliography* (1960).

Kellett, J.R., 'The Breakdown of Gild and Corporation Control over the Handicraft and Retail Trade in London, *Economic History Review*, X (1957–8).

—, 'The Financial Crisis of the Corporation of London and the Orphans' Act, 1694', *Guildhall Miscellany*, II (1963).

Knight, A.C., *Cordwainer Ward in the City of London* (1917).

Lambert, J.T., 'Notes and Reminiscences' (n.d.). Typescript in Guildhall Library

Lambert, R., *Sir John Simon, 1818–1904, and English Social Administration* (1963).

Lang, J., *Pride Without Prejudice. The Story of London's Guilds and Livery Companies* (1975).

—, *City and Guilds of London Institute. An Historical Commentary* (1978).

Laurie, P.G., *Sir Peter Laurie* (1901).

Law, F.W., *The Worshipful Company of Spectacle Makers. A History* (1978).

Lawrence, C.E., *William Purdie Treloar* (1925).

The LCC and the City (1895).

Lee, E., *Why Shouldn't London Wait? A Satire* (1884).

Letter to 'The Times' by James Beal . . . (1874).

Levin, J., *The Charter Controversy in the City of London, 1660–1688, and its Consequences* (1969).

Letters of the Rt. Hon. Sir George Cornewall Lewis, Bart., to various Friends, ed. G.F. Lewis (1870).

Lloyd, J., *London Municipal Government. History of a Great Reform, 1880–1888* (2nd edn., 1911).

London County Council. Royal Commission on London Government. Memorandum (1893).

London Government. Speech by Lord Hobhouse (1892).

London in the Age of Reform, ed. J. Stevenson (1977).

London Municipal Government. I. Opinions of the Press (1884).

London Municipal Reform. Conference of Members of Parliament and other influential Friends . . . (1881).

London Radicalism, 1830–43. A Selection from the Papers of Francis

Place, ed. D.J. Rowe (1970).

London's Heritage in the City Guilds, Fabian Tract no. 31 (1892).

'London's Rotten Borough', *Time Out*, no. 447 (1978).

Lubbock, J., 'A Few Words on the Government of London', *Fortnightly Review*, LVII (1892).

Mack, E.C., and Armytage, W.H.G., *Thomas Hughes* (1952).

'Main Points from the GLRC's Paper on the Need to abolish the City of London as a Local Government Unit' (September 1975). Typescript.

Mander, C.H.W., *A Descriptive and Historical Account of the Guild of Cordwainers of the City of London* (1931).

Marks, S., 'City under Siege', *Municipal and Public Services Journal*, LXXXV (1977).

Marsh, P., *The Discipline of Popular Government. Lord Salisbury's Domestic Statecraft, 1881–1902* (1978).

Mayer, E., *The Curriers and the City of London* (1968).

McBriar, A.M., *Fabian Socialism and English Politics, 1884–1918* (1962).

Melling, J.K., *Discovering London's Guilds and Liveries* (3rd edn., 1981).

Merewether, H.A., and Stephen, A.J., *The History of the Boroughs and Municipal Corporations of the United Kingdom* (1972 edn.).

Metcalf, P., *The Halls of the Fishmongers' Company* (1977).

Mill, J.S., *Autobiography*, ed. J. Stillinger (1971).

Moneypenny, W.F., and Buckle, G.E., *The Life of Benjamin Disraeli* (1910–16).

The Monster Municipality; or, Gog and Magog Reformed. A Dream (1882).

Morley, H., *Memoirs of Bartholomew Fair* (1874 rept.).

Morrison, H., *How Greater London is Governed* (1935).

Morrison, P., *Rambling Recollections* (1905).

Nelson, T.J., *The City of London. 'Strike but Hear'* (1884).

Newall, W., 'The Municipality of London', *Contemporary Review*, XXV (1874–5).

The New Government of London. The First Five Years, ed. G. Rhodes (1975).

Nicholl, J., *Some Account of the Worshipful Company of Ironmongers* (2nd edn., 1866).

Nicholson, F., 'The Politics of English Metropolitan Reform. The Background to the Establishment of the London County Council, 1876–89' (Toronto Univ. PH.D. thesis, 1972).

Norris, J.T., *A Letter to Sir Peter Laurie, Knight, in Reply to his Speech on the Periodical Election of City Aldermen* (1835).

Norton, G., *Commentaries on the History, Constitution, and Chartered Franchises of the City of London* (3rd edn., 1869).

Olsen, D.J., *The Growth of Victorian London* (1976).

Opinions of the Officers of the Corporation of the City of London (1847).

Orridge, B.B., *Some Account of the Citizens of London and their Rulers* (1867).

Owen, D., *English Philanthropy, 1660–1960* (1965).

— , *The Government of Victorian London, 1855–1889. The Metropolitan Board of Works, the Vestries, and the City Corporation* (1982).

Packe, M. St.J., *The Life of John Stuart Mill* (1954).

Palgrave. F., *Corporate Reform. Observations on the New Principles to be adopted in the Establishment of New Municipalitites, the Reform of Ancient Corporations and the Cheap Administration of Justice* (1833).

Pearl, V., *London and the Outbreak of the Puritan Revolution* (1972 edn.).

— , 'Change and Stability in Seventeenth-Century London', *The London Journal*, V (1979).

Perks, S., *The History of the Mansion House* (1922).

Phillips, F.T., *A History of the Worshipful Company of Cooks. A Second History* (1966).

Phillips, W., *'Home Rule for London'. An Appeal and a Warning* (1888).

— , *Sixty Years of Citizen Work and Play* (1907).

Pinto, E.H., *The Origins and History of the Worshipful Company of Furniture Makers* (1964).

Plummer, A., *The London Weavers' Company, 1600–1970* (1972).

Prest, J., *Lord John Russell* (1972).

Prevett, H., *A Short Description of the Worshipful Company of Haberdashers* (1971).

Prince, A., *The Craft of Laundering. A History of Fabric Cleaning* (1970).

Prince, L.B., *The Farrier and his Craft. The History of the Worshipful Company of Farriers* (1980).

'Proceedings in Common Council, 1827–88' (bound set of newspapers).

Proceedings in the Bills for the Regulation of the Corporation of London (1858).

Propositions for the Reform of the Corporation of London (1836).

Pulling, A., *Observations on the Disputes at Present Arising in the Corporation of the City of London and on the Power of Internal Reform Possessed by the Citizens in Common Council* (1847).

— , *A Practical Treatise on the Laws, Customs, Usages and Regulations of the City and Port of London* (2nd edn., 1849).

— . 'The City of London Corporation Inquiry', *Law Review*, XIX (1853 – 4).

A Radical Agenda for London, ed. P. Hall, Fabian Tract no. 469 (1980).

Reddaway, T.F., *The Rebuilding of London After the Great Fire* (1940).

'Reform of the City of London' (1978). Typescript in Guildhall Library.

Regan, D.E., 'In Memory of William A. Robson. *The Government and Misgovernment of London* revisited', *The London Journal*, VII (1981).

Remarks on the Speech of A.S. Ayrton, Esq., M.P., in Reference to the

Corporation of London. Observations on his Scheme for a New and Enlarged Municipality (1860).

The Reminiscences of Albert Peel, ed. T. Mackay (1908).

Report of the Royal Commission on Municipal Corporations (England and Wales): London and Southwark; London Companies (Parliamentary Papers (Cmd. 239), 1837, XXV).

Report of the Royal Commission on the Corporation of the City of London (P.P. (Cmd. 1772), 1854, XXVI).

Report of the Royal Commission on the City of London Livery Companies (P.P. (Cmd. 4073), 1884, XXXIX).

Report of the Royal Commission on the Amalgamation of the City and County of London (P.P. (Cmd. 7493), 1894, XVII–III).

Report of the Royal Commission on London Government (P.P. (Cmd. 1830), 1923, XII Part I) and *Minutes of Evidence* (1922).

Report of the Royal Commission on Local Government in Greater London (P.P. (Cmd. 1164), 1959 – 60, XVIII) and *Minutes of Evidence* (1959–60) and *Written Evidence* (1962).

Reports of the Select Committee on Metropolis Local Taxation (P.P. (Cmds. 211, 372, 476), 1861, VIII).

Reports of the Select Committee on Metropolis Local Taxation (P.P. (Cmds. 186, 452), 1866, XIII).

Reports of the Select Committee on Metropolitan Local Government (P.P. (Cmds. 268, 301), 1867, XII).

Report from the Select Committee on the London Corporation (Charges of Malversation) (P.P. (Cmd. 161), 1887, X).

Rhodes, G., *The Government of London. The Struggle for Reform* (1970).

— , and Ruck, S.K., *The Government of Greater London* (1970).

Robson, W.A., *The Government and Misgovernment of London* (1939).

— , *The Greater London Boroughs* (1961).

— , *The Heart of Greater London. Proposals for a Policy* (1965).

Ronald, P., *The Basketmakers' Company* (1978).

Rowland, W.L., 'Royal Commissions and Commissions of Enquiry touching the Corporation of London', *Transactions of the Guildhall Historical Association*, III (1963).

The Royal Commission. The London City Livery Companies' Vindication (1885).

Royal Commission on London Government, 1893–4. Report of the Special Committee of the Corporation of London (1895).

Ruck, S.K. See Rhodes, G.

Rudé, G., *Wilkes and Liberty* (1965 edn.).

— , *Hanoverian London* (1971).

Saunders, W., *History of the First London County Council* (1892).

Sayer, T.L., *Gog and Magog and I. Some Recollections of 49 Years at Guildhall* (1931).

Scott, B., *A Statistical Vindication of the City of London; or, Fallacies Exploded and Facts Explained* (2nd edn., 1867).
— , *The Municipal Government of London* (1884).
Sebastian, L.B., *The City Livery Companies and their Corporate Property* (1885).
Sharpe, R.R., *London and the Kingdom* (1894 – 5).
Sheppard, F.H.W., *London 1808–70. The Infernal Wen* (1971).
Sherwell, J.W., *The History of the Guild of Saddlers* (3rd edn., 1956).
Smalley G., *The Life of Sir Sydney Waterlow* (1909).
Smallwood, F., *Greater London. The Politics of Metropolitan Reform* (1965).
Smith J.T., *What is the Corporation of London? and who are the Freemen?* (1850).
— , *'Corporation of London Reform'. A Letter to Sir James Duke* (1850).
— , *The Metropolis and its Municipal Administration* (1852).
Smith, P., *Disraelian Conservatism and Social Reform* (1967).
Smith, R., *Sea-Coal for London. History of the Coal Factors in the London Market* (1961).
— , *The Irish Society, 1613–1963* (1966).
A Socialist Policy for the GLC. Discussion Papers on Labour's GLC Election Policy (1980).
A Socialist Strategy for London. Labour Party Manifesto (1973).
Stand Fast! Will the Citizens Consent to the Surrender of their Charters to a Foreign Body? What Says Chief Baron Kelly? (1867).
Statement as to the Origin, Constitution and Functions of the Corporation of London (1974).
Statement of the Corporation of London Read Before the Commissioners of Inquiry (1854).
Steele, A.F., *The Worshipful Company of Gardeners. A History of its Revival, 1890–1960* (1964).
— , *The Worshipful Company of Solicitors of the City of London. A Commentary on the Company's Surviving Records* (n.d.).
Stephens, A.J. See Merewether, H.A.
Stewart, J., 'Newspaper Cuttings, Pamphlets etc. relating to the Corporation Reform bill, 1856' (bound collection).
Stockdale, E., *Ptolemy Tortoise. Pages from the Life of an Alderman* (1978).
The Substance of an Address Delivered by Charles Pearson, Esq., at a Public Meeting (1844).
Summerson, J., 'The Victorian Rebuilding of the City of London', *The London Journal*, III (1977).
Sutherland, L.S., 'The City in 18th-Century Politics', *Essays Presented to Sir Lewis Namier*, edd. R. Pares and A.J.P. Taylor (1956).
— , *The City of London and the Opposition to Government* (1958).

Taylor, J.R., *Reform Your City Guilds* (2nd edn., 1872).

Taylor, R., *Lord Salisbury* (1975).

Temple, A.G., *Guildhall Memories* (1918).

Thomas, W.E.S., *The Philosophic Radicals. Nine Studies in Theory and Practice, 1817–41* (1979).

Thompson, P., *Socialists, Liberals and Labour. The Struggle for London, 1885 — 1914* (1967).

Thrupp, S., *A Short History of the Worshipful Company of Bakers of London* (1933).

Torrens, W.M., *Twenty Years in Parliament* (1893).

Treloar, W.P., *Wilkes and the City* (1917).

Tuckwell, G.M. See Gwynn, S.

Unwin, G., *Industrial Organization in the Sixteenth and Seventeenth Centuries* (1904).

— , *The Gilds and Companies of London* (3rd edn., 1938).

Unwin, P., *The Stationers' Company, 1918–1977* (1978).

Vine, G.H.M., 'The Special Committee', *Transactions of the Guildhall Historical Association*, I (1948).

Vine, G.M., 'Without the Walls', *ibid.*, IV (1969).

Wallas, G., *The Life of Francis Place* (4th edn. *1925*).

Ward, R., The City Livery Club (1971).

Warner, O., *A History of the Innholders' Company* (1962).

— , *A History of the Tin Plate Workers' alias Wire Workers' Company of the City of London* (1964).

Watney, J., *An Account of the Mistery of Mercers of the City of London* (1914).

Watson, J.S., *A History of the Salters' Company* (1963).

Webb, B., *Our Partnership*, edd. B Drake and M.I. Cole (1948).

Webb, S., *The London Programme* (2nd edn. 1895).

Webb, S. and B., *The Manor and the Borough* (1908).

The Webbs and their Work, ed. M. Cole (1949).

Welch, C., *Modern History of the City of London* (1896).

— , *History of the Worshipful Company of Pewterers of the City of London* (1902).

— , *History of the Worshipful Company of Paviors* (1909).

— , *History of the Cutlers' Company of London* (1916–23).

What is the Corporation of London? (n.d.).

White, H.C., *Lord Dickinson of Painswick. A Memoir* (1956).

Williams, M., *Leaves of a Life* (1890).

Williams, R.M., *The Tallow Chandlers of London* (1970–77).

Williams, W.M., *Annals of the Worshipful Company of Founders of the City of London* (1867).

Woolacott, J.E., *The Curse of Turtledom. An Exposé of the Methods and Extravagant Expenditure of the Livery Companies* (1894).

The Worshipful Company of Makers of Playing Cards, ed. T.W. Heather (1964).

Young, K., 'The Politics of London Government, 1880 – 99', *Public Administration*, LI (1973).

— , 'The Conservative Strategy for London, 1855 – 1975', *The London Journal*, I (1975).

— , *Local Politics and the Rise of Party. The London Municipal Society and the Conservative Intervention in Local Elections, 1894–1963* (1975).

— , and Garside, P.L., *Metropolitan London. Politics and Urban Change, 1837 — 1981* (1982).

INDEX